The Stage Producer's
Business and Legal Guide

The Stage Producer's Business and Legal Guide

by *Charles Grippo*

ALLWORTH PRESS
NEW YORK

07   06   05   04   03   02   5   4   3   2   1

Published by Allworth Press
An imprint of Allworth Communications, Inc.
10 East 23rd Street, New York, NY 10010

Cover design by Mary Belibasakis
Page composition/typography by Integra Software Services, Pvt. Ltd.,
Pondicherry, India
ISBN: 1-58115-241-8

Library of Congress Cataloging-in-Publication Data:
Grippo, Charles.
Stage producer's business and legal guide / by Charles Grippo.
p. cm.
Includes index.
ISBN 1-58115-241-8
1. Theater--Production and direction. 2. Theater management.
3. Theater--Law and legislation--United States. I. Title.
PN2053 .G696 2002
792'.0232--dc21
2002006264

Printed in Canada

FOR MY MOTHER AND IN MEMORY OF MY FATHER,
WITH LOVE AND THANKS

Contents

INTRODUCTION: WHY YOU NEED THIS BOOK

Not too long ago, a friend asked me why a producer needs a lawyer at his side.

"Because every time a producer does anything, it has legal consequences," I said.

My friend's face assumed a puzzled look.

"Well, first," I said, "there are the endless contract negotiations—with agents, play publishers, playwrights, unions, landlords, managers, suppliers, costume shops, scene shops, property houses, actors, directors, choreographers, designers, composers, lyricists. There are copyright issues and underlying rights matters.

"Then there's the fundraising: the limited partnerships, the SEC, the Attorney General, charitable solicitation laws, the board of directors. And once the producer raises the money, he's responsible for how it gets used. He's got to establish and stay within a budget. If he doesn't have enough funds, he's got to go out and raise more. If he has too much, he's got to invest the excess prudently. He's got to account for every buck to his investors, donors, the IRS, the Attorney General. He's got to keep track of even seemingly little, yet important, things, like the house seat allocation.

"Oh, and let's not forget the patron who claims she fell down in the lobby (the producer's fault, of course) and is suing for enough damages to send the entire population of a small city to Europe for a year. And then there's the producer's insurance company who says, 'Hey, we won't pay.'

"In between all this, the producer has to apply for a tax exemption and then worry about losing the tax exemption. And he has to deal with the friendly letter from the IRS that says it's going to audit the books of his last show.

"Meanwhile, the box office treasurer can't quite match up yesterday's ticket stubs with yesterday's ticket sales, and the royalty participants want an explanation today.

"The union deputy is cooling her heels in the producer's outer office; she's here to complain he violated a highly technical rule—even the union doesn't know what it means.

"But she's standing on line behind the fire marshal who's writing out a citation that the show isn't maintaining the proper number of fire extinguishers backstage.

"And wouldn't you know it? Spielberg's on the phone, offering a couple million for the movie rights to last season's comedy that the critics hated so much. But it all depends on arranging a fast deal.

"And then there's—"

"All right," my friend said. "So a producer needs a lawyer by his side."

LAWYER NOT AFFORDABLE!

Unfortunately, keeping a lawyer close by is not always feasible, and, for most producers, not even affordable. Nonetheless, a producer needs a handy source of legal advice that he can consult at any time.

It was for just that reason that I wrote this book. When I first began producing theater in Chicago in the late 1980s, I was disappointed by the lack of a central source of theater law.

In my own situation, I had one advantage over the dozens of other entrepreneurs who were hoping to be a part of the then burgeoning (now world famous) Chicago theater movement. I did not have to beg for the occasional crumb of advice thrown out by volunteer legal organizations. I did not have to ask the family lawyer to join my board and hope that she knew enough theater law to give me practical advice. As an attorney, I could wade through the hundreds of laws that regulate the theater myself. Of course, I made occasional mistakes, but I also learned a helluva lot.

But the problem remained. There was no single book to consult that brought together all of the different areas of law that the producer must know.

THEATERS AND THE LAW

Although this situation may seem odd, it is understandable, given the history of theater production. For most of the twentieth century, theater originated on Broadway. Shows opened in and around Times Square, produced by a handful of legendary names: Jed Harris, Max Gordon, Rodgers and Hammerstein, David Merrick, the Shuberts, and so on. Road companies were organized, cast, and rehearsed in the small community around 42nd Street, then sent out to tour the country and eventually the world.

In the hinterlands, theater companies were amateur, stock, or dinner operations that depended, for the most part, on reproducing the Broadway hits, once those hits had exhausted their "first class" possibilities. Few of these companies produced new works.

However, in the last three decades, regional theaters have grown up in cities, large and small, throughout the country. There are even substantial theater movements, such as the aforementioned Chicago movement. Now, more and more shows originate in the storefronts and the regionals and then move to Broadway and the rest of the world.

For example, the play *Beau Jest* originated at Victory Gardens Theatre, in Chicago in 1989. Next, producer Arthur Cantor presented the play off Broadway, where it enjoyed a long run. Subsequently, the James Sherman comedy has been performed all over the world.

With this great resurgence, tens of thousands of people are actively involved in operating the business functions of local theater. Producers, business managers, box office treasurers, artistic directors, accountants, and, yes, even volunteer attorneys. The list goes on.

And each year, thousands of young actors, directors, and playwrights graduate from hundreds of university and college theater training programs. Many such artists, frustrated by the small number of opportunities available in the established theaters, start their own companies. They have a lot of drive and talent. They know the art, but few know the law of theater.

In the last few years, as I have moved out of producing and back to my first love—writing plays—I have encountered many theater administrators who have confided in me a very deep secret. As much as they love what they are doing, they often feel overwhelmed by the utter responsibility of it all. In particular, they are frustrated by the ever-increasing number of laws, rules, and regulations with which they must comply. They need help. They need a central source that makes sense of it all for them.

If you feel overwhelmed by the complexities and contradictions of theater law, this book is for you. It is designed to help take some of the pressures off your overworked shoulders.

I have assembled together in one volume the various areas of the law the producer encounters on a daily basis. From negotiating contracts with playwrights, to choosing the right form of organization for your company, to raising funds and paying taxes—you'll find it all here. And, while many of these areas are specialties of their own, with applications to virtually every industry, I have specifically focused on the way they affect the theater business.

My goal is to guide you through murky waters. I will show you how to assert your rights, protect your company, and discharge your responsibilities. I am a theatrical attorney, producer, and commercially produced playwright. Therefore, as one who has "been there and done that," I sympathize with you and understand your problems.

I offer you practical solutions to the problems that are on your desk today. I want to show you how you can eliminate risks where possible, or minimize your exposure when risks can't be helped.

I wrote this book in plain English. I want it to be user-friendly.

Nevertheless, this book is not a substitute for legal advice. No book can— or should—take the place of a lawyer's experience and judgment. It is, instead, an educational tool, and most readers will find it very helpful if they use it in that way. For those of you who do try to use it for do-it-yourself law, be aware that neither the publisher nor myself are responsible for the consequences.

Rather than replace your lawyer, this book will teach you how to reduce your legal fees. You will learn how to recognize when paying a lawyer is less expensive than the consequences of your actions or failure to act. In addition, this book will show you how to use your attorney more effectively. It will minimize the time you will spend with her and the time that she must spend on your work.

Oh, and this book is not just for the producer in the hinterlands. For those of you who produce on Broadway, you'll find a number of money-saving suggestions you can use today.

Break a leg!

Organizing a Theater Company

Many theater companies operate quite informally. An individual simply decides to produce theater. Or several friends decide to start a theater company. Artists, such as playwrights, actors, and directors, may create their own company to showcase their work.

Unfortunately, many artistically inclined people organize theater companies very loosely. Even veteran producers may slack off. Overwhelmed by the sheer amount of work it takes to run a company, administrators may put off the pesky little details, like keeping formal minutes of their board meetings, or filing all those confusing, multi-page reports with the government.

If you intend to form your own company, this chapter will show you how to do it. If you already run a company, use this chapter to measure how closely you comply with the law.

A theater company may be organized either as a sole proprietorship, a general partnership, a limited partnership, a for-profit corporation, or as a nonprofit corporation, depending upon the intentions and resources of the producer. We will discuss each, in depth.

SOLE PROPRIETORSHIP

A *sole proprietorship* is the most basic structure under which you can operate a business. One person owns the business, which itself is not incorporated. (If you had a lemonade stand as a kid, you were a sole proprietor.) There are few restrictions or formalities. You may operate under your own name or under a different name (an assumed name). All you need to start up are business licenses from your state and local municipality. You don't even need a telephone number or bank account separate from your own personal ones, although it would be desirable to maintain a business phone number, as well as a business bank account.

The sole proprietor assumes all the risks of the business personally. If another party sues, due to actions occurring through the business, all of the sole proprietor's personal assets may be taken to satisfy a judgment rendered in favor of the suing party (the plaintiff). This includes the proprietor's personal home, autos, and bank accounts. She could be forced into filing for personal bankruptcy.

If the owner dies or is disabled, the business stops. Unlike a partnership or a corporation in which other people can carry on the business, the sole proprietorship ceases to exist if the owner can't continue to operate it. Even if the owner authorizes the executor of her will to carry on the business, this is usually not feasible. The business would have to be liquidated. Its assets may have to be sold at "fire sale" prices.

If the owner and her spouse run into marital difficulties, business assets may become entangled in divorce proceedings. The spouse may even be entitled to a share of the business.

While insurance may protect against some risks, it will not cover everything. For instance, it won't protect against a show that loses all its investment in funds. And all policies limit the amount of damages the insurer will pay.

The sole proprietor must pay taxes on all income earned from the business. This is on top of income she might have from any other sources, such as another business, investments, or wages from her job. The total of all her income might push her into a higher tax bracket. (Conversely, she can use losses from the theater company to offset her other income.)

A sole proprietor should not expect to receive large donations to help fund her productions. Even the most altruistic patron of the arts wants tax write-offs from his contributions. And one can only deduct donations to an organized, tax-exempt charity—that is, a nonprofit corporation. The only money a sole proprietor is likely to scrape up in this way is whatever she can cadge from family and friends. In that case, the motive is to help her, rather than to seek income tax benefits. So the pickings may be slim.

ASSUMED NAMES

If you choose to operate under a name different from your own, you must comply with the "assumed name" laws of your state. In some states, these laws are known as "fictitious business name" or "doing business as" statutes.

First, search your state and community's public records to determine if anyone else is using the name you have chosen. This is to avoid confusion in the public's mind. If the name is available, ask your local officials for an "Application for an Assumed Name." This form requires such basic information as your actual name, the location of your business, and the location where someone can serve you with legal process if you are sued. (Legal process consists of the complaint, which tells you that someone is suing you, the nature of his claim against you, and the amount of money damages he is seeking. In addition, a "summons" will tell you when and where you must appear in court to answer the complaint.) You file the Application for Assumed Name with the state (and often the county) in which you intend to do business. You will pay a fee. Some assumed name laws also require you to publish a legal notice of your intentions in a newspaper approved by the court, for a period of several weeks to several months before you can start doing business. That's all there is to it.

Now you have the right to operate under whatever name you have chosen—in other words, your "trade name."

If you believe the name you have chosen is unique and has the potential to be very valuable some day, consider registering it with the federal government as your "trademark." This is a highly specialized field, for which you need the services of a trademark attorney.

Even if you don't have immediate plans for a Web site, it would be prudent to register your business name as a "domain name." There are several companies authorized to register domain names for a fee. Your Internet service provider can assist you.

Be careful when you choose your name. Avoid infringing on anyone else's trademark. If you call yourself "The Disney Theater Company," even if your name is Susan Disney, you will likely get a cease-and-desist letter from lawyers for the Mouse House.

GENERAL PARTNERSHIPS

A *general partnership* is an association of two or more persons to operate a non-incorporated business for profit—regardless of whether they ever do turn a profit. Some states require a partnership to file a certificate in the county in which it will do business. Otherwise, there are no formalities required to form a partnership.

In theory, each partner brings something special to the enterprise—money, a particular talent or skill, or connections. It is often something one party possesses that the other does not. The partners pool their resources to achieve greater benefits for all.

Partners may operate their business under their own names, or, like the sole proprietor, they might do business under an assumed name. Partners also devote most, if not all, of their time exclusively to the partnership business. They do not engage in partnerships with other parties—at least not in the same line of business.

For instance, suppose David, Saul, Mary, and Patti, all of whom were classmates in the New Lincoln Theatre Training Center, decide to form a partnership to present theater. They call themselves the XYZ Theatre Company.

The advantages are that the four friends will share profits, losses, duties, responsibilities, and ownership interests, according to any formula to which they agree. Unlike a corporation, a partnership offers more flexibility to divvy up control. Changes are much easier to make. If the partners need additional capital, they can sell ownership interests in their partnership with more ease than a sole proprietor can.

But there are disadvantages as well. All of the partners have unlimited liability for the debts of the partnership. Since each partner is a co-owner, each can enter into contracts and incur debts on behalf of the partnership, for which all partners become personally liable. It doesn't matter whether all of the partners consented or even knew of any one partner's actions.

Suppose the XYZ Theatre Company decides to produce *Romeo and Juliet*. Without the consent of the others, David binds the partnership to tens of thousands of dollars of debts for costumes, theater rental, sets, and advertising. *Romeo and Juliet* bombs. The assets of the partnership are not sufficient to pay back all the debts. Even worse, David flies the coop. Saul, Mary, and Patti are personally liable for all of the debts, even though they knew nothing of what David was doing and would not have agreed if they had. All three could lose their houses, bank accounts, automobiles, and inheritances to the unpaid debts. They could wind up working for years to pay them off. If Saul dies or declares bankruptcy, Mary and Patti will still be on the hook for all of the remaining bills. Their individual credit records could be ruined for years.

Or suppose Patti hired a stage manager who was a convicted sex offender. (She didn't know of his past.) One night he accosts a patron in the theater's parking lot. The partnership is individually responsible for the acts of its employees. Again, all four could face unlimited personal liability in the civil suit that is sure to follow.

Here's a less extreme example: While driving to the costume shop to pick up Romeo's costume, Mary hits and kills a pedestrian. You guessed it. All the partners can be held individually liable for Mary's negligent driving, which occurred in the course of her duties on behalf of the partnership.

There's also the possibility of becoming partners with someone, even if you didn't intend it. For instance, suppose David, Mary, Saul, and Patti bring in a director named Michael. Because they don't have the money to pay him, they give him a share of the profits. The law may well deem Michael a partner, giving him ownership rights and making the others personally liable for his actions.

General partnerships dissolve automatically if any partner dies, files for personal bankruptcy, retires, resigns, or otherwise ceases to be a partner.

FORMAL PARTNERSHIP AGREEMENT

The way to prevent many of these problems is to draw up a formal partnership agreement. The most important terms to include are these:

1. How long will the partnership last?

2. How much money will each partner contribute to the partnership?

3. How will the partners share profits and losses?

4. How will the partners divide up duties and responsibilities?

5. For what purpose are we creating this partnership?

6. How will the partners be paid? Will they take salaries in addition to profits? Will they be permitted to withdraw money from the business?

7. How will partners who advance money for expenses be reimbursed?

8. How will we apportion voting rights? (Absent agreement to the contrary, all parties have an equal voice in the operations.)

9. If a partner dies, becomes disabled, or wants to leave the business, what will happen to the business? How will his share of the partnership be paid to him or his heirs? How will shares be valued in that event? What rights do the remaining partners have?

10. Will new partners be admitted?

11. If so, what mechanism will be put into place for admitting new partners? How do we determine what they will pay for their interests? How will the new ownership interests affect (dilute) old interests?

12. Which partners will be authorized to enter into contracts, incur debts, or otherwise bind the partnership?

13. Do we want to place dollar limits or restrictions on the debts and other obligations the partners can incur before they must seek approval of the others?

14. To how much vacation will each partner be entitled?

15. What fringe benefits shall the partners receive and in what amount?

You don't need an elaborate format. At the top of the first page, simply head the instrument "General Partnership Agreement." The first paragraph identifies all of the partners by name. The next paragraph states the purpose of the partnership—to operate a theater company. Give the name under which you intend to operate, either your own or an assumed name. Succeeding paragraphs state, in precise language, the way you have agreed to treat all of the above issues. The parties will sign and date the agreement on the last page. It's also a good idea to state, on the last page, the total number of pages of your agreement. To be extra sure, each partner should initial each page in the margin of your choice. Finally, give each partner a duplicate original—that is, a copy of the whole agreement, with original initials and signatures. That's all there is to it.

LIMITED PARTNERSHIPS

By far the most common form of organization in commercial theater, the *limited partnership* requires at least one general partner and one limited partner. Unlike the general partnership, the only thing the limited partner can lose is her investment in the partnership. She does not face unlimited liability. Since theater is such a high-risk business, it is easy to see why limited partnerships are attractive to investors.

This is the way it works. A producer wishing to put on a show acts as the general partner, bearing all of the liability. He forms a limited partnership, selling shares to a group of wealthy investors. The producer sets the price of the shares at whatever he believes the market will bear, based on the show and the amount of capital he needs.

If the show is a success, the investor, a limited partner, gets back her original investment plus a proportionate share of the profits. If the show fails, the limited partner loses her investment (or a portion thereof). In many cases, the limited partner can write off her losses against her taxes on other, more lucra-tive ventures.

Limited partners are forbidden from managing the business. In some sense, they are like shareholders in a corporation. The difference relates to losses for tax purposes: If a corporation loses money, it, not the shareholders, declares the loss on its tax return. If a limited partnership loses money, the limited partners take the loss on their personal tax returns.

ORGANIZING A LIMITED PARTNERSHIP

Organizing a limited partnership, especially one to produce a show, requires a great deal of paperwork. It is far more complicated than organizing a general partnership. The producer must comply with federal and state securities laws, as well as with the tax laws. (We will treat the securities laws in chapter 6.)

This is not a field for amateurs. A lawyer experienced in limited partner-ships, securities law, taxes, and theater law is a must.

I will reserve discussion of theatrical limited partnerships for chapter 6.

FOR-PROFIT CORPORATIONS

Corporations may be multibillion-dollar enterprises, like General Motors or McDonald's, with hundreds of thousands of employees and operations in all corners of the globe. However, the vast majority of corporations are (compar-atively) small companies, whose operations are limited in geographic scope and size.

Unlike a partnership or a sole proprietorship, a corporation is a legal entity separate and apart from its owners (shareholders) and managers (officers, directors, and those persons who actually run the day-to-day operations). This status as a separate entity makes the corporation particularly attractive to investors and entrepreneurs.

The advantages are that the shareholders of a corporation enjoy limited lia-bility. Their personal assets are not at stake. The most they can lose is their investment in the corporation. If I buy a hundred shares of New Lincoln Theatre, Inc., at $10 a share, I have invested $1,000. If the corporation goes bank-rupt or is sued, the most I can lose is $1,000. My personal residence, vehicle, and other investments are protected from the corporation's troubles.

This means that if a creditor of New Lincoln Theatre, Inc., sues for money owed out of the company's operations, he has to sue New Lincoln Theatre, Inc., not Charles Grippo personally. If he wins, he can only collect his judgment from whatever assets New Lincoln Theatre, Inc. owns.

By the same token, I (as a shareholder) cannot sue anyone who owes money to New Lincoln Theatre, Inc. It must sue in its own name. Any judgment it collects (if it wins) goes into the corporate bank account, not mine. This is true even if I am the only shareholder.

Remember that if a sole proprietor dies, the business ceases to exist. The same is true of a partnership if one partner dies or withdraws. However, a corporation continues to exist, no matter what happens to its shareholders or managers. Their deaths, personal bankruptcies, or withdrawal from management do not affect the existence of the corporation. The business goes on, uninterrupted.

Shares in a corporation are freely transferable. I can sell my stock to anyone who wants to buy it. This contrasts with the difficulty of selling ownership of a sole proprietorship or an interest in a partnership. This is why big corporations are listed on the major stock exchanges—the New York Stock Exchange, the American Stock Exchange, and NASDAQ. Their shares can be freely bought and sold by anyone.

EXCEPTIONS TO THE RULE

You knew there had to be exceptions to all of the foregoing, didn't you? Okay, here goes.

Although corporate shares are freely transferable, the shareholders may elect to place restrictions on when and how shares may be transferred. This is usually desirable in the case of small corporations, where the shareholders and managers are often one and the same or otherwise have close relationships.

Small corporations are often organized by two or more persons with unique talents or interests they bring to the business. If a shareholder desires to sell his interest, the other shareholders may want to limit his ability to sell to a third party, whom they may not know or want to have associated with their business. The remaining shareholders may wish to purchase his shares themselves, to maintain control and to keep the operations closed to outsiders.

Thus, the shareholders may agree that, if anyone wants to sell his interest, he must first offer the shares to the others either at a set price or the fair market value at the time of the proposed sale.

Most states have strict rules regarding the prohibitions that can be placed on the free transferability of shares. States want to encourage alienability of property—that is, the ease by which ownership may be conveyed between two parties.

Ordinarily, shareholders in a corporation are not at personal risk for the obligations of the corporation. Since this is no secret, lenders and creditors are aware of this risk when they make loans and sell their products to corporations.

If the corporation is a small enterprise, lenders may be unwilling to loan large amounts with only the corporate assets to serve as collateral. Lenders may also require the shareholders (who are usually also the managers) to sign personally for any loans. This means the shareholders are personally at risk if the corporation defaults and its assets are not sufficient to pay back the lender.

Another exception to a shareholder's limited liability occurs when a creditor is able to "pierce the corporate veil." In other words, the creditor can show that, even though the business was ostensibly a corporation, its managers failed to comply with the formalities required under the law of corporations. In that case, a court may deem the business as actually a sole proprietorship or a general partnership. The creditor can then enforce his judgment against the shareholder's personal assets.

Unfortunately, the managers of many small corporations leave their shareholders wide open to this risk. (I have never heard of it occurring in the case of large, public corporations.) In just a moment, I will show you how to protect yourself from this problem.

TAXES

The good news is, the corporation is taxed separate and apart from its shareholders. The bad news is, the corporation is taxed separate and apart from its shareholders.

For shareholders in high tax brackets, separate taxation is good news. By definition, they have high incomes, often from several different sources, like jobs or investments. If, atop all that other income, they also have to add the net profits from New Lincoln Theatre, Inc. (as they would have to do if New Lincoln is a sole proprietorship or a partnership), they might have to pay extraordinarily high taxes.

However—and here's the bad news, folks—the net profits of New Lincoln Theatre, Inc., are taxed twice. First, New Lincoln pays corporate income taxes on its net earnings. Then, when New Lincoln distributes those earnings as dividends, the shareholders must pay personal income taxes on them.

Here is one way to avoid the problem: New Lincoln Theatre, Inc., does not pay dividends. Instead, the corporation reinvests those net earnings into its business, thereby increasing the value of its stock. Small corporations can also pay out most of their earnings to their shareholder-managers as salaries. (The IRS must deem the salaries as "reasonable.") Thus, there will be no profits, no dividends, and no double taxation.

But there's more bad news: If New Lincoln Theatre, Inc., loses money, it must take the losses on its own corporate income tax return. Its shareholders cannot use the losses to offset other income on their personal tax returns.

For more information about corporate taxes—beyond that discussed in the sections below—refer to chapter 12.

SUBCHAPTER S CORPORATION

A corporation may elect to be treated as a "Subchapter S" Corporation. ("Subchapter S" refers to a section of the IRS Code.) To qualify, it must be a domestic, not a foreign, corporation. It cannot issue more than one class of stock. The corporation cannot have more than seventy-five shareholders. It may not own more than 80 percent of the stock of another corporation.

To make this election, all of its shareholders must sign a Form 2553. This form must be filed with the IRS no later than two months and fifteen days after the beginning of the tax year in which the shareholders want it to be effective.

The advantage to being a Subchapter S Corporation is that all of the income and deductions of the corporation are passed on to its shareholders' personal tax returns. At the same time, the shareowners still enjoy the limited liability of the corporate form. If the shareholders do not elect to become a Subchapter S Corporation, then the corporation is taxed as a Corporation—that is, it is subject to double taxation.

CLOSE CORPORATIONS

A small corporation may be treated as a "close" corporation. In a "close" corporation, because most of its shareholders also actively manage its business, the corporation is not subject to the securities laws.

THE PROCESS OF INCORPORATING

To form a corporation, one or more persons (the incorporators) must file "Articles of Incorporation" (or a "Certificate of Incorporation") with the state, and often the county, in which they have chosen to organize the corporation. Incorporators may choose any state in which to incorporate. It need not be their place of residence or even the state in which they intend to do business.

States actively compete with each other to be the preferred choice of incorporators. Many have passed very liberal corporate laws. States are anxious to collect the filing fees incorporators have to pay when they form the corporation, as well as the subsequent franchise taxes the corporation itself will have to pay during its existence.

The legal requirements to incorporate vary from state to state. However, the laws are very detailed and specific. Anyone seeking to incorporate must use the services of an attorney familiar with the laws of the state in which he wants to incorporate.

These are the general procedures for incorporating a theater company:

1. Select the state in which you wish to incorporate.

2. Your attorney will file articles of incorporation with the secretary of state of the chosen state.

3. Pay the requisite filing fee. This is usually based on the amount of stock which you initially intend to issue. If you are a small company, you can save money by issuing the minimal number of shares required by the state.

4. Issue stock certificates.

5. Establish written bylaws. (See below.)

6. Hold an initial organization meeting. Shareholders will appoint directors.

7. The directors will hold an additional meeting, during which they will authorize the actions that actually get the business up and running. These actions include opening bank accounts, issuing stock certificates, and setting the salaries of key officers.

8. Some states allow you to combine all of the business described in paragraphs 6 and 7 into one meeting. Each state has its own special requirements.

BYLAWS. The bylaws are the written guidelines for running the corporation. The following is a partial list of questions to be decided:

- *How do we issue stock?*

- *Will there be more than one class of stock?*

- *What are the voting, directorship, and dividend rights of each class?*

- *What criteria shall determine whether and when the directors may declare dividends?*

- *What are the rules for conducting shareholder, director, and committee meetings?*

- *How do we appoint and remove officers and directors?*

- *What are the duties of the officers and directors?*

- *What rights will minority shareholders have?*

CLASSES OF STOCK. Stock may be issued according to various classes, each of which has different rights. There is no requirement that a corporation issue different classes of stock. Many do, however, to encourage different types of investments.

MAINTAINING THE "CORPORATE VEIL." As I indicated, the best way to protect shareholders from lawsuits and personal judgments is to maintain the "corporate veil."

Think of the "veil" as a shield that protects your personal assets. As long as you hold the shield in front of you, your personal assets are safe. But, if you lay that shield down, you put your home and bank accounts at risk.

Fortunately, the law provides you with many ways to maintain that shield. Unfortunately, many managers fail to observe these formalities—to their profound regret.

If your company is already organized as a corporation, take a moment now to review your own procedures against the following list. How closely do your operations measure up?

1. Hold regular formal meetings. (At least once a year, you must hold a shareholders' meeting, even if you are the only shareholder.)

2. Keep written minutes of all meetings in the corporate records book. (Yes, you have one. Look for it in all your clutter. It's thick and it has a heavy red, green, or blue cover. Your lawyer gave it to you after you incorporated.)

3. Identify your business as a corporation on all stationary, business cards, Web sites, tickets, programs, press releases, and so forth.

4. Your trade name must include one of the following words: "Inc.," "Incorporated," or "Corporation."

5. In all your dealings with third parties, make yourself known as a corporation.

6. Officers should sign all contracts, documents, and so on, with their official titles. This includes ordinary correspondence, as well. Signatures on legal documents should be as follows:

> New Lincoln Theatre, Inc.
> BY: Charles Grippo (not personally)
> President

7. Don't commingle personal funds with corporate funds. Maintain separate bank accounts for each. If you withdraw money for yourself for any reason (assuming you have authority to do so), write a check on the corporate account to yourself. Then deposit the corporate check into your personal account.

8. Document that all actions are undertaken by the corporation and not by you personally.

9. Obtain a separate federal tax ID number for the corporation from the IRS. I cringe when I discover that some shareholder-owners of small corporations use their own personal social security numbers.

10. Even if you operate out of your home, obtain separate business telephone lines in the name of the corporation.

11. If you need to take major action, hold a meeting and introduce a formal resolution. Formally document the resolution.

12. Maintain separate accounting records from your personal accounts.

13. Take out all licenses, permits, and so on, in the name of the corporation.

14. If the corporation reimburses you when you advance expenses on its behalf, keep accurate records. Turn in the vouchers to the corporation. Obtain reimbursement as if you were working for a third-party employer (which you are). This is especially important if you use your personal vehicle in the business.

15. Obtain credit cards in the name of the corporation. Use only these to charge expenses and other items that are the obligations of the corporation.

16. If it is desirable or necessary to bring in new investors or capital, consult with an attorney before you talk, even informally, to anyone. Federal and state securities laws are very strict about what you can and cannot say or do. The sanctions for failing to comply range from heavy fines to jail time.

17. Pay the annual franchise taxes to the state in which you have incorporated. If you fail to pay these taxes, the state can dissolve your corporation. Your business will default to either a sole proprietorship or partnership. You will lose the benefits of limited liability for corporate obligations.

18. Once you begin formal incorporation proceedings, follow through all the way to the end. Many small businesses never achieve corporate status because their organizers failed to complete all the necessary steps to incorporate.

19. File all required reports with the state on time. This is another area in which managers are often lax.

20. Never commit fraud or misrepresentation on any documents you file with the state. If you file a document—and later discover you have innocently made one or more errors—immediately, voluntarily, file an amended document, correcting the mistakes.

21. Actively use the powers the state has granted you. In most states, the Attorney General can seek to terminate the charter of a corporation that fails to actively use its powers for a period of two years.

NONPROFIT CORPORATIONS

The choice of whether to organize as a nonprofit depends on what you want to accomplish and what sources you expect to tap for your funding. A "for-profit" corporation aims to return a commercial gain to its shareholders. A "nonprofit" does not.

For a theater company, nonprofit status is just a different way of doing business. The commercial "for-profit" producer must either fund his shows out of his own pockets or else raise money from investors. He is accountable to his backers for the money he raises, takes in, and spends. He must select shows that will attract investor interest and which will appeal to a broad audience.

The nonprofit producer raises funds from a variety of sources: wealthy patrons of the arts; individual small donors; foundations; government agencies; fundraising events; and the like. He, too, is accountable, for all the money he raises, spends, and takes in—to his board, his funding sources, and to various government oversight agencies. However, he can select shows with a more limited appeal. Since his shows don't have to show a profit, he can focus attention more on "art."

The chief business reason for organizing as a nonprofit is to qualify for financial grants from government agencies and private foundations. In addition, individuals receive tax deductions for their donations to nonprofits. It is easier to ask a large corporation to donate money or goods to a nonprofit than it is to ask the same corporation to invest in a play for commercial gain. An investment in a commercial show is a business decision that may not fit with the company's aims, as well as a huge risk to its bottom line. However, a donation to a local nonprofit falls under the heading of public relations, of giving back something to the community, of being a good corporate citizen.

Nonprofits enjoy certain privileges, such as exemptions (with exceptions) from federal, state, and local income, sales, and, often, property taxes. They receive lower rates from the post office on bulk mailings. Sometimes they receive special discounts on purchases from corporate suppliers. They may receive "in kind" donations—that is, a local printer may print up their programs or flyers for free. Nonprofits also attract volunteer labor for many positions for which the commercial producer has to pay—for instance, actors, directors, stage crew, and so on.

Organizers, directors, and managers of nonprofits enjoy limited liability from corporate obligations. The corporate veil protects their personal assets from judgments. However, delinquent taxes may become a personal liability of the officer responsible. If a manager commits malfeasance in the performance of his duties, he may become liable to the corporation for damages.

Some people believe that nonprofits cannot make a profit. That is incorrect. There is no reason a nonprofit cannot take a profit. The difference occurs in what it may do with the profit.

If a commercial theater company earns a profit on its investment, it will, normally, distribute that profit to its shareholders. However, if a nonprofit makes money, it cannot distribute its net earnings to its organizers or managers. It must retain those earnings in the business to help it achieve its goals.

A nonprofit (unless it is a co-op) cannot issue shares or declare dividends. It is not permitted to have shareholders. In a co-op, the very people or entities who use its production and distribution services also own and operate the enterprise.

When a commercial theater company dissolves or winds up its business, its assets must be sold and the proceeds distributed to its shareholders. (Or, conversely, the assets themselves may be distributed to the owners.) However, when a *nonprofit* dissolves, it must distribute its remaining assets to another tax-exempt nonprofit group.

For more information about nonprofits, see chapters 7 and 13.

CHAPTER 2

Your Performance Space

Selecting the appropriate space in which to present your productions is second in importance to choosing the right form of organization. It is akin to picking out a personal residence; it is your business home.

There are three possible roads down which you may travel. All are valid, depending on your intentions and resources. These possibilities are:

1. Show-by-show rental;

2. Long-term lease;

3. Purchase of your own space.

Each has its own advantages and disadvantages. Many of the same legal considerations apply to two of these choices: show-by-show rental and purchase of your own space.

SHOW-BY-SHOW RENTAL

Renting space on a show-by-show basis is often the most cost-effective way to present your shows, especially if you contemplate producing on an occasional basis. The advantage here: You are not saddled with the expenses of maintaining a physical plant when you do not have a show running.

THE SHOW-BY-SHOW CONTRACT

Once a producer identifies a space as suitable for his show, he must negotiate a contract with the landlord. Of course, terms will vary, depending on the size and scope of the production. Obviously, a Broadway touring company will demand a more detailed contract than a community theater or storefront production will require. However, there are many terms that are common to all kinds of productions.

LICENSE VERSUS LEASE. These agreements are usually structured as mere "licenses" for the use of the premises, rather than as "leases," regardless of how long the parties hope the show will run.

A license confers limited rights on the licensee (the producer). It is much easier to terminate than a lease. In the case of a lease, if the owner wants the producer to leave, she must apply to the courts through formal eviction proceedings. It can take weeks, even months, before the premises are restored to her.

INTRODUCTORY PARAGRAPH. The contract begins by identifying the parties: the producer, the owner, the theater, and the show. The parties may date the contract here or on the last page, adjacent to their signatures.

USE. The owner will furnish to the producer the use of the theater beginning on the date to which the parties have agreed. The parties must describe whether this use is for performance, rehearsals, or both.

Rehearsals are best held in a separate space, where the rental is much cheaper. However, as rehearsals progress, it is essential to begin holding them in the theater in which the show will perform. This allows the actors to get a feel for the space as well as an understanding of the acoustics. In addition, once the scenery has been built, it must be moved into the theater— "hung"—and adjusted until it works perfectly. Lights must also be hung. The lighting and sound plots must be programmed into the appropriate computers and tested. If the show is a musical, the orchestra must begin rehearsals with the performers. Technical rehearsals are also necessary, particularly in the days remaining before the first public performance, to bring all the components together and make final adjustments.

Make sure your contract specifies the number of performances per week for which you may use the space. Identify whether these are evening or matinee shows, or a combination of the two. You may also wish to specify that you have the right to schedule pickup rehearsals; these are for cast brush-ups or to rehearse replacement actors.

You and the owner must agree upon the date when you will first be given access to the space, to begin moving in your physical production. You should also specify the date of your first public performance, regardless of whether this is your first preview or your opening.

CLOSING DATES. The parties must decide on whether and when to schedule a closing date. This is when the producer's use of the facility for performances shall end. Some shows are scheduled for limited runs. That is, the producer intends from the beginning that the show will only play "X" number of performances, even if it is a sold-out hit. Other shows are open ended—that is, the producer does not schedule a closing date, because he hopes business will be enough to keep the show running for years.

OPEN-ENDED RUNS. An open-ended run is often a mixed bag for an owner. In the case of a hit, she can continue to collect rentals for a very long time. But at the same time, the owner doesn't want to tie up her venue with a show that may barely be limping along. It may be more advantageous to close that show and rent the facility to another show that may be a big hit. (Of course, show number 2 could be a one-night flop, too.)

Often, therefore, the parties agree to an open-ended run, providing that the show maintains ticket sales at or above a certain number. The parties decide upon that number in advance.

However, shows can dip below the minimum one week and soar well above it the following week. To obviate that problem, the producer and the landlord may agree on a specific formula to determine when the show must close. These are the two most common formulas:

> *1. Ticket sales shall be taken on a week-by-week basis over, let's say, a four-week period. Sales must meet the minimum for two out of those four weeks.*

> *2. Weekly ticket sales will be taken for a specific period of time. Gross receipts must fall below the minimum sum for two consecutive weeks to trigger termination.*

Either of these formulas make up the "stop clause" in the contract. This clause works to the producer's advantage as well. It gives him the right to close the show if the receipts fall below the stated minimum.

NOTICE OF TERMINATION. The contract must state when either party may serve the other with notice of termination and the date thereafter when the show will subsequently close. For example, commonly the parties agree that, if the owner serves the producer with a notice of termination on Monday, the show must close the following Sunday.

OWNER'S OBLIGATIONS. The "use" of the facilities includes the auditorium itself, dressing rooms, lobby, box office, patron and staff restrooms, scene storage, and so forth. Contracts rarely specifically identify these items separately, since the producer's need to use them is generally understood.

Insist that the owner furnish the theater "properly licensed." This is her assurance that the venue complies with all of the local zoning and building ordinances applicable thereto. An owner may balk at giving this warranty, since the venue may contain ordinance violations of which she may legitimately be unaware. Nevertheless, you want to avoid the "surprise" last-minute city shutdowns for zoning or licensing violations.

The producer should demand that if, during the run of the show, the theater violates any building or zoning ordinances, the owner will promptly correct them. Furthermore, the owner will indemnify the producer for any losses caused by reason of the violations (including lost box office because of city shutdowns).

The owner supplies the necessary personnel and equipment to operate the theater. Determine exactly what this encompasses. For instance, does the owner supply such front-of-the-house personnel as the house manager, ushers, and cleaning crew? What about a basic stage crew, such as the head carpenter, electrician, and property person? (A theater operating under the jurisdiction of the International Alliance of Theatrical Stage Employees must maintain these persons on the payroll.)

PRODUCER'S OBLIGATIONS. The producer supplies the production itself. This includes the play, the actors, director, and designers. It includes the physical production, such as lights, scenery, and costumes. The producer also takes care of advertising and press materials. He also furnishes the additional personnel—stage crew, musicians, and so on—needed to run the production.

STAR. The owner has a legitimate right to know whether a "star" is contracted to the production. A "star" may be one in the traditional sense of the word—a leading performer. However, the playwright may also be the star, especially if he's Neil Simon, David Mamet, or August Wilson. In the owner's mind, a star is anyone who can sell tickets and help the show to run for a long time. Long runs make money for the owner.

If the producer does not yet have a star committed to the show, he may attempt to skirt this issue by dropping the names of "stars" who, he alleges, have expressed interest in the show. Interest is not the same as a signed contract. Theater owners are wise to this subterfuge, especially because "interest" may mean the star knows nothing more about the show than what she has read in the trades. If you claim you have a star attached to your project, you'd better have a star. The owner may want you to give a warranty to that effect in your agreement. That means you are guaranteeing, in writing, that you have that star under contract to your show.

RENTALS. Small theaters are often rented on a flat, per week, fee. Whether the show sells out all or only a fraction of its available seats is irrelevant. The producer guarantees the flat fee. Period.

Larger venues often require a guarantee plus a percentage of the weekly box office receipts.

PRODUCER'S GUARANTEE. The producer pays for all of the administrative costs of operating the theater: real estate taxes, utilities, maintenance, insurance, depreciation, and interest on the mortgage. This is a fixed sum, regardless of the box office receipts. He also guarantees all other operating expenses.

The producer also pays for the owner's payroll costs at the prevailing union rates. This means that, if the rates change during the run of the show, the producer's costs change in relation to the rates.

All of these charges make up the producer's guarantee. The owner takes the guarantee out of the gross weekly box office receipts. If those receipts are not sufficient to meet the guarantee, the producer must make up the difference.

GROSS WEEKLY BOX OFFICE RECEIPTS. Gross weekly box office receipts are divided between the producer and the theater. The formula may vary, depending on the size of the house (measured by the number of seats) and the bargaining power of the parties.

Gross weekly box office receipts include all sales of tickets, wherever or however made—such as the box office, phone orders, and group sales. However, certain costs are deducted first: sales commissions, ticket broker fees, credit card company charges, and amusement taxes.

The producer keeps whatever is left out of the weekly box office receipts, after costs, guarantees, and the owner's share are deducted.

Unless the producer also furnishes the box office personnel, the theater is responsible for collecting all receipts, regardless of the source. The parties should agree on a date on which the theater will tally the weekly receipts, compare sales to tickets collected at the door, and settle up accordingly. This date is usually on Monday, for the preceding week.

DEPOSIT. At the time when the producer signs the contract with the theater, he gives the owner a security deposit, the amount of which is negotiable. This is no different from the deposit you gave your landlord when you leased your apartment. The owner holds the security deposit as a guarantee that the producer will perform all of his obligations under the license agreement faithfully. If he does not, the owner can deduct whatever sums he owes her when he vacates before she refunds his deposit.

TAKE OUT. Once the show closes, the producer must vacate the theater by removing all materials belonging to the production—such as sets, costumes, and lights. He must do so within an agreed-upon time.

This time is limited; we're talking hours, not weeks or months. Commonly, the owner gives the producer a maximum of seventy-two hours after the last performance. However, if the owner has another show waiting to go in, she may give the producer even less time.

If he fails to do so, the contract commonly stipulates (the parties have agreed in advance) that the owner may consider any property left behind as "abandoned." The owner may dispose of it as she sees fit. She may destroy it. She may sell it, applying the proceeds to her costs of removal. If she chooses to store it, she may charge all storage fees to the producer.

The reason for all this should be obvious: once a show closes, the owner has an interest in minimizing her "dark time." She wants to bring another show in as quickly as possible.

THEATER CONDITION. The producer gets the theater "as is." For some shows, the producer may need to make alterations in the facility. For instance, the producer may need to take out a couple of rows of orchestra seats, if the demands of the show warrant. A temperamental star may demand alterations to her dressing room.

If the producer wants to modify the facilities in any way, he must first obtain the owner's consent. (He may also have to obtain approval of the local building authorities.)

Upon vacating the theater, the producer must restore it to its original condition.

The producer cannot do anything to violate any local ordinances, especially such safety regulations as fire codes. He must at all times comply with the reasonable rules of the owner.

EXCLUSIVE RUN. The theater owner wants to make sure that the production playing in her theater is exclusive to her community. She doesn't want the producer opening another company at the competition's theater across the street. Usually, the parties agree to restrict the production of the play within a certain specific geographic area while the show is still running at the owner's venue and often for a certain specified time thereafter.

There are exceptions, of course. Obviously, radio stations may play the original cast album. This "promotion" is good for everyone concerned. Similarly, the producer may permit radio or television broadcasts of a limited excerpt from the play for the purpose of publicizing it.

CONCESSIONS. The owner usually reserves the exclusive right to operate the concession stand, either with her own personnel or by contracting out with a concessions company. However, the producer may sell show-related merchandise (souvenir books, original cast albums, shirts emblazoned with the show logo) out of the concession stand. The producer must pay the owner's concessionaire a royalty on all such sales.

The owner may also have an exclusive contract with *Playbill* (or one of its competitors) to supply program books for the show.

HOUSE SEATS. We will discuss house seats in chapters 4, 9, and 10. The owner will negotiate the purchase of a number of house seats for her own account. The parties usually maintain joint control over the free tickets handed out to the press.

TERMINATION. In addition to terminating the contract for poor box office, the owner can terminate in the event of fires, labor strikes, acts of God, or other unforeseen events beyond her control. She will not be liable for any losses to the producer. However, she must give the producer an appropriate, timely notice.

The owner can also terminate if the producer breaks any terms of the agreement or commits an unlawful act that would subject the owner to fine or penalty—such as storing hazardous material on the premises.

Absent permission from the owner, the producer can't shut the show down on a temporary basis, such as because of an actor's illness or for the holidays.

If the owner terminates the show, the producer must remove his property from the premises or be otherwise liable to the owner.

INSURANCE. The producer must carry adequate comprehensive general liability insurance, as well as worker's compensation. He must name the owner as co-insured on all policies and pay the premiums thereon.

HANGING PLOT. Before the producer may install any scenery or equipment, he must furnish the owner with the hanging plot. The hanging plot is an item-by-item description of the pieces of scenery and other equipment that must be attached to the theater's structure. The owner must approve. The purpose is to make sure the scenery will not damage the theater's structure or any equipment belonging to the owner.

This clause can become very detailed and technical, especially if the theater's structure demands exact specifications. In negotiating this area of the contract, it would be prudent for you to call for help from your designers.

ADVERTISING AND PUBLICITY. The theater owner may seek the right to dictate the choice of local newspaper or other media outlet in which the producer advertises. Occasionally, this works to the producer's advantage. Many theaters have long-term advertising contracts with local media, which often result in lower overall rates.

Many theaters also maintain their own local press representatives, either on staff or on retainer. Although the producer will have a national publicity director for the show, the theater's people may handle the local press. Again, this may work to the producer's advantage, since the theater's press agents usually have close working relations with the local media.

LONG-TERM LEASES

If you are planning to present one or more full seasons of shows, it may be wise to lease facilities for whatever length of time you expect to be active. This arrangement is ideal for repertory companies and summer stock.

There are advantages to presenting all of your shows in one fixed place. As a marketing tool, it helps develop long-term audiences. If you accustom audiences and the media to seeing all of your shows in the same location, it makes it highly probable that they will always know where to find you. This helps create "brand awareness" and customer loyalty.

In addition, if you can obtain "naming rights" to your facility, you can name it after your theater company. This reinforces your name in the minds of audiences and the media.

Presenting all of your shows in one facility also gives you flexibility. You can schedule your season in the most appropriate way. You do not have to wait for another producer's show to vacate the desired space before it becomes available to you. This gives you greater control over your productions.

In addition, if the space is large enough, you can build and store scenery, as well as props, costumes, and electrical and sound equipment, all in one convenient location. This saves a great deal of time. It also facilitates communication among your departments. You may even be able to maintain your administrative offices on the site.

The downside is that now you will be carrying the fixed cost of your facilities for the entire term of the lease. "Fixed cost" includes building rental, taxes, insurance, repairs, payroll for the house staff, and utilities. Most of these costs remain the same, whether you have a show on or not. Utilities (heat, electric, water) will be your only variable cost. These will likely rise when you are running a show.

Another problem arises if one of your shows is a major hit. It is hard to foresee a hit. (If it were easy, everyone would be producing nothing but hits.)

When you own or lease your own facility, it is necessary to schedule a full season of shows well in advance. This means deciding on opening and closing dates before you know what you have.

As wonderful as a breakout success can be, it can cause havoc with your season. On the one hand, you want to keep the show running as long as you can. On the other hand, you have already committed to closing it on a certain date and bringing in your next show.

In addition, you must consider your subscribers. They have bought tickets, expecting to see "X" number of shows during your season. Chances are, they have stuck with you through the flops. Once all of your subscribers have seen the hit, they want you to move on to your next production.

It can be a sticky problem. A colossal hit show devastated a dinner theater I know. It had spent years building up a substantial subscriber base, by offering five shows each season. One year it produced a gigantic—and I mean that in every sense of the word—hit. Rather than close the show down after its six weeks' scheduled run, the producer kept it running—and running—and running. For two and a half years! It was wonderful while it lasted, but, by the time it finally closed, the company had lost all its subscribers.

That's the problem with being locked into one space.

Of course, it's a happy problem that most producers would kill to have. Sometimes you can remedy the situation by moving the hit to another rented facility (assuming one is available in your town). Then you just go on with your season. However, this is risky. Audiences may become confused and not follow the hit to its new home—at least not without a lot of expensive advertising. In addition, moving a show is cumbersome, and it can cost a lot of money. It is not a simple decision.

Nevertheless, if you decide to take a long-term lease for your company, here are the factors to consider:

LEASE AN ESTABLISHED VENUE

If an already-established venue is available, this may be the most desirable solution. Out-of-date and rundown movie theaters are often available for this purpose. Some of these are architecturally significant facilities from the golden age of movie palaces. Often they need work, but their owners are anxious to move these money-draining properties off their balance sheets. Good deals are frequently available.

In recent years, large suburban malls, containing movie megaplexes, have decimated the local bijou and the adjoining downtown business strip. Many communities would welcome a theater company that wishes to renovate the bijou. Such a performing arts center often spurs redevelopment. As a result, municipalities may offer you aid in the form of tax increment financing, direct grants, low-cost loans, or other incentives.

It's also possible to galvanize the community into supporting you, particularly if the theater you've chosen has architectural or historic significance to the town. There are always arts-minded natives who look for projects like these, especially if the town lacks a performing arts facility. Don't sell these people short. Often, they can provide you with an incredible amount of help.

In one community, for instance, citizens rallied to save an Art Deco movie palace that had been a fixture of downtown life since the 1920s. The owners wanted to close the theater. By coincidence, a theater company from a nearby town had lost its lease and was seeking other facilities. It couldn't afford the movie palace on its own. So the locals organized their own nonprofit corporation. City Hall pitched in some help, too. The result: The nonprofit took over the movie palace and leased it to the theater company.

Investigate similar opportunities in your community. Often, all it takes is a little vision and a lot of enthusiasm.

RENOVATED SPACE

If an established venue is not available or is too costly for your needs, consider seeking a space you can modify to your exact specifications.

Theaters can—and do—exist in all kinds of locations besides traditional auditoriums. Church basements, old barns, retail stores, banquet halls, park district fieldhouses, and public library conference rooms are just some of the kinds of spaces in which theaters are often found.

REHEARSAL SPACE

In addition to performance space, you need rehearsal space. It may be desirable to rent space elsewhere for this purpose. Rehearsal space is less costly than performance space. Obviously, it becomes more cost-effective to hold the early weeks of your rehearsals in the less expensive space and move the company into the performance space in the later weeks, especially once the sets and props arrive. You will hold technical rehearsals in the performance space, usually in the last days before your first public performance.

Rehearsal space may be available in any number of locations. In communities that support theater, there are often many places available for rehearsal. (In New York City, for example, the area around Times Square contains so much rehearsal space, it's a mini-industry by itself.)

Many venues exist solely for the purpose of providing rehearsal space. However, space may also be available from dance studios, television broadcasters, film studios, park district fieldhouses, and public library conference rooms.

Rehearsal space is usually available for rental by the hour, day, or week. Terms lasting for several weeks can also be arranged.

Agreements tend to be informal licenses. Written contracts are rare and, ordinarily, not necessary. The producer simply reserves the time he requires, and the company shows up at the designated location. Some spaces may demand a deposit, particularly when the company expects to work there for a long period of time. However, this is not common.

The producer's main concerns here are straightforward. Is the space licensed for rehearsal use? (Rehearsal spaces are not usually also licensed for public performances.) Does the management maintain adequate security to protect persons and property, especially from outsiders wandering in off the streets? Is the space covered by adequate public liability insurance? (Performers, especially dancers, often suffer injuries during rehearsals. While some of this goes with the territory, the producer does not want to become liable for injuries caused by actions that are clearly the fault of the rehearsal space. For instance, a dancer may slip and fall on a newly washed floor.)

The amount of space the producer needs is dictated by the size of the show. A small cast comedy may require only one room. In the early weeks, musicals are usually rehearsed in separate units—the dancers in one space, the chorus in another, musicians in still another, and the principals in another room.

COMMERCIAL LEASES

If you decide to lease a storefront or industrial property, which you then intend to renovate into your performing space, there are a number of special terms to include in the lease that are unique to theater.

Make it clear in the lease that your purpose and intention for leasing the space is to utilize it as a theater, open to the public for performances, and all purposes in connection therewith.

Since you intend to renovate the space to suit your purposes, you will need the landlord's consent. In this respect, you should detail, in your lease, the specific scope, scale, and kind of renovations you are contemplating.

Herein lies a dilemma. Before you can determine whether the space is suitable for your proposed renovations, you may need to commission an engineering and architectural study of the property. Such a study may take time. It may also be expensive. All the same, it would not be wise to commit to a lease without knowing, up front, both whether the property can be renovated and what the estimated costs are expected to be.

However, few landlords are willing to remain in limbo for an indefinite period of time while you complete your analysis. The landlord's expenses of maintaining the space—even though it may be vacant—go on. She wants to generate revenue as soon as possible.

You do not have a binding agreement with the landlord until both of you have executed the written lease. You must also give her consideration—in other words, money. Until that time, you are free to commit to a different location and the landlord is free to lease to a different tenant.

Depending on demand for the space, you should be able to persuade the landlord to give you a modest period of time to obtain your study. However, her verbal promise is not binding.

There are two ways to handle this situation:

> *1. You may have to take a brief option on the space. With an option, you pay the landlord money to refrain from renting the space to anyone else for a certain agreed-upon period of time, to allow you to complete your study. The money is not refundable if you do not take the space. However, the landlord may be willing to apply the option money toward your payments under the lease, if you do take the space.*

> *2. The better alternative is to commit to the lease, making it conditioned upon the satisfactory results of your engineering study. This binds both parties to each other.*

You may have to define in your contract exactly what kinds of results you will accept. For example, the study must show the costs of renovating shall not exceed "X" number of dollars. You must also establish a time limit by which you must obtain the study and make a decision.

If the results of the study do not meet the specifications to which you and the landlord have agreed, you may withdraw from the lease without liability to the landlord. In addition, you will be entitled to a refund of your security deposit and any other money you may have paid her.

Remember, however, that there are limits to what a study can show. It is a fact of renovating life that you really don't know what you will find in a property until you actually start tearing it apart. There are often "surprises" that even the most comprehensive study could not have uncovered. These may turn out to be quite expensive. Therefore, regardless of the estimated costs of renovation that your engineers quote you, be prepared for additional expenses for "surprises."

Once you know the kind of renovations the property will require, you must provide the landlord with your detailed plans. If the renovations are to be extensive, especially involving structural components, you may need the services of an architect and engineer who are experienced in theater design. The landlord does not have to agree to your modifications, yet you need her consent before you can do any work.

LEASE SAFEGUARDS. In your lease, build safeguards against your landlord's simply being petulant. Prior to signing the lease, provide her with written specifications. Attach a list of all the modifications to which she has agreed to your final lease. Ask her to sign it, thus making her consent part of your agreement. Attach your architect's plans and have the landlord sign off on these also.

Include special language to the landlord's consent clause, as follows: "Consent shall not be unreasonably withheld." This protects against the landlord arbitrarily withholding consent.

It would be wise also to include a mechanism whereby you can obtain the landlord's consent to "necessary modifications that arise after the parties have entered into the lease." This clause covers you for the "surprises" and additional structural problems that were not readily apparent during the initial study. If such matters arise during the actual renovations, you may need the landlord's consent to deal with them.

In an ideal world, the landlord might give you a blanket consent in the original lease to deal with after-lease problems. Understandably, from her viewpoint, she may not wish to give you such broad discretion, especially when neither side knows what may be coming. Therefore, I would press to elicit after-lease consent. Again, specify that "consent shall not be unreasonably withheld."

LIMITED MARKET. Keep in mind that you are converting a space that, in its present form, might have a broad market. Once you modify it into a space for theatrical performances, it will likely have a limited market. The landlord is very justified in placing severe restrictions on you.

She would be justifiably concerned about the market for her space once you vacate the premises. A landlord may, because of the market conditions existing today, consent to your use of her space as a theater. But she may not want to be in the theater business as long as she owns the property. Once you vacate, she may demand that you restore the property to its original condition and use. These will be expenses you will have to bear at that time.

The landlord may further be concerned about your financial ability or willingness to undertake these expenses at a time that is off in the future. She may, justifiably, require that you put up either an additional security deposit or bond to guarantee that you will restore her property when you leave.

BUILDING CODE REQUIREMENTS. You and the landlord have an interest in renovating the space according to local building code requirements. This often means all work must be performed by union laborers and supervised by licensed and bonded architects and contractors. Local building codes are often tough on theaters. Compliance may be difficult and require structural changes and additional components (such as fire doors) that will add to your costs. Both parties should include terms in their contract that all work will be performed in compliance with local ordinances, using the appropriate designated materials. The party doing the work should obtain the necessary permits.

LANDLORD ASSISTANCE. It is customary in commercial leasing for landlords to assist in some of the renovations. This may mean performing or paying for some work herself or giving the tenant a rent concession. However, this usually occurs when space is being readied for retailers. Landlords will only assist you, the producer, if you commit to a long-term lease.

A theater is a unique operation. Whether your landlord will help out depends upon how much space you are leasing, the term of the lease, and demand for the space. It never hurts to ask. But don't be surprised if she turns you down.

If you are a nonprofit, often you can obtain government and foundation aid for just this purpose. Don't overlook this potential source of funding.

MARQUEE. A marquee is the most cost-effective way to advertise your show, as well as identify your location to patrons. Your landlord must understand that it is an essential component of your operations. It is the equivalent of a commercial sign for a retail business. Landlords may want the right to approve the location, size, format, and design of your marquee. You can give her this right, but make sure you restrict it as severely as you can. Of course, your marquee must comply with local zoning ordinances.

ASSIGNMENT AND SUBLETTING

If you want to leave before your lease expires, you may want to assign your rights and obligations under the lease to a new tenant. (Assignment also occurs if you sell the controlling stock in your corporation or interest in a partnership to another.)

In an assignment, the new tenant assumes your obligations under the lease to the landlord for the remainder of its term. This gets you off the hook. If the assignee (the new tenant) does not pay his rent, damages the property, or otherwise breaches the lease, that is between him and the landlord.

In a sublease, however, you find another tenant to lease part or all of your space. In essence, you become the landlord to the new tenant (subtenant). You remain responsible to your landlord under the terms of your lease, including the rent. If the subtenant does not pay you or the landlord, that is your problem. You still owe your landlord. If the subtenant otherwise violates any conditions under the lease—let's say, makes alterations without the owner's consent—you, not the subtenant, are responsible. Most leases prohibit subleasing and assignment without the landlord's consent. The landlord has a vested interest in whether the subtenant or assignee is financially responsible and whether his operations are appropriate to the property. Landlords cannot "unreasonably" withhold consent. Even if, at the outset of your lease, you do not contemplate subleasing or assigning your space, it is wise to clearly and specifically define in your original lease what constitutes a "reasonable" objection on the landlord's part.

ASSIGNMENT AND SUBLETTING VERSUS LICENSING. Now, this may put you on the flip side of our earlier discussion relating to renting or leasing an existing space for a single show or series of shows. You may be the owner or original tenant of a performance venue that you are seeking to license to another producer.

Make sure your lease with your landlord does not confuse such an arrangement with a sublease or assignment. Insert particular language that gives you the right to so license your facilities. In most instances, all you are doing is licensing your space for a single show or series of shows. Even if the show develops into a long run of years, you are not necessarily subleasing or assigning. In fact, in this kind of situation, you don't want to be put in the position of sublessor or assignor to the producer who takes over your space.

This becomes a gray area in which you must use care, particularly if the producer to whom you are turning over your facilities wants to use it for a prolonged period of time. Are you merely licensing your space for a long-run production? Or are you, in fact, subleasing or assigning?

The intention of all the parties will be the controlling factor. The duration must be secondary and perhaps even of negligible weight. To produce a show that runs for years is the dream of most producers.

Suppose you license your facility to producer Charles Grippo for the production of his show *Bedroom Follies*. The license is for the "run of the play." *Bedroom Follies* proves to be a colossal success, with a run of several years likely. (We should both be so lucky.) Although the duration of your license to me will now extend well into the future, both of us intended only an ordinary license. I didn't expect to take over your lease obligations and you did not expect to transfer them to me. Neither of us intended either a sublease or an assignment. When the show closes, I must take out the physical production and the space reverts to you.

I would make it clear in our written agreement that we intend a mere license, for the run of the play. I would further state that "nothing contained within this agreement shall be intended or construed to create a landlord-tenant relationship, sublease, or assignment of any existing leases." For good measure, I would also deny that our intention is to create a partnership or joint venture arrangement between us.

This benefits both of us. I am not taking over your lease. I am not a tenant. Therefore, I am not subject to the obligations (or protections) of the landlord-tenant laws. By the same token, you are not my landlord. Therefore, you do not have the obligations (or protections) of the landlord-tenant laws.

TAKE BACK. A "take back" clause is common in commercial leases. It is most often applied to large tenants. Therefore, if you are a large theater company, your landlord may insist upon including it in the lease.

Suppose you are interested in subleasing your space to another tenant, ABC Corporation. You negotiate terms of the sublease with ABC. Then you present your landlord with either (a) a written sublease signed by ABC; or (b) written notice of the terms of the sublease. Under the "take back" clause, the landlord has the right to recapture ("take back") the space by terminating your lease and re-leasing to a new tenant—presumably at a higher rent.

Armed with the information your sublease agreement has provided, the landlord can determine the current market rate for the space as well as the kinds of tenants who might be interested.

By terminating your lease, the landlord is relieving you of any further obligations under it. However, remember that ABC was to have taken over the space from you by virtue of your continued right to it. Once the landlord terminates your lease, ABC will have no rights to the space, unless it negotiates a new lease with the landlord.

If you sign a lease with ABC and the landlord subsequently terminates your lease and recaptures the space, you could be liable to ABC for damages. Therefore, make any agreement with ABC conditioned upon the landlord's "take back" clause.

And when, in the original lease, you consent to a "take back" clause, put a time limit on when the landlord must exercise the clause. For instance, give the landlord seven business days after written notice of the terms of the sublease to either exercise the "take back" clause or "waive it." If the landlord waives the clause, she gives up her right to take back the property. This permits you to proceed with the sublease. In either event, the landlord must do something within seven days. In this way, you and ABC do not remain in limbo for a long time until the landlord makes a decision.

CONTENT RESTRICTIONS. A landlord is justified in knowing how you intend to use her space. Merely describing your intended use as "for the purpose of presenting live stage performances to the public" may not be sufficient. The issue arises: "What kind of stage performances?"

Presenting your version of *American Buffalo* is not the same as presenting *Harvey*, which is also not the same as presenting *Oh, Calcutta!* Yet all are live stage performances. For that matter, so is presenting a line of topless dancers before a male audience.

The landlord has a legitimate concern in knowing what kind of theater company you are and what kind of content you intend to present in her premises.

The most obvious example occurs if you are leasing a church hall. Your shows must be suitable for presentation in those surroundings. Obviously, this places restrictions on the language, themes, and content that will be permissible. *Harvey* may be fine, but *American Buffalo* probably will not be. And, unless you've found an extremely liberal church, *Oh, Calcutta!* most certainly will be out of the question.

Even secular landlords may have legitimate concerns about the kinds of material a producer may be contemplating. This may have to do with making sure the theater company is an appropriate mix with other, existing tenants. It may be desirable to put a theater company into a strip mall, with a barber shop, a deli, and perhaps a takeout pizza place. But if the strip mall caters to a family business, the landlord may again demand restrictions on the content the company can present.

LOCATION DETERMINES CONTENT. Location also plays a factor. What is the character of the neighborhood surrounding the proposed facility? If it is comprised mostly of businesses, there may be fewer restrictions on content. If the residents are upscale, artsy, liberal, and for the most part, well educated, a theater company most likely can present progressive and controversial subject matter. On the other hand, if the facility is in a conservative suburb, nudity and raw language may be unsuitable.

Of course, there is the viewpoint of "wanting to shake up the status quo." Shock for the sake of shock. Bring controversy into the staid neighborhood of churchgoing people. Sometimes it works. More often, the controversy back-fires. The landlord may terminate your lease. If enough voters complain, local officials will find a way to shut you down, even if they have to send the build-ing inspectors in to cite you for every possible violation in your physical plant. That's reality, folks.

Matching content to the neighborhood is also just good marketing. You will probably draw much of your audience from the surrounding community. It just makes sense to give "the people what they want."

Therefore, before signing any lease, it is best to discuss in detail with the potential landlord the kind of material you wish to produce. Not all landlords are knowledgeable about the theater. Be specific about your intentions. In addition to creating a forthright relationship with your landlord from the beginning, you may find that she is able to clue you in to factors about the neighborhood that aid in your marketing. For instance, if you are planning to present children's theater, she may know of organizations—like parents' asso-ciations—that would distribute your flyers.

In any case, include in the written lease all agreements you make regard-ing content. This may be as broad as, "There shall be no restrictions on the content of the material the producer presents in the space." Or it may be quite specific: "Nudity in productions is forbidden."

Remember that community zoning and licensing laws may restrict the content you can present.

ZONING AND LICENSING CONTINGENCIES. Before signing a lease, it is imperative to determine whether the proposed space may be used as a performance venue, under local zoning and licensing laws. This information is readily available from the building and zoning department of your local city hall.

If the municipal authorities tell you the property is not zoned for use as a performance facility, you have two choices. The first is to find a different space that is already zoned for the performing arts. However, if you are set on the particular space, your second choice is to seek to change the zoning.

Be aware that this latter step involves the services of an attorney, may be time-consuming, may require extensive remodeling of the property, and may be very expensive. If you are willing to face all those hurdles (and you have the resources to do so), it is essential to take two steps immediately.

First, you must hold informal discussions with the municipal authorities to determine if they are willing to rezone the property in the first place. If the property is in a heavily residential neighborhood, there may be objections to rezoning it for theatrical purposes. It may alter the character of the community. Residents may not want the traffic and crowd problems a theater might bring.

Second, if the local officials are willing to consider rezoning the property, you must find out what you will have to do to rezone. Although bureaucrats are loath to commit themselves in advance of seeing your plans, they may give you an educated opinion. This will enable you to calculate a timetable for when to expect rezoning. (Add additional time to whatever schedule the officials suggest; there are invariably delays, particularly if it is possible the nearby residents or businesses may object.)

With the timetable in mind, negotiate a "rezoning" contingency into your proposed lease. This clause makes the lease conditioned upon obtaining the proper zoning. If the rezoning does not come through, you can declare the lease null and void. You can obtain a refund of any deposits you have given the landlord. This gives you an escape clause so you are not bound to the lease in case you can't get the appropriate zoning for your theater.

The timetable is important. Neither you nor the landlord wants to wait indefinitely for a zoning decision. The landlord cannot rent her property to another tenant while she awaits the results of your zoning application. A timetable sets a deadline, so both parties know what to expect and when. In addition, if you show the landlord you have held earnest discussions with the zoning board and you have constructed a reasonable timetable based on those discussions, she is more likely to agree to a contingency.

A possible simple contingency clause might read as follows:

It is agreed and understood that, at present, 125 W. Lakeport is not in an area zoned for the use for which Holiday Road Theater Company desires to lease the premises. This agreement is conditioned upon Holiday Road's obtaining rezoning of the property for use as a two-hundred-seat live-performance venue open to the public within sixty days after the date thereof. Holiday Road shall use its best efforts to obtain said rezoning. If, by the expiration of sixty days, said rezoning is denied, Holiday Road may declare this agreement null and void and obtain full and immediate refund of all deposits paid.

In other words, if sixty days go by and the zoning authorities have not given their permission to use the space for performances, Holiday Road has the right to pull out of the deal.

Contingency clauses are the best way to protect yourself over events that bear on your ability to operate but over which you do not have control.

Make use of them.

HOLDOVER. If your written lease expires and you continue to occupy the property, you are a "holdover" tenant. The landlord may begin proceedings with the court to evict you (unless the lease contained an option to renew). However, if the landlord continues to take rent from you, both of you may be renewing the lease for another term. Many leases provide that, in this situation, you are considered a month-to-month tenant, and the landlord may increase or even double your rent.

Examine these clauses carefully. They are often preprinted "boilerplate." They are negotiable.

SECURITY DEPOSIT. The purpose of a security deposit in a commercial lease is the same as in a residential lease. A security deposit is a sum of money put up by the tenant to the landlord, which guarantees the tenant will meet his financial obligations under his tenancy. It may also guarantee that when he vacates the property, he will restore it to its original condition and remove his possessions therefrom. If the tenant fails to do so, the landlord may deduct whatever he owes from the deposit before refunding any part of it back.

Many communities have passed landlord-tenant ordinances that govern security deposits, how they may be used, and under what circumstances they may be forfeited or refunded. However, almost all such ordinances apply only to residential leases and not commercial leases. This is because communities assume business people are knowledgeable and sophisticated enough to negotiate their own protections into their leases. Therefore, you are on your own here.

Negotiate specific conditions under which the landlord may claim deductions. Insert a clause giving you the option, upon notice from the landlord, to repair any alleged damages. Demand that the landlord provide you with the actual bills for the repairs. Require that the landlord refund your deposit (or provide the repair bills) within a certain specific period of time—say, thirty to forty-five days after you vacate the premises.

The landlord may balk at these conditions. There are no laws to force her to accept your terms. If she refuses, you have to choose between her property and finding another space.

OPTIONS. An *option to renew* gives you the right to renew the lease. This may be for the same terms or for different terms than those specified in the original lease.

An *option to expand* allows you to expand your operations, to help you deal with success. (Every play you present is a smash hit and audiences are clamoring for your tickets, right?) Sometimes, you have to wait until the present lease expires to exercise this option. However, you can also negotiate the right to expand during the term of your lease. Of course, this depends on whether your landlord has additional space available for you.

An *option to cancel* is a very valuable right, if you can get it. It allows you to cancel during the term of your lease if your revenues do not reach a certain dollar amount. It may also allow you to terminate your lease if a more suitable space becomes available in a different location. It is often very, very tough to get this clause, but, by all means, go for it. If the market is soft or you are a very desirable tenant, you might get it.

LANDLORD'S RULES AND REGULATIONS. Every landlord has the right to impose rules and regulations on all of her tenants, for the good of all. Often, leases make reference to rules and regulations, requiring tenants to obey them. However, they are seldom listed explicitly in leases. Rules and regulations may change, as time goes on and circumstances warrant. All the owner must ordinarily do is give you the appropriate notice of them.

At the outset, before you sign your lease, ask for a copy of the current rules and regulations. At least you'll know what you are up against.

PURCHASING SPACE

Purchasing your own space is a wonderful luxury, if you can afford it. Negotiating the purchase contract involves many of the same considerations as in leasing.

For instance, you must make any purchase contract contingent upon obtaining the appropriate zoning and licensing from the municipal authorities. Also provide a condition for obtaining a study to determine the cost and feasibility of any renovations you may have to undertake to make the property suitable for your intended use.

MORTGAGE CONTINGENCY

Chances are, you will need to finance your purchase by taking out a mortgage on the property. You will need time to obtain the mortgage.

Bear in mind that obtaining a mortgage to develop a theater is a tough proposition. It is a very specialized market in which few lenders participate.

In truth, you should begin your search for a mortgage even before you look for a theater. Your own banker may not be willing to make the loan, but she may steer you to someone who can. You may have to knock on a lot of doors before you find a lender who will even consider your application.

You may also talk to other theater companies in the area to ascertain the names of their lenders.

Another possibility is to seek out wealthy patrons of the arts, who may consider making a private loan.

Once you find a potential lender, ask for the exact requirements for making such a loan. The more you know in advance, the better you can structure your purchase to satisfy the bank.

When you are ready to sign a contract with the seller of a suitable space, make sure the contract is conditioned upon obtaining mortgage financing. Here's why: Unless you condition the contract upon obtaining a mortgage loan, you are obligated to complete the purchase, regardless of whether you get a mortgage. In other words, the contract is treated as a cash sale. You must come up with the cash, regardless of how you get it, by the date of closing specified in the contract.

By making the contract contingent upon mortgage financing, you are giving yourself an out. If, for any reason, you cannot obtain a loan, you can walk away from the contract and obtain a refund of your earnest money. (*Earnest money* is the cash deposit you give the seller at the time when you sign the contract, to bind the deal.)

A typical mortgage contingency clause may read as follows:

This contract is conditioned upon the purchaser obtaining a firm commitment within sixty days hereof for a mortgage in the amount of [X] dollars, at an interest rate not to exceed [Y]%, amortized over thirty years. If purchaser has not obtained same and notified seller in writing within the said time period, this agreement may, at the option of the purchaser, be declared null and void, and all moneys returned to the purchaser instantly.

This means that:

1. You have sixty days to obtain the mortgage.

2. "[X]" dollars represents the minimum amount of mortgage financing you need and will accept. If your lender says it will give you a mortgage for less than [X] dollars, you can refuse to proceed with the deal.

3. The interest rate cannot exceed [Y]%. Again, if the lender gives you a mortgage rate higher than [Y], you can walk away from the contract.

4. The mortgage must be amortized over thirty years. A mortgage that is amortized over less than thirty years gives you another out.

At the time when you negotiate the contract with the seller, you specify the minimum terms contained in items 1 through 4 above that you will accept.

Of course, if any of the terms do not match your specifications, you are still free to accept the nonconforming terms and proceed with the contract. It's your choice.

Be very careful about time limits and notices. Remember, the contingency called for you to notify the seller, in writing, within sixty days if you have not obtained the mortgage. Many people get tripped up by these clauses, both in commercial and residential mortgage contingencies. They fail to give the proper notices, on time, and, as a result, give the seller the right to hold them to the contract as if they had actually obtained the mortgage.

Keep track of the days. If you are approaching the deadline and your lender still has not given you a firm commitment for a mortgage, you have two choices:

1. When the deadline arrives, notify the seller in writing that you have not obtained the mortgage financing and you wish to declare the contract null and void.

2. Ask the seller for an extension, the duration of which depends on what your bank thinks it will need to complete the processing of your application. (The seller need not give you the extension, though she might if the time period is not unreasonable and she is anxious to sell.)

Do not sit back and do nothing. You will get into a lot of trouble with that approach.

Whether the producer chooses to license space on a show-by-show basis; lease and renovate a space on a long-term lease; or purchase a permanent home for his company, it is important for him to make sure the space is suitable for the kind of productions he intends to present. Before beginning his search, the producer must carefully evaluate his short- and long-term plans and take these into consideration when he negotiates any agreements for his performance space.

CHAPTER 3

Licensing Plays

Once you have organized your company and arranged for a performance space, it is time to select the show you will do.

There are three ways of finding shows:

1. License well-known scripts.

2. Present original plays—world premieres or second productions.

3. Create your own material either through commissions or company-generated pieces.

We will deal with options 2 and 3 in chapters 4 and 5, respectively. For now, let's concentrate on licensing well-known scripts.

There are several methods of finding a well-known play, and all of them are equally valid. The simplest way is to select plays with which you are already familiar. If you are seriously interested in theater, you already have favorite shows, types of shows, or a favorite playwright. Perhaps you even own published editions of the scripts.

Another way is to attend as much theater as you can. When you see a play you would like to produce with your own company, take note of it.

Finally, you can search publishers' catalogs for shows that may fit your needs. All of the major play publishers issue catalogs on an annual basis, which list the shows they represent, including new additions to their lists. Each entry describes the play in one or more paragraphs, together with its cast size (broken down by the number of women, men, and children) and technical requirements. Often the amateur royalty fees for the particular show are also listed. (We'll discuss royalties shortly.) If you are not familiar with the show, yet it sounds intriguing, you can purchase a copy of the script from the publisher.

In selecting a script, there are several questions to consider:

1. Does my company have the resources to present this show successfully?

2. Does it fit with our artistic goals?

3. Is it financially feasible for us to produce this show?

4. Are the rights to this script available to us?

5. From whom do we license the rights?

Only you can answer the first three questions. The fourth and fifth questions are easily answered with a modest amount of effort.

LICENSING AGENTS

Most published scripts are represented by a licensing agent who acts on behalf of the copyright holder, who is usually the author, or, if she is dead, her estate.

There are usually two kinds of published scripts. The first is a trade edition, which is the kind of hardcover or paperback book you might buy at your favorite bookstore. It is printed on good quality paper. It may contain photographs from the Broadway production. It is the kind of book you'd display on your bookshelf in your living room.

The second kind is the acting edition, which is usually less expensive than the trade edition. It has a plain cover. It often contains staging suggestions instead of production photographs. It is printed on cheaper paper. Usually the publisher of the acting edition also acts as licensing agent for the script.

In either case, look on the reverse side of the title page. Here you'll find the copyright notice, followed by legal boilerplate that warns you not to attempt any kind of production or copying without obtaining permission first. Next, you'll find the paragraph that tells you what you want to know:

The amateur performance rights to *Sex Marks the Spot* are controlled by XYZ, Inc.

This information will be followed by the licensor's address. Then, a few lines down, another paragraph will read as follows:

For all other rights, contact the author's agent, 15% Incorporated, New York, N.Y.

Unless you are seeking the movie rights or are planning a major Broadway production, this last bit does not affect you. Instead, you will deal with XYZ, Inc.

In fact, most non-musicals that have run on Broadway or at the leading regional theaters are represented by one of several licensing agents. The biggest ones are Samuel French, Dramatists Play Service, Dramatic Publishing Company, and Broadway Plays. There are also a number of smaller agencies. Some of them deal with particular niches—such as high school or church plays. (For a complete list of the major play licensors and their contact information, see appendix A.)

Play licensing agents are not the same as the author's agent. They are publishers who act as subagents for the playwright in all markets except First Class Productions (Broadway) and film rights. These exceptions are handled by the playwright's personal agent. Concordantly, the playwright's agent, with few exceptions, does not ordinarily deal with anything other than First Class productions and film rights. (The money isn't worth his time and effort.) So, to keep our discussion simple, when we say *licensing agent*, we are referring to publisher-licensor, as opposed to the playwright's agent.

Licensing agents greatly simplify your life. The procedures at all the agencies are the same. The agents can supply you with scripts. They can offer you insights and valuable tips on how other companies have staged the particular show and have solved particularly knotty technical or budgetary problems. They are used to dealing with all kinds of requests—even unusual ones. With one or two inquiries, they can tell you whether the rights to a show you want to present are available to you. They will quote you royalties based on the kind of theater company you operate. They act as buffers between you and the author.

In addition, licensing agents are easily accessible by phone, snail mail, e-mail, and fax. Playwrights usually aren't. The agents are business enterprises who work out of a central location, and they are well experienced with dealing with your concerns.

LICENSE APPLICATIONS

The procedure for licensing a show is quite simple. You submit a written application on a form supplied by the agent. You tell the agent which show you want to do, followed by the dates and number of performances you are contemplating. Give basic information about your theater:

1. Seating capacity;

2. Admission fee;

3. Amateur or professional (you are professional if you pay your actors, amateur if you don't);

4. Number of copies of the acting edition of the script you will need to purchase.

The agents will notify you by return mail whether the rights are available.

But, you protest, the play is in the catalog. Doesn't that mean that the rights are automatically available? Not by a long shot. Agents often list new shows in their catalogs as soon as they obtain the rights. This is to let you know they will be representing the script when it becomes available to your market.

The play may still be in its initial run on Broadway. A national tour may be planned to pass through your town. Another local presenter may have beaten you to the exclusive rights. In the case of an older play, a major national revival may be in the works and the copyright holder may have withdrawn the rights. Any one of these scenarios is possible. If you are denied the rights, you can ask the reason.

CAUTIONARY NOTE!

Always inquire about the rights available for your theater before you hold auditions, expend any money, advertise a production to the media and the public, or otherwise begin production. The agents are not required to license a show to you just because you asked. And they are not responsible for any expenses you've incurred or embarrassment you've suffered because you've jumped the gun and promoted a show without first nailing down the rights.

ROYALTY RATES

Assuming the rights are available, the agents will quote you a royalty rate for your production. These royalties will be quoted in writing, as agents do not give verbal quotes over the phone. An inquiry into availability and royalties does not bind you to present the show. When you receive the royalty schedule, you are free to say, "Thanks, but no thanks."

Since royalties for previously produced shows are similar to royalties for original works, I will defer further discussion until chapter 4.

LICENSING AGREEMENTS

In addition to the royalty quote, the agencies will send you a license agreement. If you choose to produce the show, you must sign and return the agreement, together with your check for the guaranteed royalties, not later than ten days before your first performance before an audience.

Licensing agreements are uniform from agent to agent. Let's examine one.

The agreement states that the agent is giving you a revocable license to present the show on the dates and for the number of performances you have requested. (Remember, the agent is acting under the authority from the copyright holder.) In return, you undertake certain obligations:

*1. **Royalties**: You must pay the quoted royalties. As I indicated, guaranteed royalties are due at least ten days before your first performance. If you owe additional royalties above the guarantee, you must pay these on a weekly basis.*

*2. **Author Credit**: You must give proper authorship credit on all your programs, advertising, publicity, posters, and other promotional materials. (For more information, see chapter 4.)*

*3. **No Changes in Script**: You must present the play exactly as written—you must stick to the text. This is a pitfall for many producers, even experienced ones. Sometimes the problem arises because of artistic interpretation. Virtually every play, even if presented exactly according to the text, lends itself to a wide variety of interpretations. An actor in one production may recite a line of dialogue with a different emotion, speech pattern, or emphasis than an actor in another production. Directors are also notorious for ignoring stage directions and inventing their own. This is one of those gray areas for which there are no right answers. It is sufficient to say that you have met this obligation as long as you have affirmatively presented the author's material as he or she wrote it. If you still wish to make changes to the script, the appropriate procedure is discussed in the next section.*

*4. **No Recordings**: No recordings, video or audio, are permitted of the show (see chapter 4).*

*5. **Licensing Agent Credit**: You must give due credit to the licensing agent in your advertising and programs. This stipulation is satisfied by including the line, "Presented by special arrangement with XYZ, Inc."*

*6. **Copyright**: You cannot do anything to impair the copyright of the show.*

*7. **Extensions**: If your production is a hit and you wish to extend, agents are happy to accommodate you. An extension means more royalties to the author and more commissions to the agents. Just be sure you put in your request in time for them to send you an amended application.*

If you must cancel your production for any reason—poor ticket sales, loss of your lead actor, lack of funds—notify the agents at once. Do not delay. Once the agents disburse your advance payments to the copyright holders, they cannot give you a refund. That money is lost, regardless of the circumstances.

CHANGE REQUESTS

Sometimes artists attempt to create their own personal vision of the material. They rearrange dialogue, omit scenes or incidents, change characters radically, or even attempt to transpose locations. Unless they obtain permission first, they are violating the author's copyright and jeopardizing their license to present the show.

One director had a radically different vision of the John Steinbeck story *Of Mice and Men*. As originally written, it is a story of two itinerant farm laborers in California in the 1930s. My friend wanted to update the play, making the men homeless in 1990s New York City. However, before he booked a theater, auditioned actors, or notified the press, he was wise enough to seek permission first.

The licensing agents consulted the Steinbeck estate, which issued a resounding "No!" The estate was well within its rights. The only cost to the director: the price of mailing his detailed proposal to the agents—a first-class postage stamp.

Recently, a nationally known regional theater found itself in hot water over the show *Side by Side by Sondheim*, a revue of some of the works of Stephen Sondheim. According to *Backstage*, the theater weekly, the artistic director changed the order of the songs and added other songs not in the revue. He also incorporated material out of a recent biography of Sondheim without obtaining permission from its author. Neither Sondheim nor his agents even knew of this, much less consented.

However, in one of those quirks of fate, three of Sondheim's closest friends attended the opening night: actress Lauren Bacall, producer Harold

Prince, and Joy Abbott (widow of director George Abbott). They notified Sondheim, whose licensing agents shut down the show and levied a hefty fine against the theater.

The moral: present your production exactly as written.

If you wish to make changes to the script, however, you must prepare a specific, detailed proposal, outlining exactly what changes you wish to make. Support your proposed changes with solid reasons. (Do not criticize the play or the author.) Submit this proposal, in writing, to the agents, with a request that they pass it on to the author or her estate.

Give yourself plenty of time. Don't wait until the day before your opening. It may take months to receive a response. The author may not be easy to reach. If she is preparing another show, your request will go to the bottom of her "to do" pile.

Actually, the best time to submit your proposal is concurrent with your request for availability of rights and royalty quotes. This should be months before you actually intend to present the show.

When you receive the playwright's response, you are legally and morally bound to honor it. Don't assume you know better than she what is best for her script. If the author says, "No," that means no. She does not have to give you a reason. If you can't live with a negative response, pick another play.

If you do not receive a response and you are nearing production time, you may follow up with the agents. However, if you still don't receive a response, take that as a "No." You cannot go ahead and change the author's play, just because she has not responded.

Again, as a playwright and as a producer, I strongly discourage requests to change an author's script.

MUSICALS

The procedure for licensing a musical is not that much different from the procedure for a straight play—expect, however, that you will pay higher royalties for musicals than for straight plays.

PRODUCTION MATERIALS

With the exception of Samuel French, the major musical licensing agents do not publish and sell acting editions of the books (librettos). (A few of the smaller, niche-oriented agents do.) In fact, unless the musical has been published in a trade book edition, it's nearly impossible to purchase the book.

Instead, the musical agents will supply you with the book in manuscript form. If you wish to determine whether a show is right for you, the agents will loan you a manuscript for a limited period. The amount of perusal time you will be given varies from agent to agent. All you have to pay is postage and handling. At this time, only Tams-Witmark will also loan you the vocal score. This is the entire musical score, including songs, overture, as well as incidental and dance music, reduced to a piano arrangement. It is several hundred pages in length. The other agents will send you the vocal selections, which are the most popular songs from the show in a piano arrangement with guitar chords. (Actually, for most shows, you can buy both the published vocal scores and the vocal selections at many large music stores. Vocal scores may cost anywhere from $50 to $100.) Some agents will also loan you the original cast recordings in cassette form.

TWO ROYALTIES

If you apply to license a musical, you will be quoted two royalty fees. The first is the ordinary royalty to present the show itself. The agent deducts a commission, then sends the balance on to the authors. The second is a rental fee for the music scores, orchestrations, chorus parts, librettos, and so forth. These fees are retained by the agents, who pay to have these materials prepared. The rental fees depend on how long you will need the materials and whether you require full orchestrations or piano arrangements.

You will also pay modest charges for the cost of shipping the scripts and scores to you. Once your rental period is over, you must promptly return all of the materials, at your own expense.

CHOREOGRAPHY AVAILABLE

For many musicals, you can also license the original Broadway choreography. Some agents also provide study guides, videotape discussions with the authors, and such publicity materials as T-shirts with the show logo. Check with the agent for availability of these products for the individual show.

A complete list of the major musical agents is included in appendix A.

CHAPTER 4

Producing Original Plays

Imagine that one day an original manuscript crosses your desk that absolutely knocks your socks off. It's the best play you've read since *Death of a Salesman*. The author is unknown and the script has never been produced. You are euphoric. Even as you read the last pages of the manuscript, you begin thinking what it would mean for you and your company if you produced it.

For you, there would be the prestige of discovering the next Arthur Miller. It might even lead to a job at a top talent agency or with a Broadway producer.

For your theater, this might be the breakthrough hit you've been struggling to find. Today your company is a small nonprofit, struggling to make ends meet, desperate for any publicity you can get. You are always in need of funds, but they are hard to come by. But if you produce this play, word of mouth is sure to open the floodgates. Audiences will clamor for tickets, critics will call you, and potential donors will stuff your mailbox with checks. (Everyone wants to grab the coattails of success.) Your company may even become famous.

And, of course, there is the artistic satisfaction of finding and nurturing a great new talent.

Well, okay, you've found the play. Now what do you do? You're used to dealing with the major licensing houses for plays somebody else produced first, such as recent Broadway hits. Now you must negotiate with an unknown author for the rights to an unknown masterpiece.

Unless you have to run your choice of play past a committee, call the author and license the play right away. Most unknown playwrights submit the same play to many theaters at the same time. This is made necessary because theaters are notoriously slow in reading and selecting plays. (We all know how overworked you are.) If an author mails her play to one theater at a time, she could wait a lifetime for a production. So, multiple submissions are the rule.

The problem is, several other producers may be reading that masterpiece at the same time as you. If you want the rewards of presenting the premiere production, you must act now before someone else beats you to it.

But you still need to draw up a fair contract. Fortunately, unless you're presenting a first-class production on Broadway, this isn't as much of a problem as you may think. This chapter will show you how.

(Instead of dealing directly with the author, you may have to deal with her agent. The only difference is that agents are more experienced in negotiating contracts than most playwrights. The author may be more concerned about her artistic vision, while agents tend to focus more on the financial terms.)

THE DRAMATISTS GUILD

Many playwrights belong to the Dramatists Guild. Unlike Actors' Equity, the Guild is not a labor union. This is because playwrights are ordinarily considered independent contractors, not employees. (This is different from the situation in Hollywood where film and television writers are viewed as employees. They are represented by the Writers Guild—which is a labor union.)

Instead, the Dramatists Guild is an organization, founded by playwrights, which audits royalty statements, gives business advice (to its members), publishes form contracts for use between producers and playwrights, and conducts various forums and seminars on the craft and business of writing for the theater. Its Approved Production Contract (APC) is the standardized agreement in general use on Broadway. It negotiates this contract with the League of American Theatres and Producers. (There is an APC for straight plays and another for musicals.)

Since it isn't a labor union, the Guild can't force any theater or producer to use its contracts (including the APC). However, the Guild's power is derived from its membership, which includes most of the biggest names in the theater—like Neil Simon and David Mamet. Individually, these playwrights can write their own tickets. But they have chosen to place their muscle behind the Guild, to protect their less powerful colleagues. These playwrights can choose to withhold their own works from theaters that refuse to model their contracts along the Guild's own contracts.

For a complete list of current Guild contracts, see appendix B. Only playwrights who are members of the Guild are entitled to use their contracts.

If your playwright does not belong to the Guild, you can draw up your own contract.

THE CONTRACT

Before you contact and contract the playwright, however, you must determine a myriad of factors, ranging from the payment of actors to complimentary tickets. Obviously, the producer of an amateur company cannot give the same terms as a major, equity house, and he should not expect the author to give him the same rights a large production could demand. Each of the factors discussed below must be outlined clearly in your contract with the playwright.

OPTIONS

A producer may seek to obtain an option from the author, giving the producer the exclusive right to present the play in a specific geographic territory or a specific level of production (or both), for a specific time period. An option is not the same as a full production agreement (or even a license) in which the producer guarantees the production of the play at a particular time. With an option, the producer promises only that he will *try* to begin performances in the agreed upon level of production or territory within the particular time frame.

Options are desirable when the producer is seeking to present either the world or area premiere of the play, but he is uncertain he will be able to do so. Options are unnecessary if the level of production is relatively small, such as filling a slot in a summer stock or amateur season. In those circumstances, authors want guaranteed productions, and they are unwilling to grant exclusive rights. Broadway producers, on the other hand, always take options on scripts.

The chief reason a producer may take an option on a play is the money factor. Until the producer can raise the necessary funds, he cannot guarantee he can produce the play. Another reason is that the producer may be seeking a particular star or director for the script; until he actually has the star or director under contract, he cannot make guarantees.

The producer options the play in order to sew up the exclusive rights to present it. He is contracting for the author to take the play off the market, so another producer won't present the play in competition with him. (See "Exclusivity of Run," later in this chapter.)

In exchange for the exclusive rights to present the play, the producer pays the author a fee at the outset. The author takes the play off the market in the territories she has granted the producer for the duration of the option period.

The time frame under which the producer has the rights to present the play is negotiable and depends on the producer's intentions. Authors know it takes one to two years (or more) to mount a Broadway production, so they will likely grant the producer this time period. On the other hand, it may take six months to a year to present the play at a regional theater, so the parties will agree on the time frame accordingly.

The producer may want or need additional time, especially if he is planning a substantial production (like Broadway). The parties may agree on option periods in increments. For instance, the first option period may expire in six months; the producer may want to give himself a second option period for another six months, which he may choose to exercise when the first option period expires. He may seek a third, fourth, and so forth. The parties are free to negotiate as many option periods over as much of a time frame as they desire. However, playwrights are ordinarily unwilling to take their works off the market for too long. So the overall time frame must be something both parties can accept.

A producer may also seek to mount a production at different levels. For instance, the first production might be a workshop; if that goes well, the producer may seek an option to move the show up to a regional theater mainstage production; if that works, he may want to go to Broadway. In this way, the producer can protect himself. He does not have to expend millions on a Broadway production without testing the play out first. At each successive step, he will choose either to exercise his option to take the play to the next level or simply let his rights expire.

Each time the producer exercises an option—whether because he needs more time or wants to move the production up a level—he must pay another fee. Option fees are payable at the time the producer chooses to exercise the option, not at some later date. These fees are nonrefundable. If at some point the producer chooses not to proceed further, the author retains those fees. If the producer does present the production, he may, ordinarily, recoup those fees out of the author's royalties.

If the producer fails to exercise his options at the time when they come due, his rights to present the show expire and revert back to the author. The author is free to find another producer.

It is best to negotiate the full production agreement at the time of taking the initial option. You can iron out the details at a time when both you and the author are enthusiastic about presenting the piece. If you wait until you are ready to exercise your option for a full production, either of you could hold the other over a barrel. Delays, disagreements, and numerous problems could jeopardize the production. Instead, negotiate the full production contract according to the following model.

LEVEL OF PRODUCTION

Your contract should begin by describing the kind of production the parties are contemplating—regional, summer stock, dinner theater, or community, for example. (If you are offering Broadway, you will, of course, use the Dramatists Guild APC.) The kind and level of production will determine the terms of the agreement you will negotiate.

For the purposes of our discussion, let's assume you will be presenting the world premiere of the work. Second, and all other subsequent productions (except moves from the nonprofit regional to the commercial sector), usually fall under the procedure for licensing plays, even if the script has not been published.

EQUITY OR NON-EQUITY?

It's important to note whether the actors will be paid. This is the industry standard for determining whether the company is professional or amateur. In a professional production, actors are paid. A related factor is whether the production will be a signatory to Actors' Equity contracts. If the production is "non-equity," the actors are not members of Actors' Equity. Non-equity actors can be paid, though usually not at the union rates. Sometimes actors in non-equity shows receive only a small stipend. If the actors are not paid at all, the group is amateur or community theater. And, of course, some productions are performed by school and university groups. Except as noted in the next paragraph, actors in these productions are usually not paid.

A variation is the Equity Guest Artist Agreement (GAA), under which a college, university, or community theater may engage an individual Equity actor to perform a specific role in a particular play. The Equity actor is compensated for his services.

The contract should clearly state the particular case.

SEATING CAPACITY, LOCATION, AND ATTENDANCE

The seating capacity of the performance facility must be disclosed. This may determine the kind of contract to use. (For example, the Dramatists Guild has different contracts for different sizes of production facility.) It also helps determine the size of royalties.

The location and purpose of the production may matter. The Dramatists Guild has different contracts, such as the Model League of Regional Theaters Agreement, the Small Theatre Contract (National), and a Form Licensing Agreement. These take into account the special needs and financial capabilities of the intended production.

In addition to seating capacity, if a theater has been operating any length of time, it's fairly easy to determine average attendance for the kind of play to be produced. A frothy Neil Simon type of comedy will likely draw more attendance than an absurdist Beckett piece. The producer should give the playwright an idea of what kind of attendance to expect.

ROYALTIES

Royalties may be a flat sum, a percentage of ticket sales, or a combination. Just as in dealing with licensing agencies, the amount of royalties depends on whether the company is professional or amateur.

Amateur companies ordinarily pay a flat royalty for each performance. For a well-known, full-length play, the licensing agencies charge amateurs based on seating capacities: for seating capacities of 350 or less, the fee is usually $60 for the first performance and $40 for each subsequent performance. Royalties for shorter plays are usually $25 for the first performance and $20 for subsequent performances. (Today, there is a trend towards one-acts—or "intermissionless plays"—that constitute an entire evening performance. The same length of time used to be occupied by two or three acts. For royalty purposes, such a one-act would be considered a full-length.) Higher royalties apply to theaters with seating capacities above 350.

There is no substance to the argument that an amateur company should pay an unknown author less than it would pay for a Broadway hit. Royalties are so low that it would be criminal to undercut an author merely because she is unknown.

Professional companies usually pay a guaranteed royalty against a percentage of gross ticket sales. Here, the producer pays the author a flat fee for each performance week of the run, against a percentage of ticket sales. The amounts of the flat fee and the percentage are negotiable. However, the percentage should not be less than 6 percent.

Here's how it works. Suppose the facility has a seating capacity of three hundred and the ticket price is $10. The producer plans eight performances each week for two consecutive weeks. The total potential weekly revenue is 300 x 10 x 8 = $24,000.

The contract guarantees the playwright $1,000 per week against 6 percent of ticket sales. Now, the $1,000 is nonrefundable. Whether the show sells 100 percent of the tickets or 10 percent, the playwright keeps the $1,000. (This is part of the producer's risk, just as it's also his risk to bear the costs of sets, costumes, salaries, facility rental, and so forth, even if no one comes to the show.)

Suppose, during the first week, the show plays to 90 percent capacity. So, we calculate: 90 percent of $24,000 equals $21,600; 6 percent of $21,600 equals $1,296. The producer has already paid the author $1,000, so now he owes her $296.

If the budget is hard-pressed to offer guarantees, it is borderline acceptable to ask the author to share the risk of producing the play. Instead of giving a guarantee, the producer may offer her a higher percentage of the gross—perhaps 8 or 9 or even 10 percent. The risk here is upside; if the production is a gigantic hit, the producer has committed himself to paying significantly higher royalties.

Royalties should be based on sales from all sources, including single tickets at the box office and subscription, phone, and mail sales. They should be based on the gross ticket price, not on any discounts or special promotions. Royalties are due for all performances before an audience—even free ones, such as previews for the board. (You have to pay your actors, technical crew, and so forth. Why shouldn't you also pay the author?)

Royalties should be paid to the author on a weekly basis. Commonly, royalties are paid on the Wednesday following the performance week for which they are earned.

COPYRIGHT

The copyright should always belong to the author. No exceptions.

AUTHOR COMPS AND HOUSE SEATS

An author is certainly entitled to see all performances of her show for free. At the non-equity or amateur level, she may also ask for a reasonable number of comps for friends, family, and professional attendees.

Comps are distinguishable from house seats. Comps are free and given to the artists and staff in many non-equity and regional houses. They are designed to make up for the theater's inability to pay decent salaries. Often, the artists use them to invite agents and producers who can further their careers.

House seats are the best seats in the theater. They are for the producers, theater owners, artists, and anyone else who can negotiate them into their contracts. Very common in the Broadway theater, house seats are passed on to friends, relatives, and so on. If, for example, Mel Brooks's dentist wants to see *The Producers*, Brooks, as a courtesy, might get him house seats. But they are not free. Someone must pay for them; either Brooks himself or the dentist who receives them. They are held in reserve (from the general public) until a certain specified time before the performance. (On Broadway, this time is commonly 6:00 P.M. before an evening performance and 12:00 P.M. before a matinee.) If they are not used, they are released for sale to the general public. (That's why it's often possible to obtain excellent seats at the last minute for even the biggest Broadway hits. These are seats no one connected with the show is using for that particular performance.)

Any contract should specify the number of comps or house seats the author gets for each performance. The author should get at least the same number as the producer holds for himself.

The contract should also limit the number of comps the producer is permitted to pass out. Some theaters use comps as a marketing device. For instance, theaters may induce people to buy a season subscription by offering them one or more shows for free. Nonprofits frequently give free tickets to large donors or board members.

These are very legitimate uses for comps; they help the theater meet its goals. However, each free ticket represents lost royalties to the author. The person who sees the show for free today is not likely to purchase a ticket to see it again in the future, even at a different theater. Fairness demands full royalties for authors, even for free tickets. As long as the producer pays full royalties for comps, the author need not put a limit on the number of free tickets the producer can distribute.

RUN OF THE PLAY

The contract must specify the exact date the play is to open (including previews) and the exact date it will close. It should specify the number of performances, breaking this down to matinee and evening performances.

If the run is to be open-ended, then, of course, a closing date will be omitted from the contract.

EXTENSIONS

If the run is for a limited time, and yet the show is a major success, it may be desirable to extend the show. The contract should provide that the parties will negotiate in good faith any extensions by a separate agreement at the appropriate time. Of course, if the play is a hit, the author will be entitled to better terms.

CASTING

Authors are entitled to casting approval. An exception would be if the actors are hired for the entire season to appear in several plays, such as a repertory company or summer stock.

DIRECTOR APPROVAL

Likewise, the author is entitled to director approval. This is especially important with a new play. The first production is artistically the most important. This is when the author gets to experience her work for the first time, in rehearsal with actors, and in performance before an audience. A good director helps the author determine the play's strong points, as well as its weaknesses. The author and the director absolutely have to be able to work together.

Presenting a brand-new play is an arduous process in which the author should be involved in as many areas of production as possible. Frequently, changes must be made in the script as the rehearsal process continues. (With a previously produced play the script is usually frozen by the time you have licensed it.) Plays evolve in the production process. Often, a playwright will see things in rehearsal she didn't know were in her play, sometimes for the good, sometimes for the bad. As the actors and directors bring her manuscript pages to life, they may have ideas and suggestions either for the good or the detriment of the work. Finally, the early audiences will tell the author what she has. It is essential to have the playwright on hand.

But, as in all creative endeavors in which there are many artistic hands at work, these situations are fraught with potential conflicts. (There is hardly a success in the history of Broadway that didn't have its share of artistic disagreements.) These can easily get out of hand and torpedo an otherwise promising production.

The producer should discuss the choice of director early with the playwright. If the playwright and director haven't worked together before, the producer must bring them together and make sure they share the same artistic vision for the script.

OTHER PERSONNEL APPROVAL

Authors are also entitled to approve the designers of the scenery, lighting, and costumes.

If the show is a musical, the author also has the right to approve the selection of the choreographer, and the composer has the right to approve the musical arrangers, orchestrators, and conductor.

APPROVALS NOT UNREASONABLY WITHHELD

Producers are naturally concerned that, by giving authors approvals of all of the major personnel, they are putting themselves at the author's mercy. If the author has unlimited power in this direction, she can act arbitrarily and capriciously to veto any of the producer's choices.

To circumvent this problem, producers often try to insert a provision in their contracts that the "Author will not unreasonably withhold approval." Unfortunately, such a clause is wide open to interpretation. What exactly constitutes "unreasonably" withholding approval? An author with a bit of imagination can find any number of "reasonable" reasons to withhold approval of any particular person the producer wishes to hire. Similarly, a producer with a bit of imagination can find any number of reasons why an author's rejection of an artist is "unreasonable" withholding.

It might take a court to decide "reasonableness," and, by the time the parties litigate the issue, the show will be well up and running. (Or it will have gone up and have bombed.) In either case, by the time the matter gets to a judge, the issues may be moot.

Authors will, justifiably, resist such a clause.

A compromise might be to ask for "mutual approval" between the author and producer. However, what happens if the parties cannot agree? Then there is no "mutual" approval.

A reasonable limitation upon the author's approvals of the various artistic personnel is possible when the theater is a repertory or summer stock organization, which uses the same artists for all productions within its season. In that case, the theater is justified in restricting the author's approval to the artists within the pool from which it draws. This gives the theater freedom to select artists with whom it is used to working, while at the same time allowing the author reasonable approval rights.

ARTISTIC CHANGES

In Hollywood, the screenwriter receives only slightly less respect than the custodian who sweeps the stage at night. A screenwriter may be fired on the whim of the director or star, regardless of the quality of his work.

In the theater, the playwright, traditionally and justifiably, holds the muscle. Her position is even higher than the director's.

This means, contractually, historically, morally, and ethically, the playwright's vision should prevail. No artistic changes should be made in her script without her consent.

Again, of course, one faces the issue of "unreasonably" withholding consent. However, in this matter, the author's rights are absolute.

OWNERSHIP OF ARTISTIC CHANGES

Any artistic changes that the playwright does choose to adopt belong to her as her sole property. It doesn't matter whether the actors, director, or the producer thought up the ideas. The playwright owns them outright. She does not have to compensate anyone for them.

There are sound reasons for this. Obviously, during the course of production, many people will offer suggestions, invent bits of business, or find new facets to characters. Historically, all ideas discovered during production, regardless of the source, have been recognized as belonging to the playwright, to do with as she sees fit, even to retain in her script. After all, their ideas wouldn't exist if her play hadn't been the blueprint in the first place.

As a practical matter, it's often difficult to determine exactly who contributed what. Often the artists themselves won't remember. Sometimes one actor might throw out an idea, which triggers a better idea from the director, which itself might spark an even better idea from the playwright. The burden of attributing payment and credit would be too great. Too much time would be consumed in rehearsal trying to keep track of who contributed what.

In addition, for the creative process to work effectively, artists need absolute freedom. They must feel free to contribute ideas, as well as to accept them. Keeping a running tally would unnecessarily bog down the process.

Moreover, such a process could be taken to absurd lengths. Suppose the seamstress who sews the costume for the female lead's gown suggests to the costume designer that a particular brooch would look good—and the author, upon seeing the brooch, decides it so reveals character she incorporates it into her script. Does this mean the author owes credit (and royalties) to the seamstress?

Do you see how an author could easily end up paying out 150 percent of her copyright and credit to literally dozens of people, some of whom have only the remotest connection to the piece?

Here are two real life examples. When Neil Simon was out of town with the original production of *The Odd Couple*, he was having trouble with the third act. Finally, Elliot Norton, a Boston critic who hosted an arts television show, suggested to Simon during an interview that he bring back the Pigeon sisters. Hmmm, thought Simon, that sounds right. He rewrote the third act, bringing back the Pigeon sisters, and this is the third act we know today. Does anyone seriously think Simon owed Norton royalties for the suggestion?

Another Simon *Odd Couple* story: During the second act, one of Felix's lines was not working. Walter Matthau, who played Oscar, begged, cajoled, and finally tricked Simon into changing the line. Does Simon owe Matthau for his idea?

I dwell on this subject at great length, because, right now, it's a vein-buster of an issue. Increasingly, directors and dramaturgs (whose jobs in the first place are to help authors develop their plays) are seeking co-ownership of copyrights, royalties, and credits from playwrights. (The Lynn Thompson *Rent* case is one; the Gerald Sachs *Most Happy Fella* case is another.)

Under the Dramatists Guild APC for both straight plays and musicals, authors, composers, and lyricists respectively own, automatically, any material they have approved, which the producer or any other persons have contributed to the show. They do not have to compensate the contributors, unless they have made a separate agreement with them to do so.

PRODUCER, PROTECT THYSELF

Producers are increasingly finding themselves in the middle of this tug-of-war between artists. As a consequence, many playwrights are demanding, in their contracts, that producers hold them harmless and indemnify them against any claims by anyone connected with the production for ideas the playwrights incorporate into their script. This is not unreasonable. After all, the producer hired the alleged claim-jumpers. So authors want producers to make it clear to all their employees that all ideas and suggestions become the author's sole property. If any person has a problem with this, perhaps he should not work on an original script, unless he enters into a separate contract with the playwright.

Producers can protect themselves by requiring all of their employees to waive, as part of their written employment agreements, any and all claims they might have against authors for any ideas or suggestions they contribute or claim to contribute. This would be strong evidence in any subsequent controversy that the producer did his part.

MERCHANDISING

As an additional revenue source, some theaters sell merchandise with the play's title and logo on it—T-shirts, buttons, and jackets, for example. The author must consent, and she is entitled to a percentage of the profit. The terms are negotiable.

REHEARSALS

Authors are always entitled to be present at all rehearsals. No one may exclude them.

For his own protection, a producer of a world premiere may wish to insert a clause committing the author to attend a certain minimum number of rehearsals and previews, or otherwise to be available for rewrites, as necessary. If the producer expects an out-of-town author to attend rehearsals or previews, the producer must pay for the author's reasonable travel and living expenses. See below.

AUTHOR TRAVEL AND HOUSING STIPEND

Out-of-town authors are entitled to reasonable travel and housing expenses.

If the budget is tight, there are ways to minimize housing costs. Either the producer or a generous board member could give the author room and board. A local hotel may be coaxed into exchanging a room for advertising space in the program, or co-sponsorship of the show.

VIDEO AND AUDIO TAPING

Many theaters automatically assume their license to produce the play also gives them the right to videotape the show "for the archives." No! The license to produce the play is only that: the right to present the show, live, in front of an audience for whatever number of performances the author has granted. Any taping—even if "for the archives"—without the author's consent is a violation of copyright.

Authors properly have many concerns with taping. In most instances, the taping is done by someone else. The author has no quality control over the recording or the edit. Even worse, taping creates a record of a show that may still be a work in progress. The author should have a chance to fix any weaknesses in her script before a record is made of it.

In addition, the author can't control where, how, or to whom the tape is shown. "For the archives" is meaningless. The author may not want certain people to see a tape of the play, at least in its present stage of development. And any commercial use of the tape may interfere with the author's ability, at a later time, to sell the film or TV rights to her script. It may hinder her chances of getting a major production, since the sale of movie rights is a major inducement for investors to back the play. The author is also entitled, of course, to additional compensation from any recordings made of her play.

If taping "for the archives" is desired, the author may place as many restrictions on its use as she wants. It is reasonable to seek permission to show a brief excerpt from the play (measured in seconds) for use in TV or radio commercials promoting the production. But the recording must be used only for that purpose.

Of course, no member of your audience should be permitted to audio- or videotape a performance for any reason. (I don't care if their precious eight-year-old daughter is in the show.) The taking of photographs or recording of a show is also prohibited by Actors' Equity. And if the show is recorded, the theater can't sell or rent any tapes without the author's consent and without paying her additional, corresponding royalties.

FIRST PRODUCTION CREDIT

Ordinarily, published versions of playscripts contain a page describing the first (and sometimes also the second) production of the play, giving credit to the theater, initial cast, director, and so forth. I would hesitate to expect an author by contract to guarantee this credit. The author has to negotiate her own contract with the publisher, and it's unfair to tie her hands any more than necessary.

It's acceptable to ask an author to merely use her "best efforts" to secure first production credit. But, as a matter of course, publishers usually give the credit anyway, so it's not necessary to haggle about it.

BILLING

The author is always entitled to credit whenever the title of her play appears—programs, publicity, advertising, handbills, and so on. The credit usually appears on a separate line, thusly:

SEX MARKS THE SPOT
by Charles Grippo

The author's name should appear in a type at least 75 percent of the size of the typeface used for the title.

The parties should agree upon what action must be taken if a mistake occurs in billing, due to printer's error, oversight, or other causes. Sometimes an insert into the program can solve the problem. If the author's name is misspelled or left off a subscription brochure, the error is more serious and can be expensive to correct.

Whatever the nature of the billing mistake, the responsibility for correcting it belongs to the producer. In your contract, you must agree to correct the mistake promptly or upon notice from the author.

INTERPOLATING OTHER COPYRIGHTED MATERIAL

Occasionally, a play may require the use of material created and copyrighted by persons or entities other than the playwright. The most common example is using a song or snippet of a popular song.

For instance, in the Neil Simon play *Last of the Red Hot Lovers*, one character sings two lines of the Bacharach-David song "What the World Needs Now Is Love." In this instance, the theater is now seeking to use material copyrighted by someone other than the playwright. This requires special permission and licensing from the appropriate copyright holders.

A playwright may take care of this issue before she begins circulating her script to producers. She may already have obtained a blanket license from the copyright holders to use their material in all productions of her play. In that case, she should furnish the producer with a copy of her signed licensing agreement with the copyright holders. Of course, the author may, quite properly, charge the theater the appropriate royalties for the use of the interpolated copyright material, which she will then pay to the copyright holders. This charge is in addition to royalties for the play itself. Another alternative is to require the producer to pay the interpolated royalties directly to the copyright holder. (This assures the producer the royalties have in fact been paid.)

There is an alternative way to handle interpolated material—one that I much prefer, both as producer and playwright. Instead of the playwright's obtaining a blanket license to use other copyrighted material in all productions of her play, the individual producer obtains a license directly for his own production.

The advantage here is that, as producer, you may be able to negotiate lower royalties by dealing directly with the copyright holder yourself. You may have special circumstances or special needs that the copyright holders can take into account in setting the amount of royalties. You may even have a prior relationship with the copyright holder that might entitle you to special considerations. The trouble with a blanket "one size fits all" license is that it isn't practical. The royalties for a five-hundred-seat equity house should be appropriately higher than those for a fifty-seat storefront manned by volunteers, yet under a blanket license both may pay the same amount.

While it may be one more thing to think about—and we know you already have lots on your mind—licensing a song from a copyright holder is no different from dealing with a play licensing agency. Large music publishers get these kinds of requests all the time and are well equipped to deal with them. Simply submit the same information you would give a play licensor—seating capacity, dates of performance, equity versus non-equity, amount of the song you wish to use (measured in bars or in seconds), and they will respond.

You may, however, encounter certain problems. If the copyright is held by an individual, instead of a corporation, he may be hard to find or a difficult negotiator. (Irving Berlin owned the copyright to his own songs. Even in the waning years of his life, he turned down Steven Spielberg for the use of the song "Always" for a film.) If the copyright holder is an estate, or, worse still, the heirs of a deceased creator, you may have a helluva time tracking down all the owners and negotiating a license with them. Or, even with a large publisher, the rights may simply be unavailable or the fees exorbitant.

In that case, you must simply tell your playwright the circumstances. The playwright must then either pick a different song or secure the rights herself. If she refuses, you may need to choose a different play.

A related issue arises when the script calls for using a particular recording of a specific song—for instance, Frank Sinatra's recording of "New York, New York." In that case, you must obtain two licenses: one from the owner of the song, and the second from the company that issued the recording. (Ask the recording company if they have authority to act on behalf of the artist; most do. However, if the particular company cannot give you that assurance, you will also have to obtain a license from the artist.)

Insist that the publisher or recording company warrants, in writing, that it has the right to license the material to you.

Another alternative is to use public domain material, such as "The Battle Hymn of the Republic." However, this is an author's choice and much depends on what she wants to accomplish by her choice of song.

EXCLUSIVITY OF RUN

If you are presenting the first production of a brand-new play, tie down the exclusive rights to the world premiere. After all, you can't take the credit for the world premiere of a play if another theater presents it first.

Remember, due to the long waits for theaters to read and make decisions about plays, authors commonly send the same script to many theaters at one time. If you're interested in a hot play, several other theaters may also be interested.

Of course, you must give the author solid reasons why you should be first. Can you get your production up before anyone else? Do you have a very visible venue or strong reputation? Are you personal friends with the playwright? Can you offer her more money?

If you can't offer the playwright a significant enough first production, then ask for the exclusive rights for the run of the play in your area. If the play is a hit, you don't want another theater down the block to mount a production while yours is playing. This is a reasonable request only if yours is the first production. With previously produced plays, licensing agents and authors rarely give exclusive geographic rights, unless it's a really major production.

Ask the playwright for exclusive rights to the play within a fifty-mile radius of your theater for ninety days prior to your run.

Be reasonable with your request. Unless you are offering a very significant level of production, it's unfair to ask the playwright to pass up other opportunities so you can have exclusivity.

SUBSIDIARY RIGHTS

The life of a successful play may extend for decades. From its first production in a regional theater, it may get a commercial transfer to on- or off-Broadway. Afterwards, there may be the sale of the movie rights, as well as amateur and stock licensing. All of these constitute the subsidiary rights, which the author owns. Producers who can offer the playwright a *significant* level of production may occasionally share, on a limited basis, in the author's future income from these sources.

I emphasize "significant" because just any old production won't do, even if it's the world premiere. A community theater in a small farming town may present the world premiere of a play, but that is hardly a significant production on the level of, say, the Mark Taper Forum. To be "significant," such as to entitle the producer to share in the subsidiary rights income, the production must make a substantial contribution in the development of a play. The most obvious contribution is exposing the play to important media outlets.

(As part of the APC, Broadway producers routinely receive a substantial share of the subsidiary rights. However, Broadway still remains the production gateway to the world for a play, so this is not unreasonable.)

Artistic development is also a major factor, of course. But here again, reasonableness should prevail. Certainly it helps the author to see her play performed even by a community theater. But no one would seriously compare the theater's artistic contributions to those offered by, say, the Goodman in Chicago.

The test should properly be whether the production contributes "significantly" (there's that word again) to the *market value* of the work. In truth, few productions can honestly make that claim. Broadway and off-Broadway obviously do. A *major* regional production that attracts national attention may also qualify. Most other productions do not qualify for any participation at all.

And if you are taking a mere license to present a production—even if it is a world premiere—you are not entitled to share in the subsidiary rights. Period.

If a share of subsidiary rights is deserved, it should be reasonable and limited in time and scope. A regional theater mainstage premiere might be able to justify taking a share of as much as 5 percent, though personally I believe any theater that takes that much is robbing the author and should be ashamed of itself. Lesser productions will be entitled to correspondingly smaller percentages and, again, most productions will not qualify at all for subsidiary rights participation.

Note that, whatever the share, it is net of agent's commissions. In other words, if the author's gross income, which is subject to the regional's share, amounts to $100,000, her agent's commission must first be deducted. That's 15 percent, or $15,000, leaving the author with net earnings of $85,000. The regional's 5 percent is calculated as followed: $85,000 x .05 = $4,250.

SCOPE OF PARTICIPATION. Subsidiary rights can be broken down into kinds and geographic territories.

The *kinds of rights* refer to all of the various possible uses of the material: first-class (Broadway), off-Broadway, second-class, stock, amateur, foreign-English-language and foreign-language productions, radio, audio, audio-visual, motion picture, videocassette, DVD, television, concert versions, musicals or operas based on the work, merchandising of products, sequels, prequels, and so on and so forth.

Geographic territories refers to the United States (and various regions therein), Great Britain, Australia, Canada, and, of course, every other nook and cranny of the world.

Unless he has produced the first-class or off-Broadway production, the producer of the significant world premiere will not share in all of the author's net earnings from dispositions of these various rights. Instead, he may only share in earnings from the United States and Canada, and lesser productions may be even more restricted in geographic scope.

DURATION. The period of time in which the initial producer shares in the disposition of subsidiary rights is also limited. Again, except for first-class and off-Broadway productions, this time period is usually restricted to not more than five years after the close of the world premiere at a *major* regional house.

The important thing here is that the contract for the disposition of the rights must be entered into within the five-year period. It doesn't matter when the income is earned. As long as the author signs the contract disposing of the particular rights within that time frame, the producer receives a share of the author's income from that contract, regardless of when she actually receives the income.

Why five years? Well, that's the norm that has come out of industry practice. The closer in time to the original production, the more likely that someone became interested in the particular subsidiary rights because of that production. Conversely, once you get past the five- year point, it becomes harder to link the purchase of the subsidiary rights to the first production. Lesser productions may be entitled to a share of the subsidiary rights for a correspondingly shorter period of time.

VESTING. Subsidiary rights do not vest—that is, inure—in the producer automatically. Commonly, the producer's production must run for twenty-one consecutive performances before the producer becomes entitled to any share of subsidiary rights. These must be paid performances of a full production before an audience. The producer cannot count more than eight previews into the total number. One performance must be designated as the official opening.

ALTERNATIVE SUBSIDIARY RIGHTS FORMULA. Today it is common for plays to originate in regional productions and then move either on or off Broadway. Commercial producers are often willing to give the originating theater a small percentage of the weekly Broadway gross. This is to compensate the regional theater for undertaking the risk of mounting the first production, something the Broadway producer would otherwise have had to do. This is in lieu of not in addition to taking a percentage of the author's subsidiary rights.

This is the way it works: The regional theater agrees to take a smaller percentage of the Broadway production's gross weekly box office receipts than it would take from the author's net earnings. Because the gross weekly box office receipts will always be considerably higher than the author's royalties, the regional stands to profit more from its smaller percentage than it would from its higher percentage of the author's income.

UPPING THE LEVEL OF PRODUCTION

If your production is a big, blooming hit, you may want to move it up to a higher level of production.

In your initial contract, try to get your playwright to give you an option to move the play up to a higher level of production. As with extensions, these terms are best left open to negotiation, at the appropriate time. At the outset of producing a brand new play, neither you nor the playwright really knows what future it might have. So settling terms without sufficient information can result in a bad contract for both of you.

Instead, if, in your original contract, you seek options to move the play up to a higher level, you should state that the parties will negotiate a full production contract at the appropriate time. Both parties should act in good faith. When the parties cannot agree on terms, it is reasonable to fall back on industry custom.

However, as with options for extensions, you will still have to give your playwright additional incentives. So, if you seek an option to move the play up, be prepared to pay more.

Be realistic in your approach, however. If you are seeking options for additional productions, you must show the playwright you have the ability and the resources to move the show up to a higher venue.

Don't expect the playwright to give you a great deal of time to make up your mind, after the first production closes, whether to exercise your option. Most playwrights will only give you from thirty to sixty days. If you don't exercise your option within that time period, the rights revert back to the author.

The duration of the option period that you can negotiate depends on the level of production to which you want to move up. The higher the level, the longer the option period you can request, with one year being the outside time limit.

If you believe you may need more than one year, or you wish to give yourself the extra time in case you do need it, you may have to request additional option periods. However, authors are not likely to grant them.

Remember, also, that options are not free. Each time you exercise an option, you must pay the author an additional sum of money. The amounts, of course, are negotiable. They are payable each time the producer seeks an option or seeks to extend the option.

You should specify the venues or at least the level of production to which you want to take the show.

Each level of production will demand different terms in the full production agreement—the higher the level, the higher the terms both parties may expect from each other.

AUTHOR WARRANTIES

It is reasonable to ask the author to warrant that she is the owner of the work; that it is original with her (except for public domain material); and that she has the sole right to contract for production with you. She should also represent that she has already copyrighted the work or will do so before your production. If she has used material from another source, she should represent that she has the right to use such material. She should hold you harmless and indemnify you, if her warranties prove to be untruthful.

Here's why this is important. Suppose you have contracted with Author A to produce a play she claims to have written called *Love Chimes*. In your contract, she warranted the piece was original with her and agreed to hold you harmless and indemnify you, if it was not.

You produce *Love Chimes*.

Subsequently, Author B sues you, claiming that he, in fact, wrote the play. If a court finds for Author B and awards him a judgment against you, Author A is responsible to pay that judgment because her warranties of authorship were false.

ASSIGNMENT OF CONTRACT

As a producer, you may wish to assign your rights to present the play to another producer. Authors are justifiably leery of such clauses.

An author-producer relationship is, in some respects, like a marriage. Both parties should be committed to each other and to the work. It is a relationship based on trust and shared vision for the future. A producer wishing to assign his rights to another is like a fiancé wishing the right to substitute his best man in his place at the altar at the time of the marriage ceremony.

There are only two circumstances under which a producer may justifiably assign his rights: first, when he needs to bring in a co-producer to help him present the work; or when he is assigning the rights to the limited partnership that will provide the financial backing. In both events, the producer remains with the show.

TERMINATION

An author has the right to terminate the contract if the producer fails to live up to his obligations thereunder. An example might be if the producer fails to pay royalties on time or does not pay the proper amount of royalties. Another example would be if the producer improperly assigns the contract.

CHAPTER 5

Commissions and Company-Generated Works

Instead of producing a script that has already been written, you may wish to create your own play from scratch.

Unless you are also a playwright yourself (and have the time outside of your producing duties), there are two ways to create your own work:

1. You can commission a playwright to turn your idea into a finished work.

2. The members of your company can collaborate to create a brand-new script.

COMMISSIONS

The advantage to commissioning a play is that you are involved from the beginning in shaping and structuring the piece according to your own vision and needs. You are not restricted by the demands or the form of a script that has already been written.

If you operate a nonprofit company, many foundations and governmental agencies make funds available to help develop new works. In recent years, funding sources have become especially interested in supporting plays that dramatize certain social issues—such as child sexual abuse or gay rights. Special consideration is often given to female playwrights or members of minority groups.

A commission can occur in any one or combination of several ways:

- *You (or a member of your company) have an idea you wish to develop into a full work.*

- *You have obtained grant money for that purpose.*

- *A playwright approaches you with an idea (but not a finished script) and seeks a commission.*

- *You are particularly anxious to work with a certain playwright and want her to create a work especially for you.*

- *You have acquired the rights to dramatize a particular property from another medium, such as a novel.*

However you initiate the project, the process and the legal requirements are the same: You are paying a playwright to create a particular work for you.

CONTRACT DETAILS

Once you have decided on a project and selected a playwright, both parties must negotiate two separate, yet interdependent, contracts between them:

1. The commission agreement

2. The full production contract

The commission agreement is a simple document that sets forth the terms of the arrangement between the producer and the playwright to create the work. The full production contract sets forth the terms of production, once the play has been written and the producer is ready to present it. The full production contract is the more complicated and should be based on the model I have described in chapter 4.

I recommend negotiating the "full production" agreement at the beginning of the relationship. The less desirable approach is to put off finalizing the agreement until after the writer has completed her script and you have decided to present it. It is better if both parties have a clear understanding of the terms of the production before the playwright actually begins work. If you wait until the script has been completed and the two of you cannot reach a satisfactory production agreement, both of you may find that all of your work, time, and expense has gone for naught. If you are hopelessly deadlocked, at least one party (and probably both) will lose.

In addition, the production negotiations will demonstrate how well you and the playwright can get along and reach agreement on substantive issues.

If you can't even agree on the terms of production, how will you work together to create a finished play? And how will you work together during the actual production process?

If you choose to wait to negotiate the production agreement until the script is finished and you have decided to produce it, then all you need do is prepare the commission agreement. Add a clause therein, such as the following:

> In the event the producer deems the work satisfactory, then, prior to any production, the parties shall negotiate in good faith an additional agreement, setting forth the terms of the production.

RISKS. The commission agreement is an option to produce a work that is yet to be written. This distinguishes it from producing an already-completed script, as discussed in chapter 4. Unlike an already-completed play, you have no way to judge its quality, playability, or suitability for your needs. But you can minimize your risks. You can work with a playwright with whom you have worked before or with whose work you are familiar.

However, this in itself may be a risk. The well-known playwright may be "written out" by the time you commission her. She may lack the fresh perspective or vision that a newer playwright may bring to the piece. And, while using a well-known playwright may help sell tickets, it forecloses your chance to discover a new "star."

FEES. It is customary to pay the writer half the commission fee when she signs the contract. The writer receives an additional one-fourth when she turns in her first draft. It is likely at this point that you will conduct readings with actors, to give you and the writer a chance to hear the words. You may ask the writer for rewrites.

You will pay the author the balance of her fees when she turns in her rewrites. You are not actually paying the writer for the rewrites. You are in fact simply paying her the balance of the agreed upon fees. She has completed her work. Whether it is suitable or not, she is entitled to be paid.

Commission fees are never conditioned on the acceptance or quality of the final work. You are taking the risk that the work may be not be suitable or satisfactory.

The size of the total commission payment is negotiable. It may depend upon external factors, such as how much grant money you have received or the restrictions placed on that money by the donors. It must be sufficient that the writer feels reasonably compensated for her time and effort.

If the playwright must travel to research the project, the commission fees should include reasonable reimbursement for her expenses. If she must acquire materials for research—such as copies of old documents—you must reimburse these charges also.

If it is any consolation, higher commission fees look good on grant applications. And it may be money well spent.

Commission fees are always nonrefundable, even if the work proves unsatisfactory. Unlike regular option fees, they are also not recoupable out of royalties, unless they are unusually large.

COPYRIGHT. Regardless of who generated the idea, the copyright always belongs to the playwright, even for commissioned works.

SCHEDULE. Provide for a specific schedule to which the writer is expected to adhere in turning in her drafts. The schedule you negotiate will depend upon the work that is to be done, how quickly the writer works, and whether travel or substantial research must be done. Also factor in the time it may take to arrange readings and to complete the rewrites that will surely occur as a result.

Ask the playwright whether external factors might interfere—such as family or job responsibilities. You are entitled to know if the playwright has prior obligations to other producers. Inquire whether she is under contract to write a screenplay for a film company. Under the Writer's Guild contracts with film companies, a screenwriter's services are exclusive to the studio until she has completed the contracted screenplay. Therefore she cannot begin work on your project until that time.

Factor in when you would like to present the play as part of your own schedule.

SATISFACTORY WORK. When the script is completed satisfactorily, you will choose to go ahead with production. The terms of the full production agreement will kick into effect. At this point, you are taking an option to present the work. You owe the writer an "option" payment (separate and apart from the commission fees).

UNSATISFACTORY WORK. After all is said and done, you are free to choose not to present the play. Although you commissioned the work, the writer is free to take the play elsewhere, with one exception.

The exception occurs if you own the dramatization rights to the underlying work, such as a novel. In such an event, unless you release the rights, the project is dead in the water.

It may be fair to negotiate a mechanism by which you will assign your underlying rights to the playwright (or her subsequent producer) in consideration of a fee. Certainly it would be reasonable to expect reimbursement of whatever money you have paid for the dramatization rights. This arrangement allows the writer to salvage her work product, which, without the underlying rights, would otherwise be unproducable. And it compensates you for fees you paid for the underlying rights for a project you have, in the end, chosen not to do.

In the case of a satisfactory script, you will always assign your rights to the underlying work to the playwright.

EXCLUSIVE AND NON-EXCLUSIVE RIGHTS. By commissioning the author and paying the subsequent option fees, you are purchasing the rights to present the "world premiere" of the work.

You may reasonably request the right to present the play more than once—perhaps several times over a period of years—at your venue, exclusively in your geographic area. (A "geographic area" is usually defined as within sixty miles of your location. I have seen it stretched to as much as two hundred miles—with, however, a corresponding increase in fees and royalties to the author.)

However, it is unreasonable to demand the "exclusive" right to present the play anywhere in perpetuity. After the initial run, the playwright should have the right to take the work to other producers, especially outside of your geographic area.

COMPANY-CREATED WORKS

Some companies create their own works. This is especially true of actor-driven and improvisational groups.

However, true improvisations are not written down in playscript form. Usually, all that is reduced to writing is an outline of the direction in which the piece is supposed to go. Companies may occasionally generate formal, written scripts out of improvisations.

Often, the director may create the written script, based on the material the entire company creates. More often than not, the company will bring in a playwright. In some cases, the playwright may be nothing more than a glorified transcriber. Or she may be asked to use her craft to bring sense and structure to what may be a great deal of loosely connected material.

Whatever the case, company-generated works require a great deal of careful legal thought before work begins. Unfortunately, many companies do not consider the legal consequences of what they are doing, until they are too far along in the process to stop, or until the members have a falling out among themselves and someone calls in a lawyer. That's when the project becomes subject to the presumptions of the copyright laws. These presumptions are often not what the parties intended.

For just these reasons it is crucial that the members decide all of the major issues at the outset. Then they must reduce their agreement to a formal, written contract.

I know that it is sticky to even bring up the need for a contract, especially since the members may often be good friends. It requires tact and diplomacy. Nevertheless, it must be done.

THE SOON TO BE FAMOUS PLAYERS

To illustrate the issues and pitfalls that arise when a company wants to create its own piece, we'll use the fictitious theater company, the Soon to Be Famous Players.

Its members are all good friends. They are recent graduates from the same theater school: the John Barrymore College of the Performing Arts.

The cast of characters is as follows:

ACTORS: MAX
JUNE
PHIL
SUSAN
ART
ELAINE
NEIL
DIRECTOR: ROSS
PRODUCER: AGNES

The company rents a small store that they convert into a fifty-seat theater.

The company has decided to develop an idea Max has had for a two-act romantic comedy to be called *Love Chimes*. They will create the work in a series of improvisational workshops, which Ross will direct.

The first issue the company must decide is what they intend to do. Do they intend to jointly author the piece? Are they simply going to use the workshop to toss out ideas? Or are they expressing those ideas in such a form as to constitute authorship? Merely participating in a series of workshops does not, by itself, constitute a collaboration, unless it is clearly the intent of the parties.

The company understands also that, while they don't need a written agreement to establish joint authorship, such an agreement will protect all of them from the vagaries of the law and will evidence their intentions.

By voice vote, the Soon To Be Famous Players decide they will all become joint authors of *Love Chimes*.

In addition, the company decides to call in a professional playwright, Sheila, to help them. Sheila will give them the benefit of her knowledge and craft and shape their loose improvisations into a properly structured play. They agree Sheila will function as a true playwright, not merely as a transcriber of their ideas. Accordingly, she will be a joint author of the work.

Thus, there will be ten authors of *Love Chimes*. The parties must now negotiate the nitty-gritty terms of their agreement.

COLLABORATION AGREEMENTS

When two or more persons agree to jointly author a work, they become "collaborators" with each other.

Throughout theater history, there have been many famous collaborations: Rodgers and Hammerstein, Kaufman and Hart, Gilbert and Sullivan, Lerner and Lowe, as well as many lesser-known partnerships. In fact, some of the greatest shows have been created through collaborations. Musicals, in particular, are most commonly written by several people—a book writer, a composer, and a lyricist. Often, these are ongoing partnerships. Two or more artists join together to create more than one show—like Rodgers and Hammerstein. In other cases, the parties collaborate to create one specific show.

With the explosive growth of regional theater companies over the last three decades, it has become quite common for the members of a particular company to create their own works—as the Soon to Be Famous Players have decided to do. In such an instance, the parties become "collaborators," regardless of whether they use that word or think of themselves as such. Therefore, their efforts are governed by the law of "collaboration." The agreement they draw up among themselves is a "Collaboration Agreement."

Here are the terms the Soon to Be Famous Players must include in their written agreement.

COPYRIGHT. Since copyright always belongs to the author—and the parties have agreed to be joint authors—copyright will be taken in all ten names. It is unusual to have so many copyright holders for a single work, but it is perfectly legal. A better alternative, however, might be to create a corporation and hold copyright in the corporation's name.

It is important, at this point, to understand copyright law.

At common law (law that is not created by statute), an author automatically owns all of the rights in a play (or any work of art) as soon as she creates it. This includes the right to authorize its production, publication, or conversion into film. The author does not have to formally register the work with the U.S. Copyright Office to own or maintain ownership in her material.

However, registering the work with the Copyright Office gives the author rights that are so valuable it is foolhardy not to register. The registration procedure is simple and the fees are very low, compared to the benefits bestowed on the registrant.

If someone infringes on the author's copyright, the author must prove that (a) she was the original author of the piece; and (b) she created it before the act of infringement took place. Without copyright registration, this proof may be difficult, if not impossible, to establish. She will need witnesses to prove they read or viewed a staged reading of the material before the act of infringement occurred. The witnesses may not be available, or their memories might be faulty. Even if witnesses can be found (without undue expense), the author must still persuade a judge and jury that she created the work first.

However, when an author registers a work, the Copyright Office issues a Certificate of Copyright. This certificate is the strongest possible proof that the author created the work first. As long as the author registers the work before or within five years of its first publication, the court must accept the registration as valid.

Timely registration gives the winner in a copyright infringement case the right to recover attorney's fees and costs—which can be substantial.

It is frequently hard to prove the amount of damages the winner has suffered when her copyright has been infringed. Timely registration gives her the right to statutory damages, which can be any amount between $200 and $20,000. If the infringement was willful, the winner can recover damages up to $100,000.

Do you understand now why registration is such a smart move?

Just make sure you register the work in a timely fashion. If you have not published the work, you must register before the act of infringement occurs. If you have published the work, you gain important benefits if you register within three months of first publication.

Under current law, the term of copyright, for works created since January 1, 1978, lasts for the rest of the author's lifetime, plus an additional seventy years after the author's death. Then it will fall into the public domain. Thus, the copyright on this book will last for the rest of my life, plus seventy years after my death. After that time has expired, it will enter the public domain.

When a work is created by two or more authors (as in the case of the company-created work—the collaboration), the term of copyright lasts for seventy years after the death of the last surviving author. (They must not have created the work for hire—as employees.) That can be a pretty long time.

BILLING. Billing is not simply a matter of ego. In the theater, billing can open doors and advance careers.

When two or more authors create a work, billing should be fair to all. Equal billing is usually fairest. The order of billing is often determined alphabetically, by last name.

Occasionally, there are sound reasons for unequal billing. For instance, Sheila may be a playwright of national repute. Her name sells tickets and attracts media attention. The members of the company are still relative unknowns. It may be wise to let Sheila's billing stand out, so the other authors and the work can ride on her coattails. For instance:

LOVE CHIMES
A play by SHEILA
And also AGNES, ART, ELAINE, JUNE, MAX, NEIL, PHIL, ROSS, and SUSAN

Besides, if Sheila is well known, she may demand separate billing anyway.

There may be strong feelings whether billing is horizontal or vertical.

All of the authors should receive billing whenever the others do. Unless, again, you have one author whose name means more than the others, the size and typeface should be the same for all.

For our purposes, we will say that Sheila has no better or greater reputation than the others. Therefore, what applies to everyone applies equally to Sheila. Also, we will refer to the entire company as the "Authors" or the "Collaborators," since that is their intent.

DECISION-MAKING. Determining which of the parties makes decisions for the group may be the toughest issue to address. Someone has to make the many artistic and business decisions that will affect any piece the members of your company create. The absolute worst case occurs when one person decides, unilaterally, to be the decision-maker for all. At the outset, all parties may be comfortable with this arrangement. Sooner or later, however, bad feelings will develop. Unpopular decisions will be made. Sides may be taken. Disaster will result.

The collaborators must agree how decisions are to be made. Majority vote is often desirable, but the parties must understand that, occasionally, they will be outvoted. Decisions will not always go their way.

Unanimity is the other alternative. But what if the parties can't reach full agreement? Much time may be wasted while the collaborators argue. And what if they can't ever reach agreement? Deadlock will result, making a bad situation worse. Emotions may get out of hand. The parties may fail to think with rational, clear minds.

There is no right or wrong answer to how decisions should be made. Your group must consider the possibilities that exist among your members. You may even discover that making a decision about making a decision will be your first serious bone of contention. If that is the case, ask everyone to step back and consider how much tougher it will be to resolve other issues if you can't figure out this one.

But what happens if the parties can't agree and they become hopelessly deadlocked? In that case, it is wise to provide in your collaboration agreement that you will leave the decision-making to a neutral third party—preferably someone whom all the collaborators can respect. For business decisions, a theatrical attorney might be selected as the third party tie-breaker, while artistic deadlocks may be broken by a playwright or director of note.

Your agreement should provide for arbitration and mediation, in the event of a disagreement. This process is less expensive than litigation, but I recommend it only if all else fails. It is still time-consuming and can hold up your show.

If you are creating a musical, some members of your company may be responsible only for contributing certain elements of the project, such as the book or the music or the lyrics. Commonly, the composer and lyricist should retain decision-making power over musical elements like the arrangers, orchestrators, and musicians. The book writer should have decision-making authority over the book. If your project lends itself to this kind of decision-making, it simplifies your agreement.

In the case of *Love Chimes*, a straight play, the collaborators have decided that the actors, playwright, and director will make the artistic decisions by a majority vote. Each artist will have one vote equal to the others. Agnes, the producer, will make all of the business decisions.

ROYALTIES. In the case of a straight play, like *Love Chimes*, royalties are usually divided equally among all the collaborators. Some theater companies try to determine who contributed what and how much. (Max, for instance, might argue that since it was his original idea, he should receive slightly higher royalties.) This may often become a fruitless effort, especially if your company is generating a script out of improvisation workshops.

How do you measure individual contributions in a straight play? By logging the time one invests in it?

All right. Let's go down that road. Suppose, in our example, all of the parties, except June, attend every workshop and put in the same number of hours. By the measurement of time, they are entitled to a greater share of the royalties than June.

However, although June misses five out of the seven workshops, she contributes an idea, a character, or a speech that single-handedly transforms a modest show into a blockbuster hit. (Don't think that can't happen. Remember what the title song did for *Hello, Dolly!*) Maybe June didn't give as much of her time as the others. Yet her brainstorm may mean a movie sale, as well as hundreds of thousands of dollars in additional licensing fees. Does June have an argument for a greater share of the royalties?

Even in a musical, it may become difficult to quantify the individual elements. No one can put a percentage on which element is the most important—the book, the music, or the lyrics. The book contains the underlying elements—character, incident, and story—out of which the songs are created. Yet, by its definition, a musical is not a musical without the music. And the tunes need the lyrics to advance the story and illuminate character. And, again, using the *Hello, Dolly!* example, what if you have one song that completely defines the show?

With a musical, I would treat each element as a separate component. Therefore, each element receives its own share of the royalties. If one person creates more than one element, such as a book writer who also writes the lyrics, she receives separate royalties for each element.

With a straight play, it is fairest to divide the total money earned into as many equal shares as there are collaborators. Give each collaborator one share.

MERGER

Playwrights and producers tell me this is the single most confusing legal concept in company-created works. As you might expect, it follows that it is also the most important to understand.

Let me make it simple.

"Merger" occurs when two or more elements, which could exist independently of each other, join together to form a unified whole. Once those elements link with each other, they cannot be separated without damaging the unified whole thing they have formed.

MERGER OUTSIDE OF THE THEATER. By jumping out of the theater element for a moment, I can clarify merger very easily.

If John Jones and Mary Smith marry, they have "merged" with each other. Until the marriage ceremony declaring them "Husband and Wife" (or whatever is politically correct these days), John and Mary have led independent lives. They have existed separately. However, their marriage vows join them together into one unified whole—emotionally, sexually, and legally. John and Mary have become a couple who are now indivisible. (Oh, all right, until divorce makes them independent again!)

The United States of America was originally a group of independent colonies and territories, until, one by one, they all joined together — "merged"—to form one union, which now consists of fifty states.

If you decide to build a house on land you own, you hire a carpenter who brings lumber, an electrician who brings wiring, a brick layer who brings bricks, a plumber who brings pipes, and so forth. Each tradesperson dumps individual materials on your land. At this point, all of the elements exist separately from each other. If, for instance, you fire the carpenter, he can haul his lumber away to another construction site.

However, once construction begins, each element—wiring, pipes, bricks, lumber—is joined with the other elements to form one unified structure. Once the house is built, you can't remove the bricks or the pipes without damaging the finished product.

MERGER IN PLAYWRITING. "Merger" works the same way in the writing of a play or musical. Each collaborator brings to the project elements that exist separately from each other until they join together to form a finished show.

In the case of *Love Chimes*, Max had the original idea, which is the basis of the play. Susan contributes the female lead whose actions drive the plot. Phil offers many one-liners. June contributes the second act speech that transforms the play. The others contribute their own individual ideas. (I am oversimplifying, of course. In truth, it is usually difficult to determine who contributed what, especially in the case of a straight play.) All of these individual ideas and elements come together to form a unified whole—the finished script.

WHEN DOES MERGER OCCUR? As part of their agreement, the collaborators must decide, "When do we want merger to take place?"

In other words, when do all of the individual contributions become so intrinsically linked to one another that removing one or more of them would destroy the entire fabric of the piece?

Merger never happens on its own, in an arbitrary fashion. Merger occurs only when the collaborators say it happens.

At some point, the piece must exist on its own, without regard to what its collaborators are doing or how they are getting along. The piece must cease to be merely a collage of independent elements. It must become a unified whole, just like all the construction materials must join together to form a house.

If the collaborators fail to decide this point, disaster is sure to follow.

CONSEQUENCES OF FAILING TO SPECIFY MERGER. Let's suppose *Love Chimes* is up and running. The reviews are great. Performances are sold out. The show is sure to run a long time. Broadway producers are circling the project. But the collaborators failed to decide when "merger" was to occur.

Susan, who has created a wonderful character that drives the piece, has a falling out with Agnes, the producer. In a snit, Agnes fires her.

"Fine," Susan says, "and I'm taking my character with me!"

Oh, boy, is the company in trouble!

Since merger never took place, Susan's character never became part of the unified whole. The character belongs to her. If she leaves the show, she can take the character with her. The problem is, since the show revolves around Susan's character, the whole enterprise collapses.

Take a musical example. No doubt much of the enduring appeal of *Mame* is due to Jerry Herman's title song. Suppose, however, that in creating the show, Herman and book writers Jerome Lawrence and Robert E. Lee failed to select a date when "merger" was to occur. Now, some thirty-five years later, Herman decides to yank his title song out of the score. He doesn't need a reason. He just got up on the wrong side of the bed. Without merger, he has the right to take back his song. But if he did, the market for *Mame* would probably dry up.

Of course, Herman, Lawrence, and Lee were Broadway professionals with experienced attorneys and agents. No doubt they addressed "merger" in their collaboration agreement. Besides, Herman didn't get where he is by being dumb. Even if he had the right to withdraw his title song, he's far too smart to do so.

MERGER KEEPS THE SHOW ALIVE. Merger keeps the show living, no matter what the collaborators are doing or how their relationship changes over time. Disagreements, personal strife, death, and disability don't affect the show's ability to go on and earn money for its authors.

But you must address merger in your collaboration agreement. Membership in a theater company is usually not permanent. Artists move on to other things. However, if you've created a show together, you must have the ability to continue that show as long as the market demands.

WHEN MERGER OCCURS. When does merger occur? Whenever the authors say it does. On Broadway, it is usually the first press preview. Your company can decide for itself. Perhaps it is the final technical rehearsal before opening. Perhaps it is your opening night. The choice of date doesn't matter so much as actually choosing a date.

Want a simple guideline? Merger occurs whenever removing any material would seriously undermine the fabric of the show.

There is an exception, however. (Are you surprised?)

In the case of a musical, certain elements can exist outside of the unified whole. (Are you thoroughly confused yet?) Let's take a real life example: *Guys and Dolls*. Abe Burrows wrote the book (based on stories by Damon Runyon), and Frank Loesser wrote the music and lyrics.

Up until "merger" occurred, the Burrows book and the Loesser songs existed independently of each other. Suppose, during this time, Burrows and Loesser had an argument that was so serious they decided to go their separate ways. This means that Burrows could collaborate with a different composer-lyricist, and Loesser could take his songs into another show.

Here's why this part of the concept is so important. Merger affects only that material that the authors intend to be part of the show on the date that merger occurs. Any other material—even though created specifically for the show—does not become part of the unified whole. It belongs to its creator, who may do with it what she pleases.

This situation exists with the carpenter who has brought lumber for the house. Once the house is finished, he may take his leftover lumber with him and use it for another project.

With musicals, collaborators often create more material than winds up in the final show. Most often, this material consists of additional songs. Once merger occurs, the authors can take any excess material and use it in any way they choose.

There is an additional twist to musicals. Songs can exist independently of the book. Although at present there are few songs out of musicals that make it outside of the show, for decades, show songs have been recorded over and over by many different artists. (Think of how many show songs Frank Sinatra recorded on his albums over the years.)

Yet musical books rarely exist, in any effective way, without the score. Imagine the book for South Pacific without "Some Enchanted Evening."

Here's another, crucial reason your company absolutely must agree on merger. Broadway producers and Hollywood film companies demand it. They won't even consider your show unless you can show explicit agreement on merger. No one wants to produce a show if one of its collaborators can remove her material at any time.

REMOVAL OF A COLLABORATOR

Collaborators often don't remain with a project through to completion.

An actor-collaborator may leave the company for greener pastures. Personality conflicts may cause one or more persons to leave. The producer may decide an actor-collaborator does not fit with the company.

Since the actor is also a joint author of the show, he has certain rights, regardless of the circumstances of his departure. If he leaves after "merger" has occurred, his material remains with the show. He is still entitled to royalties, authorship credit, and voting privileges. By the same token, he cannot take his material out of your script.

You must, however, prepare for removing and replacing a collaborator before merger occurs. This system must be fair and applicable to all. If his departure is voluntary, the other collaborators are entitled to reasonable notice and an opportunity to determine how to replace him. If he is asked to leave, he is entitled to notice, as well as the reasons he is being terminated.

In case you wish to ask a joint author to leave, you must agree on who makes the decision. The fairest way would be a vote of the collaborators. In addition, you must set specific criteria, so that all of the authors know the standard to which they will be held. Specific criteria also help the collaborators determine when a party has fallen short.

When an actor-collaborator leaves before merger occurs, two issues arise. First, the material he has already contributed must be considered. At this point, he has the right to take this material with him. But does he want to? Is it of any value to him outside of the immediate project? Do the collaborators want to give up those contributions?

If he wants to leave his material in and the others wish to keep it, appropriate arrangements must be made for compensation, voting rights, billing, and so on. Otherwise, depending on the people involved, either side could hold the other hostage. This could create high emotions and result in great expense. There may be great pressure to meet deadlines, especially if the show is already on the schedule.

The second issue involves bringing in a replacement. Suppose the Soon to Be Famous Players have voted Susan out of the company, yet they want to retain some of her material for *Love Chimes*. To complete her work, they want to hire Thelma.

Suppose Susan and Thelma contribute material in uneven proportions. Remember, in the past, Susan received equal billing, as well as equal royalties and an equal vote. But now Susan is gone. Yet some of her material remains. Thelma replaces her. So how much of a share does Thelma receive? The others balk at giving Thelma an equal share, because this would reapportion everyone's share. Instead of one-tenth, each person would receive one-eleventh. Yet Susan is entitled to something for her material, and so is Thelma.

You must ask these questions. Where is the work in the development process? How much work still needs to be done? How far away from opening night are we? What kind of emotional situation are we facing? Has the company divided into a "Susan" camp and a "Thelma" camp?

In addition, how are decisions to remove and replace to be made? Should we set forth objective criteria in our agreement? But this means a measurable standard to which everyone must adhere. How do you quantify such a standard? Is it even possible to do so? Should we count up hours devoted to the project? But June missed most of the workshops, yet contributed the stunning idea that put the show up over the top—what should we do?

Oh, the questions are tough, aren't they?

But you know what? If you don't decide at the outset, if you wait until crisis time, they get impossible. And I can't give you answers. You have to discuss each of these issues, one by one, and decide the answers for yourself.

DEATH OF A JOINT AUTHOR

Just when you thought things couldn't get any thornier, they can.

The truth is, all of the collaborators are gonna die at some time during the life of the copyright. Remember, we said that under present law the copyright exists for the remainder of the author's life, plus seventy years. The author's life refers to the last of the authors to die.

For the Soon to Be Famous Players Company, this is good. It means their copyright does not expire until seventy years after the last of them dies. This may stretch into the next century.

While that may seem a looooooooooooonnnnnnggggg way off, you've got to consider all the ramifications now. Just about everyone wants her heirs to benefit from the work she has accomplished during her lifetime. If there are no direct heirs, such as spouses, children, siblings, or parents, people usually want a favorite charity or close friend to benefit.

I don't know of anyone who, if she thought about it, actually would want her property to escheat (that is, pass) to the state upon her death.

The problem is, people often procrastinate planning their estates. Young people, in particular, think death is very far off in the future.

However, your company is now creating a work of value. Especially at the outset, no one can quantify that value. Each collaborator, regardless of age or health, must protect her ownership interest in the copyright.

ESTATE PLANNING FOR COLLABORATORS. As producer, you should strongly urge your joint authors to see an estate planning attorney, regardless of what other assets they may have. This should be done contemporaneously with the drafting of the collaboration agreement.

If the holder of an interest in a copyright dies, without designating by properly prepared will or trust to whom she wants her interest to go, the state of her residence at the time of her death will make the determination for her. Each state has its own laws of descent and distribution. These determine how property passes when its owner dies without a will or trust (meaning, he dies intestate).

A collaborator may designate in her will or trust to whom she wants her interest in the show to go. She can also designate who will take over her voting rights. Sometimes the two are the same. Sometimes a spouse or children may actually inherit the property, while an attorney or a bank will act as the executor or trustee who will actually make the decisions.

ESTATE PITFALLS FOR THE COLLABORATION. Without careful planning, the death or disability of a joint author can create pitfalls for the collaboration. Designees who take over voting rights are rarely artists. They may not have the same knowledge as the deceased. Chances are, they will not share her artistic vision (which may have been in perfect sync with the rest of the company). This is especially true of lawyers and bankers.

In addition, if a collaborator dies while the work is only partially finished, she must be replaced. Her designee may not be qualified to vote on an appropriate replacement.

I would explicitly cover this contingency in the collaboration agreement. I recommend designating the remaining collaborators as the decision-makers for the work—at least artistically. However, you must bring in the deceased's heirs or legal representative into any business matters.

DISABILITY OF A COLLABORATOR

Suppose Elaine has an automobile accident in which she suffers brain injuries, or Max is felled by a stroke, which affects his reasoning capabilities. In both instances, the doctors predict that Elaine and Max will live long lives; however, they are incapable of managing their affairs, as well as participating in the artistic and business decisions for *Love Chimes*.

Unless Elaine and Max have properly prepared for these contingencies, while they were still mentally able to do so, the courts will intervene. A judge will appoint a guardian to take charge of their physical persons, as well as a conservator of their respective estates. (An "estate" is all the property a person owns, or in which she has an interest.) This would, of course, include their respective interests in *Love Chimes*.

Now here's the major difficulty: absent a written direction from Elaine or Max, the judge may appoint anyone he chooses as conservator. He doesn't have to appoint Elaine's friend or relative, or Max's friend or relative. The conservator may be someone whom Elaine or Max would not have chosen themselves, if given the choice. In fact, the court is very likely to appoint a complete stranger to Elaine, Max, and the Soon to Be Famous Players.

Many courts are required to appoint a state official known as the Public Guardian (or Conservator) for persons deemed incompetent to manage their own affairs. Other courts appoint conservators from a list of (often politically connected) professional conservators. Although Elaine and Max will continue to receive the income from their respective shares of the show (net of the conservator's fees and costs), which may be necessary for their care, the conservator will step into their voting and decision-making shoes with the rest of the collaborators.

In other words, your company will have to deal with a complete stranger whom no one would have chosen. The stranger may not know or care about theater or what you are doing. He may be a career bureaucrat.

This is a grim scenario, indeed, yet well within the realm of possibility. It is still another reason all of the collaborators must consult their own estate planning attorneys.

There are several possible solutions, provided action is taken in advance. Using an instrument called a "Power of Attorney for Financial Affairs," (which is available in most states), a collaborator appoints a friend, relative, or co-collaborator as her attorney-in-fact, to make business and artistic decisions in her place if she is unable to do so. (She can have a separate power of attorney for her financial affairs other than the collaboration, if she chooses, naming a different attorney-in-fact.)

Or she could convey her interest into a living trust, with herself as trustee. She names a successor trustee to take management of her affairs if she dies or is disabled such that she cannot manage her own affairs herself. Most attorneys will recommend both the living trust and the power of attorney for financial affairs.

Similarly, the collaborators should provide in their collaboration agreement for this kind of contingency.

The collaborators must also decide how they wish to handle the death or disability of one of their members if the death or disability occurs while the work is still being written. The same considerations apply as in the removal of a collaborator. However, since the death or disability was not caused by any fault of the person, they may not wish to treat this as a true removal. Yet it may be necessary to bring in another collaborator to finish the work

Again, there are no easy answers. Each group must discuss these issues in depth and create a solution that works for its particular membership.

REPRESENTATION

Under the copyright laws, all of the authors have an equal right to grant non-exclusive licenses for the material. However, if everyone can be out there marketing non-exclusive rights, confusion can result. Moreover, commercial producers would likely refuse to become involved in a show that ten collaborators are hustling at the same time.

It greatly simplifies matters to designate one person as the representative for the work. In the case of a company-created piece, the producer is the most likely choice. The representative must present all offers to the others for vote before binding the project.

A variation is to select an agent to represent the work. Sometimes it's desirable to place the work on an exclusive basis with one agent. It facilitates negotiations with third-party producers or film companies.

However, if several of the collaborators have agents, it is permissible for all to represent the work. (In musicals, for instance, usually the book writer, the composer, and the lyricist have different agents.) This is distinguishable from the case in which all of the authors market the work themselves at the same time. Unlike artists, agents are accustomed to working with other agents both in marketing scripts and negotiating production contracts.

EXPENSES

All projects incur expenses. The parties must decide how expenses will be handled.

Usually, it makes sense to give the representative the authority to incur expenses, in her discretion, up to a certain dollar amount without having to first seek permission from all the collaborators. The parties should decide on that dollar limit.

Once the representative reaches that limit, the parties must put into place a mechanism so that she can obtain permission to incur additional expenses, if the need arises. If one party advances expenses out of expected future income, how is that party to be reimbursed? What if the future income never materializes? Should the company establish a petty cash fund out of which expenses can be withdrawn? Until money starts to flow from the project, how will the group fund the petty cash account? How much initial capital may be needed? What will be the sources of that capital?

Logically, it would seem that the collaborators should kick in something. But how should the parties apportion each collaborator's contribution to petty cash?

DRAMATISTS GUILD CONTRACTS

If all of the joint authors are members of the Dramatists Guild, state that all contracts for productions of the play shall be based on the Guild models for the particular class of production. This should eliminate most potential bickering among the collaborators.

CHANGES TO THE WORK

No changes may be made in the script without the consent of all of the other authors. If the show is a musical, no changes may be made in the book without the consent of all the book writers. No changes may be made in the music and lyrics without the consent of the composer and lyricist.

REPRESENTATIONS AND WARRANTIES

All of the collaborators represent and warrant (guarantee) to the others that all material they contribute shall be original with them. They own the material and therefore have the right to put it into the show. This material does not violate or infringe on the copyright of anyone else. It also does not defame any person, product, or entity. Finally, it does not invade anyone's right of privacy.

Emphasize the meaning of this clause to all the collaborators. This is an important undertaking. If any collaborator violates this clause—that is, passes off someone else's copyrighted material as her own—she could be liable in damages to the others.

What are these damages? Well, if your finished product contains someone else's copyrighted material, all of the collaborators will be sued by the aggrieved party. All may be held liable for financial damages, even though only one of them appropriated another person's work. All will have to pay attorneys fees and court costs. Under this clause, the "truly guilty" party must reimburse the others for all their expenses.

MUSIC AND LYRICS

If your show contains music and lyrics, ordinarily, the copyright for these will be taken out in the names of the composer and lyricist alone and not also the collaborators on the book. In the case of a company-generated work, all of the members may have written the lyrics and composed the music. In that case, of course, copyright would be taken out in all the names.

The composer and lyricist retain the publishing rights to the music and lyrics. The composer has the right to approve of the music director, arrangers, and orchestrators.

SMALL VERSUS GRAND RIGHTS

"Small performing rights" are the non-dramatic rights to the musical compositions. The dramatic rights are the "grand rights." It is often tough to distinguish between the two, but it's important if your show is a musical.

If you license *Bye Bye Birdie* from Tams-Witmark, you are obtaining a license for the grand rights to present the musical as a full dramatic production—the book, music, and lyrics. There is a plot, which is depicted by action and characters. The music and lyrics are interwoven with this plot in such a way as to carry it forward and to define character. In other words, you are presenting *Bye Bye Birdie* as a fully realized show.

However, if you are merely recording or performing one of the songs from the show—let's say, "Put On a Happy Face"—you are licensing the "small performing rights."

It gets a little trickier if you are performing "Put On a Happy Face" in much the same way as it is presented in the show—that is, a character named Albert Peterson sings and dances to the song with a "sad girl" in a train station. Now you are moving into grand rights territory.

In your collaboration agreement, the composer and lyricist will retain the "small performing rights" to the musical compositions. For simplicity's sake, this means the right to license others to record or perform any of the songs outside the show. (Let's say Barbra Streisand wants to record your show's big love song "I Suck Your Navel." This is a "small performing right.")

When you are creating a company-generated musical, it is important to distinguish between the "small performing rights" and the "grand rights" in your agreement. It is reasonable (and standard) to allow the composer and lyricist to license the small rights, even while your production is playing at your theater.

However, licensing the grand rights should require everyone's consent—since this is allowing a full dramatic production of the material. In addition, you may not want to license the grand rights to another producer while your production is still running.

OPTION TO PURCHASE COLLABORATOR'S INTEREST

It may happen, down the line, that one of the collaborators wants out. He needs money. He wants to sell or pledge or lease or otherwise dispose of some or all of his interest. The others may not want a third party to purchase these rights. They don't want a partner they don't know suddenly stepping into the arrangement. Or they simply would prefer to own these rights themselves.

Establish a mechanism so that the selling party must give the other collaborators a chance to buy the rights themselves. He must give advance notice. This notice must be in writing and delivered to the others by registered mail. The notice must set forth the terms on which he wishes to sell. These terms should be determined by the price and other particulars which a third party has offered for the rights. The other collaborators have an option to match those terms and purchase the rights themselves. Set a time limit during which they must exercise the option; a reasonable time might be fourteen days after receipt of the notice. If they fail to exercise the option, the selling party is free to accept the third party's offer.

If you have a lot of collaborators, this may get sticky. What if each of the others wants to buy the selling party's interest for themselves? This could lead to friction or a bidding war. You must decide upon a fair system. Perhaps you can require that the selling party notify all the others at the same time. The first one to match the other offer can purchase the rights. Or perhaps you do want a bidding war. There is no single right way to go.

CHAPTER 6

Financing Commercial Theater in a Limited Partnership

The most popular vehicle for raising funds in the commercial theater is the limited partnership. Except for those wholly financed by deep-pocketed, international corporations (like Disney), most shows are financed in this structure.

This is an area that is heavily regulated by the federal, state, and, in some cases, local governments. All of your efforts to raise funds from investors will be scrutinized carefully by one or more government agencies. The laws are very detailed and specific.

Backers invest in shows in the commercial theater with the ultimate aim of making a profit. "Angels" who finance shows on a regular basis know the odds are against them, but they also know that, when a show becomes a hit, they stand to make enormous profits. A blockbuster hit can gross hundreds of millions of dollars. (Andrew Lloyd Webber's *Phantom of the Opera* has grossed over $3 *billion*.) Some do it for love of the theater, or glamour, or tax losses. All must be gamblers at heart.

On that note, let's examine the legal hoops a commercial producer must jump through in order to raise money to finance his shows.

The limited partnership combines the corporation's advantages of limited liability to its investors with the tax benefits of the general partnership.

Here's what I mean. If you organize as a corporation, the stockholders (investors) enjoy limited liability. As I indicated in chapter 1, they are not responsible for any obligations or debts of the corporation beyond their original investments. However, if the corporation makes money, its profits are taxed twice: first as income to the corporation, and then as dividends to the shareholders. And if the corporation loses money from its operations, the corporation, not its investors, gets the tax benefits. Moreover, the corporation must first have income, against which it may take the losses.

If you organize as a general partnership, the partner-investors get the tax benefits from any losses on their individual tax returns. But they also risk unlimited personal liability for partnership debts.

The limited liability partnership gives investors the benefits of limiting their risk for partnership obligations to the amount of their investments, while allowing them to take any tax losses to offset income from other activities on their individual returns, subject to the passive-activity-loss rules of the Tax Code. Profits are taxed only once—to the individual partners.

In a highly speculative business, such as the theater, in which losses are more common than profits, the limited liability partnership is the ideal vehicle for most investors.

REQUIREMENTS

A limited partnership requires at least one general partner and one limited partner. The general partner is the producer; the limited partners are the investors.

This is the way it works. A producer wishing to put on a show acts as the general partner. He bears all of the liability. He forms a limited partnership with a group of wealthy investors, who each buy shares in the partnership at whatever price the producer has set. This is how the producer raises funds.

If the show is a success, the investor, or limited partner, gets back her original investment plus a proportionate share of the profits. If the show fails, the most the limited partner can lose is her initial investment, which she may then write off her taxes as a loss. Limited partners are forbidden from managing the business.

A limited partnership agreement must be drawn up very carefully to distinguish the partnership from a corporation. Otherwise, if the IRS deems the venture as a corporation, the investors will lose the tax benefits.

Before the investors are obtained—and before the limited partnership agreement is drawn—the producer must familiarize himself with a myriad of factors, ranging from the total amount of money he will need to raise, to the procedures taken in the event of death, disability, or bankruptcy. These factors, among others, will be addressed in the limited partnership agreement put together by your attorney.

ESTIMATED PRODUCTION REQUIREMENTS

The producer must disclose the minimum amount of money he needs to raise in order to mount the show. This figure protects the investors in case the producer raises less than the minimum he was seeking. For example, suppose producer David Belasco estimates he needs to raise $1.5 million to open his show on Broadway (not an unusual figure for a non-musical these days). If he raises only $1.2 million, he is short and therefore cannot begin to use the limited partners' money without their written consent.

To avoid tying his hands to a specific dollar amount, a producer may target a range from minimum to maximum. In our example, Belasco may define his estimated production requirements as a minimum of $1.4 million and a maximum of $1.5 million. Now, if he raises only $1.4 million and he believes he can produce the play for that amount, he can draw on the investors' money.

OPTION PERIOD

The producer must disclose the period of time he has taken the play under option from the author. For example, the author may have given him eighteen months either to raise the money or to open the show on Broadway. The investors are entitled to know the time frame within which the producer must work.

SINKING FUND

No matter how successful a show may be, producers rarely pay out all of the profits right away. Theatrical grosses can vary wildly from week to week. Yet the show's running expenses must be met. Each week, the producer will deposit a certain amount of the profits (assuming there are any) into a "sinking fund." During weeks when the box office receipts are less than the show's nut (its weekly expenses), the producer may draw on the fund to make up the difference.

GROSS RECEIPTS

Gross receipts are the total of all of the money taken in by the partnership from any source. Ticket sales are the most obvious. But, remember, the partnership also owns a share of motion picture rights, as well as a share of such subsidiary rights as amateur licensing and original cast albums. And once the show closes, the producer will dispose of the physical production—sets, costumes, and so forth. These are all part of the gross receipts.

PRODUCTION EXPENSES

All of the costs it takes to actually mount the show are its production expenses. This includes fees to the various artistic personnel; rehearsal expenses; attorneys and accountants fees; the cost of sets, costumes, props, and so on; publicity and advertising; bonds and deposits with the various unions; and theater rental.

RUNNING EXPENSES

Running expenses are the costs of actually operating the show once it is up. These include royalties, payroll to the performers and the other personnel it takes to put on the show, publicity and advertising, and theater rental.

NET PROFITS

Start with the gross receipts. Subtract the amusement taxes, ticket sales commissions, running expenses, production expenses, producer advances (prior to the formation of the partnership), and all of the other costs involved with presenting the show. Anything that's left over constitutes net profits.

FILM AND RECORD COMPANY INVESTMENTS

Back in the days when Hollywood regularly purchased film rights to shows, studios often purchased limited partnership shares. Sometimes film companies made substantial investments in shows. Hollywood hoped, in this way, to get first crack at the movie rights.

Similarly, in the days when original cast albums could sell millions of records, record companies sought the options on the cast albums. (CBS financed the original Broadway production of *My Fair Lady* and made a mint, both from the album and from its investment in the show.)

At present, both Hollywood and the record companies are lukewarm to downright cold on film and cast album rights. (Actually, at the moment, Hollywood is more interested in producing stage versions of their more popular films, since they can be quite lucrative. But that's another story.)

In any event, if a record company or a film producer does invest in a show, in the hopes of nailing down the film or cast album rights, the investors must be told.

PRODUCER FEES

In order to attract capital, producers must keep the fees they propose to pay themselves out of a production within reasonable bounds. What constitutes "reasonable bounds" basically depends on what the marketplace will bear— that is, how much the investors are willing to compensate the producer for his services.

It is customary for a commercial producer to receive 1 to 2 percent of the gross weekly box office receipts. Obviously, this fee begins once there are actual box office receipts, or once patrons start purchasing tickets.

In addition, the producer receives a weekly "cash office charge," which reimburses him for that portion of his weekly office expenses used by the production. This amount can range up to several thousand dollars, weekly, if the show runs on Broadway. This fee usually begins two weeks before the first rehearsal and terminates two weeks after the show closes.

The producer is entitled to receive both the fee and the cash office charge for each company of the play under his management. In other words, suppose there are three companies of the play *Sex Marks the Spot* running: the original Broadway production, the first national touring company, and the second national touring company. All are under the management of Charles Grippo Productions, Inc. My corporation would receive a fee and a cash office charge for each of the companies—or three fees and three cash office charges.

The producer commonly receives 50 percent of the net profits, while the limited partnership receives the other 50 percent. The individual limited partners split that 50 percent among themselves, according to their pro rata share of the partnership.

Some producers wear more than one hat. For instance, a producer may operate a theatrical publicity and advertising agency in addition to his production company. Naturally, he will hire his agency as the press representative for the show, paying it a fee. As long as the work would be farmed out to a third party anyway (as in the case of publicity), the fee is reasonable, and he fully informs the investors, there is nothing wrong with this arrangement.

NET PROFIT SPLIT

Investors are entitled to know the formula for splitting net profits between the general partner and the limited partners. Commonly the division is fifty-fifty. However, I have known of sixty-forty splits (in the investors' favor).

RETURN OF CAPITAL TO INVESTORS

Investors want to know when they can expect a return of their capital, once the show opens. First, the producer must pay all of the expenses of the show. He must set aside money to cover any contingent expenses. The producer must also establish a cash reserve for the sinking fund, as discussed above. If he intends to tour the original company, he must have money for that purpose. And, finally, the producer must fund any additional companies of the play he intends to create. It is only after all of these needs are met that the producer may return capital contributions to the investors.

RIGHT OF RECALL

Here's a twist investors accept but rarely like. Suppose the producer has returned capital contributions to the investors, as well as some profits. Subsequently, the producer discovers the partnership needs additional funds.

He has the right to recall both the net profits and the capital contributions from the investors.

In other words, if you're an investor, just when you think you've gotten your money back and even made a profit, the producer can demand that you fork that money back over to the partnership. Investors return profits first, followed by their capital contributions. The amounts are pro-rated in proportion to the profits the individual investors have received.

ADDITIONAL GENERAL PARTNERS

The producer always reserves the right to bring in additional parties as general partners. These persons or entities will have the same rights and obligations as the original producer. If the producer takes in other general partners, he still remains obligated to the limited partners as before. The producer will pay the additional general partners out of his fees and share of the net profits.

ADDITIONAL LIMITED PARTNERS

The producer reserves the right to sell partnership shares to additional persons. During the time when he is endeavoring to raise all of the initial capital, he must retain this right so he can sell additional shares.

However, once the producer raises the initial capitalization, he may find he needs additional capital. Thus he needs to bring in additional limited partners. At this point, if he does so, he will dilute the interests of the original subscribers.

Here's what I mean. David Belasco sells ten shares in the *Sex Marks the Spot* partnership, at $100,000 per share. Each limited partner, at this point, owns a one-tenth interest in the partnership. Subsequently, Belasco discovers he was way off in his initial estimates and now he needs an additional $500,000 to mount the show. (I didn't say he was the smartest producer in town.) If he sells five more shares at $100,000 per share, there are now fifteen shares outstanding. This means that now each limited partner's share has been diluted (reduced) to one-fifteenth interest in the partnership.

Do you think the original subscribers like to see their shares diluted through no fault of their own? Not a chance.

Dilution means that each subscriber sees less of the profits. If the limited partners originally owned one-tenth interest in the partnership and it takes in net profits of $1,000,000, each limited partner receives one-tenth of those profits, or $100,000.

However, if the shares have been diluted to one-fifteenth interest, then each limited partner receives one-fifteenth of the profits or $66,666.67. Aside from profits, with more partners, the show must take in more money to pay back its capital investment. That means it may have to run longer—which is by no means guaranteed. That's still another reason investors hate dilution.

To solve this problem, the limited partnership agreement will permit the general partner to take in additional limited partners (after the original capital has been raised). However, he must pay them out of his share of the net profits.

Obviously, this puts the onus on the producer to estimate his capital requirements carefully and raise what he needs at the outset—not to mention staying within budget.

PRODUCER REIMBURSEMENT

The partnership must reimburse the producer for all legitimate expenses he has incurred prior to formation of the limited partnership—option fees to the author and attorneys fees, for example.

PRODUCER ASSIGNMENT OF RIGHTS

Remember that, at the very beginning, the producer took an option with the author for rights to the play. Subsequent to formation of the limited partnership, the producer assigns all of his rights to the play to the partnership.

ADDITIONAL COMPANIES

The general partner may use limited partnership funds to mount other productions of the play—such as road companies. He may also organize productions in other territories for which he has the rights—Great Britain, for example. He may present these productions on his own or in partnership with other general partners or firms, including some in which he may have an ownership interest. Some Broadway producers own or co-own production entities in other countries. Many American producers have ongoing production arrangements with producers in London, by which they jointly present West End productions of the New York producer's latest Broadway show, and vice versa.

DEATH, DISABILITY, AND BANKRUPTCY

The limited partnership terminates if the general partner dies, resigns, becomes disabled or insane, or is adjudicated bankrupt.

If you recall our discussion of corporations and partnerships in chapter 1, I said that a corporation goes on even if its principal shareholder dies, becomes insane or is otherwise disabled, or is adjudicated personally bankrupt. A partnership dissolves, however, if one of the partners suffers one of the foregoing events. This clause covers one of the four factors that, in the view of the IRS, distinguishes a limited partnership from a corporation, thereby allowing the investors to reap the tax benefits.

Of course, the limited partners do not want to see the partnership dissolve if any of these contingencies happen to the general partner. This is especially true if the partnership is presenting a hit show. Therefore, most partnership agreements provide a mechanism whereby any one of the remaining general partners may continue to operate the business. The partnership will not dissolve as long as he does so, within a certain specific time limit, usually thirty days.

PRODUCER CORPORATION

Many general partners are, understandably, reluctant to subject their personal assets to unlimited liability. To obviate this problem, they form corporations, which then act as the general partner.

This is acceptable to the IRS—up to a point. You can't just form a shell corporation (one that has no assets) for the purpose of acting as general partner for a theatrical limited partnership. If you do, the IRS would likely declare the whole partnership as a corporation. Your producing corporation must have substantial assets.

LIMITED PARTNER'S ASSIGNMENT OF INTEREST

Another factor distinguishing a corporation from a partnership is that corporate shareholders may freely transfer their shares. (That's why you can easily buy and sell shares in Microsoft or Disney or any of thousands of other corporations over one of the stock exchanges.) Therefore, to maintain the tax benefits of the limited partnership, the producer will restrict the right of the limited partners to transfer their shares.

Producers also curtail transfer of shares in order to ensure that the limited partners are persons (or entities) with whom they want to do business. This is not elitist; it is sound management.

Some partnership agreements allow an investor to assign his interest in the profits to another person—his assignee. However, the producer must give his consent. The assignee does not become a substitute limited partner.

If a limited partner dies, becomes disabled, or is declared insane, his executor or representative has the same rights he had. The same is true of the representative of a corporate limited partner that is dissolved. The representative is likewise bound by the same terms and obligations under the agreement as his principal.

ARTISTS CONTRACTS

The agreement must set forth, in specific detail, the contract terms of any artists who are entitled to percentages of the gross. These include royalties to the author, as well as to the director, scenic and lighting designer(s), and the choreographer. Stars usually receive a guaranteed weekly salary against a percentage of the gross receipts. The formula for determining these payments must be disclosed. In addition, if any of the parties have agreed to deferred or reduced royalties, this information must be set forth.

TERMINATION OF THE PARTNERSHIP

The partnership terminates under any of the following scenarios:

- *The general partner dies, becomes disabled or insane, or is adjudicated a bankrupt;*

- *If the general partner is a corporation, upon its dissolution;*

- *The partnership's rights and interest in the play expire;*

- *The general partner abandons the production;*

- *An event occurs that would dissolve the partnership under state law.*

Even so, termination does not occur automatically. The general partner must file a certificate of dissolution with the state and, in some locales, the county or municipality.

In addition, its assets must be distributed.

For more information on termination of the partnership, see "Limited Partnerships" in chapter 13.

LEGAL BOILERPLATE

The closing clauses in a limited partnership agreement are legal boilerplate: definition of terms; designation of the state whose laws govern; provisions for binding arbitration in the event of a dispute; the who, when, and where of sending legal notices; terms binding upon heirs and administrators and assignees. Once the producer's attorney has prepared the limited partnership agreement, the producer is ready to start raising funds, right?

Well, not quite, as the rest of this chapter will demonstrate.

SECURITIES LAWS

Prior to the stock market crash of 1929, the federal government paid only lip service to regulating trade in securities. Unfortunately, this left the door wide open for swindlers to market fraudulent securities to gullible investors.

During the "get rich quick" frenzy of the 1920s, investors purchased more than $50 billion of new, largely speculative securities. About half of all that money was lost in such worthless ventures as nonexistent gold mines, dry oil wells, and shell corporations that had no assets or operations.

Not all the investors were naive or babes in the woods. Many highly sophisticated investors who should have known better got caught up in the greed of the times and lost great fortunes. Even banks lost vast sums of money, which was why many depositors, fearful of losing their savings, created a "run" on the banking system. Unable to meet all those demands for withdrawals, many banks failed, thus turning their account holders' fears into self-fulfilling prophecies. Many investors committed suicide when they found themselves wiped out.

To help restore public confidence in the capital markets, Congress passed the Securities Act of 1933 and the Securities Exchange Act of 1934. Both were designed to assure integrity in the financial system. Both are based on the following principles:

- *Investors are best served when they are fully armed with factual information about the enterprise in which they are considering purchasing securities. Investors need to know the financial risks and the various other factors that might affect the business offering the securities.*

- *Investors must be treated honestly and fairly by the sellers of such securities—the brokers, dealers, and exchanges.*

SECURITIES AND EXCHANGE COMMISSION

To enforce the laws, Congress created the Securities and Exchange Commission, which, as you might have guessed, is headquartered in Washington, D.C. At present, it also has eleven regional and district offices throughout the country. Since much theatrical financing originates in New York City, the SEC's office there specializes in theatrical limited partnerships.

By law the U.S. President appoints five commissioners to run the SEC. One commissioner is designated as chairman.

The SEC has four divisions and eighteen offices. For our purposes, the most important division is that of Corporation Finance. If you are a producer seeking to raise money for your show, this is the division that will oversee your efforts. Contrary to popular belief, the staff is not your enemy. Actually, the employees are quite helpful. They can offer you valuable guidance to help you comply with the law.

The other division that can have great bearing on what you do is Enforcement. This, however, is the division that hopes not to hear from you and from whom you hope not to hear. They investigate violations of the law, and, if necessary, bring administrative actions before either a federal or administrative court judge. In case of criminal violations, the staff will cooperate with the appropriate law enforcement agencies to bring criminal prosecutions.

NECESSITY OF LEGAL COUNSEL

If you remember nothing else from this chapter, there are two crucial rules you must retain.

This is the first: *Do not attempt to raise money without the benefit of legal counsel experienced in securities law.* Next to taxation, this is the most complicated and confusing aspect of theatrical law that you will encounter. In putting together a financing package for a show, there are many decisions that require legal experience and advice.

And penalties for violating securities laws can be quite severe. If a producer fails to comply with what can be very technical rules, he may become personally liable to his backers for their investments. As I indicated above, under some circumstances he could also face criminal prosecution.

DISCLOSURE

The second rule you must remember may be summarized in one word: disclosure.

All of our securities laws (and the regulations issued thereunder) are based on one key element: Investors must be given full and complete disclosure of all the facts relevant to the security, which is being offered to them. The producer who wishes to raise money for a theatrical enterprise is responsible for fully disclosing to prospective backers all information that might affect the investment. In all of the following discussions, this principle prevails.

Once again, Class, what is it?

"Disclosure."

REGISTRATION AND FILING

The Securities Act of 1933 was designed to accomplish two things, based on the two principles mentioned earlier of full disclosure and fair treatment:

> *1. To make sure that investors receive accurate and full information about the securities being offered; and*

> *2. To outlaw fraud, deceit, and other misconduct, whether verbal, written, or by action, in the sale of securities to the public.*

To achieve these objectives, everyone wishing to sell securities (such as shares in a theatrical limited partnership) must first either submit the shares to full registration with the Securities and Exchange Commission or obtain an exemption from full registration. Its Corporate Finance staff will review the documents and either "approve" them for sale or send them back for more information and revision. Until the SEC issues its approval, the producer may not sell any shares. Under some conditions, however, he may advertise that shares will be available for sale shortly.

It's important to note that just because the SEC has approved shares for sale does not mean they are a good investment. The SEC does not pass judgment on the merits of the securities or the enterprise being undertaken. Nor does the SEC guarantee that the information being provided in connection with the sale is truthful and accurate. Approval means only that the securities meet the SEC's requirements for registration. If, in fact, the promoters have provided false or deceptive information, the law gives investors certain rights to recover their money.

A producer who "cooks the books" in an effort to defraud investors may be found personally liable to them. In addition, he may go to jail.

Full registration is expensive and time-consuming, and we will discuss it later in this chapter. However, under our securities laws, some theatrical offerings may be exempt from full registration. Let's examine the exemptions first, since they offer the producer the most benefit.

The SEC recognizes that full registration is often burdensome, especially when the amount of funds the producer wants to raise is not very large. (In the capital markets today, an offering under $1 billion is not even bus fare.) Therefore, certain small offerings may be exempt from full registration. The promoters of small offerings still must file for this exemption. These filings are simpler and require less time for the production's lawyer to prepare and for the SEC staff to review. Most theatrical offerings may fall under one or more of the following exemptions:

- *Private offerings to a limited number of persons or institutions.*

- *Offerings whose size is limited.*

- *Offerings made to investors entirely within one state.*

Exempt securities are exempt only from full registration. They still must comply with the securities law, especially as it relates to fraud. Their promoters are still subject to civil liability, as well as criminal prosecution.

REGULATION D

For many producers, Regulation D is a godsend. It enables the producer to raise the money he needs in a reasonably timely and cost-efficient manner. It gives him three choices under three different rules:

RULE 504. Under Rule 504, of Regulation D, the producer may offer and sell up to $1,000,000 of limited partnership shares during any twelve-month period.

In computing the total amount of securities the producer can sell within the twelve-month period, one must look at whether the producer has also sold shares privately during the prior twelve months. If he has, the aggregate offering of all of the securities must be taken into account and applied against the total he will now be permitted to sell over the current twelve-month period, under Rule 504.

Here's how it works. Suppose on January 2, 2001, David Belasco sold $50,000 of shares in the *Sex Marks the Spot* limited partnership to private investors. On June 2, 2001, Belasco sold an additional $50,000 of shares to private investors. On July 1, 2001, Belasco began offering shares under Rule 504. Between July 1, 2001, and June 30, 2002, Belasco may only raise another $900,000. This is because in the January 2, 2001 sale ($50,000) and the June 2, 2001 sale ($50,000), he already raised $100,000. This aggregate total must be applied toward the offering he may make under Rule 504, in the twelve-month period between July 1, 2001, and June 30, 2002—that is, $1,000,000 less $100,000 – $900,000.

There are other restrictions. First, the producer may not sell or advertise the shares to the general public. Second, the shares are "restricted" securities. That means that the purchasers may not, in turn, sell the securities to anyone else unless they are first registered or unless the SEC staff approves them for exemption. Restricted securities must bear a legend across their face that states clearly that they may not be resold to the public unless the sale is exempt. This usually means the purchasers must hold them for at least one year after purchase. A transfer agent must remove the restrictive legend, but none will do so without authorization from the issuer.

In practice, this does not come up often. Under the terms of most limited partnership agreements, shares in theatrical ventures are not transferable anyway.

At least $500,000 of the shares must be sold pursuant to a registration under the securities laws of the states in which they are offered. Thus, the producer must still comply with state blue sky laws. (See "Blue Sky Laws," later in this chapter.)

Within fifteen days after the producer makes the first sale of his securities, he must file Form D with the Securities and Exchange Commission.

RULE 505. Under Rule 505, a producer may offer and sell up to $5 million in aggregate limited partnership shares within any twelve-month period.

He may offer these shares to an unlimited number of "accredited investors." What is an accredited investor? Any of the following as defined in Rule 501 of Regulation D:

> • *A bank, insurance company, registered investment company, business development company, or small business investment company;*
>
> • *An employee benefit plan, within the meaning of the Employee Retirement Income Security Act, if a bank, insurance company, or registered investment adviser makes the investment decisions, or if the plan has total assets in excess of $5 million;*
>
> • *A charitable organization, corporation, or partnership with assets exceeding $5 million;*
>
> • *A director, executive officer, or general partner of the company selling the securities;*
>
> • *A business in which all the equity owners are accredited investors;*
>
> • *A natural person who has individual net worth, or joint net worth with the person's spouse, that exceeds $1 million at the time of the purchase;*
>
> • *A natural person with income exceeding $200,000 in each of the two most recent years, or joint income with a spouse exceeding $300,000 for those years and a reasonable expectation for the same income level in the current year; or*
>
> • *A trust with assets in excess of $5 million, not formed to acquire the securities offered, whose purchases are made by a sophisticated person.*

In addition, the producer can offer the securities to up to thirty-five other persons who do not meet the above qualifications.

Opens up a lot of opportunity, doesn't it?

The producer also has the freedom to decide what information he will provide to the "accredited investors," as long as he complies with the antifraud prohibitions of the law. However, he must give "nonaccredited" investors the disclosure documents that are required in registered offerings. And he cannot withhold information from nonaccredited investors if he gives it to the accredited investors.

Of course, he must inform the investors that the securities are "restricted."

RULE 506. You're going to like Rule 506. Rule 506 allows a producer to raise an unlimited amount of money without full registration of the limited partnership shares. Again, the securities must be "restricted."

Like Rule 505, the producer may offer the securities to an unlimited number of accredited investors and up to thirty-five other purchasers. However, under Rule 506, all of the nonaccredited investors must be sufficiently knowledgeable and experienced in financial affairs. In other words, they must have the capability to fully evaluate the investments and the attendant risks.

REGULATION D, OTHER PROVISIONS. In addition to the restrictions specific to each of the above rules, Regulation D also contains certain other limitations applicable to all of the rules.

First, Regulation D is designed to permit private offerings. This means the producer cannot offer, sell, or advertise these shares to the general public.

Second, the producer must be available to answer questions by prospective purchasers.

Under Rules 505 and 506, the producer must comply with certain requirements for financial statements, which must be certified by an independent CPA.

Regardless of the rule under which the producer hopes to fall, under Regulation D he must still comply with the securities laws of each state in which he is offering the securities.

REGULATION A

Regulation D allowed a producer to sell limited partnership shares in a private offering—an offering not made to the general public—without registering the securities. However, under Regulation A of the Securities Act of 1933, a producer may offer limited partnership shares to the general public without registering them, provided he meets certain conditions. He may sell up to $5 million in total securities within a twelve-month period.

To do so, the producer must first file a Form 1A with the SEC. This is an offering statement that sets forth, at a minimum, the following information:

- *Name of the producer, or general partner;*

- *Name of the corporation or partnership;*

- *Date and state of its organization;*

- *State in which it carries on its principal business; and*

- *Name of anyone owning 10 percent or more of producing company.*

During the twenty days following the filing of Form 1A, the producer may advertise that he is offering the securities for sale, provided his advertising only contains the following information:

- *The name of the partnership;*

- *The title of the security;*

- *The amount being offered;*

- *The offering price of each unit (share) to the public;*

- *The general type of business, such as theatrical limited partnership;*

- *A brief statement as to the general character and location, if any, of any property it owns.*

The producer's advertising must also inform investors from whom they may obtain an offering circular (see below).

During this twenty-day period, prospective purchasers may make oral or written offers to purchase the securities. However, the producer may not accept them. Instead, he must wait until his offering statement is "qualified." Qualification occurs automatically on the twentieth calendar day after the filing, provided the SEC does not delay or suspend the offering. Once the offering is qualified, the producer may accept offers and otherwise sell the partnership shares.

Why might the SEC delay or suspend the offering? Information might be missing. Or the SEC might find misstatements of fact. That's why you must make sure that you have included all of the required information on Form 1A. And you must take care not to misstate any facts.

PRELIMINARY OFFERING CIRCULAR. Before the producer's offering statement becomes qualified, he may give prospective purchasers a "Preliminary Offering Circular." It must be labeled as such on its outside front cover. It must also contain the following statement along the left-hand margin, perpendicular to the text:

> An offering statement pursuant to Regulation A relating to these securities has been filed with the Securities and Exchange Commission.
>
> Information contained in this Preliminary Offering Circular is subject to completion or amendment. These securities may not be sold nor may offers to buy be accepted prior to the time an offering circular which is not designated as a Preliminary Offering Circular is delivered and the offering statement filed with the Commission becomes qualified. This Preliminary Offering Circular shall not constitute an offer to sell or the solicitation of an offer to buy nor shall there be any sales of these securities in any state in which such offer, solicitation or sale would be unlawful prior to registration or qualification under the laws of any such state.

The Preliminary Offering Circular may omit the offering price and other information related thereto. Instead, on the outside front cover, the producer must include a bona fide estimate of the maximum offering price and the maximum number of shares to be offered.

FINAL OFFERING CIRCULAR. As I mentioned above, the producer gives out the Preliminary Offering Circular while he awaits approval of his offering statement. Once, however, his offering statement has been "qualified," the producer must give the Final Offering Circular to prospective purchasers at least forty-eight hours before he sells shares to that person. He should keep a detailed record of each person to whom he gives a prospectus.

The cover page of the final offering circular must bear the following legend, printed in boldface type, in capital letters, at least as large as that used in the body of the circular:

> THE UNITED STATES SECURITIES AND EXCHANGE COMMISSION DOES NOT PASS UPON THE MERITS OF OR GIVE ITS APPROVAL TO ANY SECURITIES OFFERED OR THE TERMS OF THE OFFERING, NOR DOES IT PASS UPON THE ACCURACY OR COMPLETENESS OF ANY OFFERING CIRCULAR OR OTHER SELLING LITERATURE. THESE SECURITIES ARE OFFERED PURSUANT TO AN EXEMPTION FROM REGISTRATION WITH THE COMMISSION; HOWEVER, THE COMMISSION HAS NOT MADE AN

INDEPENDENT DETERMINATION THAT THE SECURI-
TIES OFFERED HEREUNDER ARE EXEMPT FROM
REGISTRATION.

OFFERING CIRCULAR CONTENTS. In addition to the differing elements described above, both the Preliminary Offering Circular and the Final Offering Circular must contain the following information:

- *The name of the producer, or general partner.*

- *His financial contributions to the partnership, if any.*

- *The formula for sharing profits and losses between the producer and the limited partners.*

- *The minimum amount of capital each purchaser must invest.*

- *The maximum amount the producer intends to raise.*

- *Risks to the investor (see "Risks," later in this chapter).*

- *The name and the track record of the author.*

- *The producer's professional experience and detailed five-year track record of plays produced; the number of performances; and the gain or loss to investors.*

- *The name and a brief description of the play the limited partnership intends to produce.*

- *Names and track record, if any, of the artistic staff: director, designer, and so on.*

- *If any important actors will be cast in the show, the circular must disclose the details of their employment. (Remember that stars command substantial salaries, as well as a percentage of the gross; these factors will affect the ultimate economic success of the investment.)*

- *Provisions, if any, for overcall. (This is discussed later in the chapter.)*

- *Producer fees (see "Producer Fees," as was discussed earlier in this chapter).*

- *Estimated weekly budget.*

- *Subsidiary rights granted by the author to the producer, who will sign these over to the limited partnership.*

- *Production budget.*

- *The manner in which net profits will be computed; this formula is set forth in the limited partnership agreement discussed earlier in this chapter.*

- *Terms of the Limited Partnership, as we have discussed earlier in this chapter.*

FULL REGISTRATION

A producer should file a full registration with the SEC if he:

- *Intends to offer shares to the general public; and*

- *Intends to solicit purchasers in interstate commerce—that is, intends to offer the shares in more than one state; and*

- *The offering is for more than $5 million.*

As soon as the producer files for registration, and while he is awaiting SEC approval, he may circulate to potential subscribers a so-called "red herring" prospectus. It must bear the following legend in bold red ink across its face:

PRELIMINARY PROSPECTUS——ISSUED
A registration statement relating to these securities has been filed with the Securities and Exchange Commission, but has not yet become effective. Information contained herein is subject to completion or amendment. These securities may not be sold nor may offers to buy be accepted prior to the time the registration statement becomes effective. This prospectus shall not constitute an offer to sell or the solicitation of an offer to buy nor shall there be any sales of these securities in any State in which such offer, solicitation or sale would be unlawful prior to registration or qualification under the securities laws of any such State.

As the legend states, the producer may not sell any of the shares until the SEC approves the offering. Once it does so, he will provide potential investors with a final prospectus. Both the "red herring prospectus" and the "final prospectus" are similar to the preliminary offering circular and final offering circular used for exempt securities; however, the prospectus, coming in conjunction with full registration, discloses, in a much more detailed way, all of the information we have previously discussed.

RISKS

Theater is, by nature, a highly speculative venture with a very high risk of loss. The producer, as general partner, must fully disclose all foreseeable risks of the investment, regardless of whether he must register his limited partnership shares or whether they are exempt from full registration. In his offering documents, the producer must provide investors with statistics that show just how chancy their investment is. He sets forth details of the previous theatrical season, showing the number of plays that lost money. In addition, the following facts of risk must be included for prospective investors' consideration. The following is by no means an exclusive list of the risks inherent in theatrical investments. They are the most common, however.

PRESTIGE VERSUS PROFIT. Even if the play receives critical acclaim and wins all the major theater awards, it may still lose money. Investors stand to lose all of their capital. They must be willing and able to withstand such losses.

ABANDONMENT OF THE PROJECT. The producer may, for any reason, decide to abandon the play at any step in the production process. If he does so—and the decision is his to make alone—the investors may still lose part or all of their money.

FORESEEABLE RUN. The producer must disclose the number of weeks the play must run at full capacity to earn back its capitalization, based on the contemplated ticket prices. The play may not last that many weeks. It also may not run at full capacity, which means it will take longer to recoup its investment. The producer must provide statistics from the prior season showing the number of productions that ran for the necessary number of weeks.

INCOMPLETE CAPITAL. The producer may not raise the full capitalization necessary to put on the show by a certain specified date. If he does not, he must return any funds previously subscribed to the respective investors (together with accrued interest).

ADDITIONAL LOANS. Even if the producer raises the full capitalization, it may not be enough to produce the play. The show may run over budget or the producer may have erred in calculating the original budget. Whatever the cause, the producer may, in his sole discretion, advance or borrow such additional funds as he needs. Repaying these advances or loans takes priority over recouping partnership capital. In other words, the production must pay back these advances or borrowings before it pays back the funds contributed by the original partners. The investors will have to wait even longer for the return of their capital. The show may not run long enough for that to happen.

NONTRANSFERABLE INTERESTS. Theatrical limited partnerships are, ordinarily, not freely transferable. In other words, a limited partner may not resell or otherwise assign his share to another investor without first obtaining the general partner's consent. Even if the general partner gives his permission, secondary markets for theatrical shares are rare to nonexistent. Thus, a limited partner is likely to be locked into his investment for the life of the partnership, regardless of whether he needs or wants the funds for other purposes. In short, these are very illiquid investments.

In addition, once a limited partner signs the limited partnership agreement, he may not withdraw. He is responsible for his entire share of the capital.

PROFIT RECALL. The producer has the right to recall any net profits or capital contributions he has distributed to the limited partners. Suppose the show is up and running and, out of the weekly box office receipts, the producer has paid back to the limited partners all or part of their investment. Perhaps he has also distributed net profits to them. However, the limited partnership incurs debts, taxes, or other obligations. To pay these bills, the producer may demand that the investors return both their capital contributions and the net profits.

RETURN OF CAPITAL AFTER PRODUCTION. Even if the play is successful, the producer need not necessarily return, in full, all of the initial capital contributions. He also does not have to distribute all of the net profits. Instead, he may choose to deposit some or all of these funds in a reserve, to invest in additional companies of the show. Obviously, this will delay the money from being passed back to the investors. Furthermore, there is no guarantee that any of the additional companies will be successful. They may lose some or all of the reserve funds, thus reducing capital contributions or profits.

ADDITIONAL GENERAL PARTNERS. The producer may bring in co-producers or associate producers, who will, of course, also act as general partners. There are two conditions. First, he must bring in the additional parties before the limited partnership is formed. Second, he must offer investors a chance to rescind any purchases they made before he brought in the new general partners.

TAXES. As we will discuss in chapter 12, limited partners are taxed on their share of the net profits of the partnership, regardless of whether they actually receive any net profits. Thus, investors must have the cash from other sources to pay taxes on net profits they may not actually have received.

SPECIFIC ARTISTIC PERSONNEL. The producer must disclose whether or not he has contracted for any of the artistic personnel for the show. This is particularly true if the show is built around or needs a star. Furthermore, if the star dies, becomes ill or is injured, or otherwise leaves the show during its run, the producer must describe the likely effect on the box office and the investment in the production.

REFUND WAIVERS. A refund waiver is a risk factor that deserves special treatment. From the time the first investor purchases a share in the limited partnership until the last subscriber comes on board, the producer must deposit all incoming funds into a special escrow account with a bank. He may not begin to use this money until he has raised all of the capital and he can form the limited partnership. Until that time, he is holding that money in trust for the benefit of the investors.

If he abandons the play, he must refund all previously raised funds to the investors. In other words, if the producer cannot complete the offering, for any reason, the early subscribers have the right to get their money back.

During the time the producer is seeking backing, he needs funds for production-related expenses. Perhaps he has the chance to engage a major star, but the star's agent demands a substantial advance before he will permit the star to sign a contract. Or the producer needs funds to book a desirable theater. We could conjure up a host of reasons why the producer needs immediate cash.

Early subscribers may let him tap into some of their funds. However, this is a very risky proposition. They expose themselves to unlimited personal liability for any debts the production incurs before the partnership is formed.

At the time when the early investors consent to the use of their funds, they must choose whether to retain or waive their right to a refund if the producer abandons the play prior to production. If they waive their right, they may lose all or part of their investment. If they retain the right, they cannot look to the partnership for refund, since the partnership was never formed. Instead, they must look to the producer (general partner) for a refund. However, he may lack the resources to reimburse them.

It's a knotty situation. Investors should consider their options carefully.

The offering circular must state clearly that an investor obtains no advantage allowing her funds to be used in this way, unless she has otherwise negotiated such an advantage with the producer.

FRONT MONEY

A producer incurs various expenses in preparing a show for production. These preproduction costs may include the option for the play itself or rights to the underlying work, such as a novel on which the play may be based; advances to various artistic personnel, such as the director and choreographer; attorneys' fees; deposits on the theater; advance advertising and press materials; and so on. In recent years, producers have taken to conducting "workshops" to develop new material. These cost money to mount. Finally, the producer needs to pay the cost of preparing the offering documents, for the limited partnership.

Some of these expenses arise before the producer even begins to raise capital for the show. Some occur during the period when he is selling shares but before the time the money can be released for his use. These are called "front money" expenses.

Some producers have pockets deep enough that they can advance this money themselves. In that case, since they are expenses of the partnership (once it is formed), the producer is entitled to be reimbursed, out of the investor's capital, for his advances. (He may not be reimbursed for funds he has advanced for the purpose of raising money.)

Other producers lack the resources to bear these expenses themselves. They may need to take in an associate producer or co-producer to help out.

Front money investors take a big risk. If the show is not produced, for any reason, they may lose their entire capital. (See also chapter 8.)

OVERCALL

When a show goes over budget, it may also have to go into "overcall." This means the producer has to go to the investors and ask them for more money, to meet the unexpected expenses. Overcall is a very sticky situation, both for the producer (the general partner) and the investor (limited partners).

When a producer is preparing his production budget, prior to attempting to raise money, he must estimate how much money he will need to mount the show as closely as possible to the actual costs. However, no matter how careful the producer may be in his estimates, occasionally shows run over budget.

A show running over budget may be due to any number of factors. The most frequent causes are changes made during the rehearsal and tryout process. The author may create entirely new scenes, taking place on different sets than those originally planned. (When *Hello, Dolly!* was in tryouts, director Gower Champion scrapped whole sets, and, with producer David Merrick's blessing, had replacements built in a hurry—at great additional cost.) Tryouts and previews may eat up more production dollars than expected. Perhaps ticket sales are moving slowly, thereby not generating as much revenue as the producer had hoped. Performers may be replaced; this can be expensive, particularly if the performer being replaced is a star. Of course, the producer's original estimates may simply have been wrong. There can be a hundred reasons why a show goes over budget.

An investor who is asked for more money beyond his original investment is not gonna be a happy camper.

The producer may insert a provision into the limited partnership agreement, giving him the right to ask investors for additional funds for "overcall." The amount is usually expressed in percentages in relation to the investor's original investment.

For example, suppose the producer sold a hundred investment shares at an original offering price of $10,000 per share, raising $1 million. He needs overcall of 10 percent from each investor. In other words, for each share an investor has purchased, the producer is now asking her to ante up another 10 percent—or $1,000 per share. If all the investors comply, the producer raises an additional $100,000.

Unfortunately, some investors may balk. So what does the producer do? He needs $100,000 to pay the over-budget costs. He can't go to the compliant investors and ask them to make up the difference; that wouldn't be fair, and he would catch hell from some of them. Of course, he could take the money out of his own pocket, but that's only if he has the jack to invest. And that's risky for him.

The alternative is to sue the reluctant investors. But litigation takes time and the show needs the money *now*.

There is no easy solution.

You see why overcall can make a producer reach for the Maalox?

NEW YORK STATE THEATRICAL FINANCING

Since so much financing for theatrical ventures originates in (and is often confined to) New York, it is instructive to review that state's theatrical financing laws.

Specifically, let's look at the New York Arts and Cultural Affairs Law, art. 23, Ch. III, part 50. You can say that one out loud twenty times, or you can simply call it by the name by which it is known: "Theatrical Syndication Financing Act." (Okay, that one's not so easy either.)

Many of its requirements for offering circulars and limited partnership shares duplicate the SEC regulations we have already discussed. There are, however, certain provisions that bear particular examination.

BLIND POOL

It often happens that a producer seeks to organize a limited partnership to invest in more than one specific named show. He may be contemplating investing a substantial amount of the proceeds in several nonspecified shows. If the producer intends to invest 75 percent or more of an offering's proceeds in the nonspecified shows, he is making a "Blind Pool" Theatrical offering. (Without knowing the titles or other particulars of the plays that their money is backing, the subscribers are essentially investing "blind.")

The following language must be typed in boldface capitals on the outside front cover page:

BECAUSE LESS THAN 75 PERCENT OF THE PROCEEDS OF THIS OFFERING ARE NOW ALLOCATED TO SPECIFIED PRODUCTIONS TO WHICH THE ISSUER OR OTHER OFFEROR HOLDS THE PRODUCTION RIGHT OR RIGHTS TO INVEST, THIS OFFERING IS DEEMED TO BE A "BLIND POOL." A "BLIND POOL" IS A THEATRICAL OFFERING WHICH DOES NOT SET FORTH EACH SPECIFIC PROPERTY WHICH WILL BE PRESENTED AND WHICH WILL ULTIMATELY BE A SOURCE OF THE THEATRICAL PRODUCTION COMPANY'S PROFITS, IF ANY.

TWO OR MORE PRODUCTIONS

A producer who intends to invest the proceeds from an offering in more than one show must disclose a risk particular to this kind of venture: specifically, that profits and losses from the various productions may offset each other.

For instance, the producer invests $100,000 in Show A; $100,000 in Show B; and an additional $100,000 in Show C. The results are as follows:

SHOW NET PROFITS
A $50,000
B $50,000
TOTAL NET PROFITS $100,000

However, Show C is unsuccessful and loses money, as follows:

SHOW NET LOSSES
C ($75,000)

The loss of $75,000 must be applied to the Total Net Profits ($100,000) generated by Shows A and B. It wipes out three-quarters of the net profits, leaving the investors with total net profits (from all three shows) of only $25,000.

The producer must disclose these risks, in the following legend, printed in boldface capitals across the cover page of the circular:

SPECIAL RISKS:
THE PROCEEDS OF THIS OFFERING WILL BE USED FOR MORE THAN ONE VENTURE. THEREFORE, WHILE THE LOSSES FROM AN UNSUCCESSFUL PRODUCTION MAY BE OFFSET IN WHOLE OR IN PART BY THE PROFITS OF A SUCCESSFUL PRODUCTION, INVESTORS SHOULD NOTE THAT PROFITS FROM A SUCCESSFUL PRODUC-TION MIGHT BE DIVERTED TO AN UNSUCCESSFUL ONE.

STATE BLUE SKY LAWS

In addition to federal regulation of securities, most states also regulate securities offerings made within their borders, under "Blue Sky Laws." Because little theatrical financing is done outside New York, other state regulators may not be as knowledgeable or experienced in theatrical financings.

Usually, the Attorney General's office of the state supervises securities offerings, and it is with that office the producer must deal. Some states will accept the Federal filings, and others require separate documentation. Again, your counsel is the best person to advise you what you must do in your state.

Financing commercial theater is a legal minefield. But, with all the money that's at stake, would you expect anything less?

CHAPTER 7

Managing the Nonprofit Theater Company

By its nature, the nonprofit theater company presents management challenges of its own. Since its aim is not to make a profit for investors, its producers have the freedom to select scripts with a more narrow appeal than commercial producers. While this approach may be satisfying artistically, it usually results in a wide gap between ticket revenues and budgetary expenses, thereby leaving the nonprofit's managers scrambling endlessly for additional funds.

In addition, producers, artistic staff, and the board must meet the organization's goals. Unlike the commercial producer, they have fewer resources at their disposal.

Nonprofits face heavy scrutiny from a variety of government sources. Their producers walk a narrow legal tightrope. These pages will show the nonprofit's managers how to keep their balance. (Information on tax exemption for nonprofit organizations can be found in chapters 1 and 12.)

FUNDRAISING

Not-for-profit theater companies raise funds through a variety of sources. The most prominent of these are the following:

- *Government agencies;*

- *Private foundations;*

- *Bequests in the wills of wealthy supporters;*

- *Appeals to the general public;*

- *Ancillary businesses—gift shops, restaurants, etc.; and*

- *Corporations.*

Of these, we will concern ourselves with appeals to the general public, since they are the areas most heavily regulated.

APPEALS TO THE GENERAL PUBLIC

Nonprofits use a variety of techniques to raise money from the general public:

- *Telemarketing;*

- *Direct mail;*

- *Door-to-door solicitations;*

- *Fundraising events—bake sales, dinner dances, auctions, and so on; and*

- *Raffles, bingo games, Las Vegas nights, and the like.*

It is not within the scope of this book to evaluate the effectiveness of these methods of raising funds. Instead, we will concern ourselves with the laws that apply thereto.

REGULATION

Virtually all states regulate the fundraising activities of not-for-profit organizations. The states have two concerns:

1. To protect the public from fraud and misrepresentation by less-than-honest charities and their fundraisers;

2. To ensure that a substantial portion of the dollars donated actually go to the cause they are supposed to help.

REGISTRATION

In order to regulate nonprofit corporations, states require such enterprises to register with one or more governmental agencies. This registration is in addition to the requirements for organizing and operating as a corporation in the first place.

The particular agency with which the nonprofit corporation must register varies by state, but usually it is the Attorney General's office. Most Attorney

General's offices have special divisions that concentrate on nonprofit matters. In addition, many municipal governments require nonprofits to register with their offices, especially if the charity wants to solicit funds on a door-to-door basis. The charity must register with the appropriate agency before undertaking fundraising of any kind. The agency charged with regulating nonprofit corporations will provide the appropriate registration forms upon request.

All states provide penalties for failing to register. These sanctions are often monetary fines imposed against the organization and the persons responsible for registering. However, there may be other remedies available to the state's chief law enforcement officials. The Attorney General can seek injunctive relief. This means a court may (a) order the charity to register; or (b) remove from office the organizers, trustees, or directors charged with registering the charity; or (c) do both. In extreme cases, the court may even order the dissolution of the corporation. In short, the laws offer a wide range of potential penalties for failing to register, depending on whether the failure was inadvertent or intentional.

On the other hand, some charities may be exempt from registering at all, if they solicit less than a certain specified dollar amount in any twelve-month period.

ANNUAL REPORTS

Nonprofit organizations must file annual reports with the regulatory body. The annual report is the yearly accounting of the charity's fundraising and financial activities.

In its annual report to the state, the nonprofit must disclose the amount of money it received during that year. It must also report how it used or spent the donations it received. Of particular concern are the salaries, benefits, and other compensation the charity paid to its highest-paid officials or employees. In addition, it must disclose the fees it paid to professional fundraisers. The organization must reveal the total value of its assets and liabilities at the end of the year. The charity must also identify its major funding sources, whether government, corporate, foundation, or individual, and specify their respective contributions in dollars.

Once filed, this information is available to the public. This allows persons who are solicited for donations to determine if the charity is legitimate and to see what portion of their dollars actually benefits the nonprofit's purpose.

In addition to filing reports with the state and municipality, all nonprofits must file an annual Federal return (IRS Form 990 or 990PF) with the Internal Revenue Service. This, too, is public information. And if the charity uses professional fundraisers, it may have to provide audit reports by a CPA.

PROFESSIONAL FUNDRAISERS

Some people make a living out of raising funds for charities. The nonprofits pay them fees, the size of which may be tied to the amounts raised. States are particularly interested in these arrangements, particularly if the fundraiser receives inordinately high fees in relation to the dollars raised. Then the question becomes whether the professional fundraiser is using the charity to actually raise funds for himself. Therefore, if a person conducts or manages a fundraising program on behalf of a nonprofit theater company and is compensated therefore, he must register with the state as a professional fundraiser.

To further ensure that the money raised does not go into the wrong pockets, states often require the professional to also file a written accounting of all funds raised. He may have to put up a corporate surety bond, to protect the donations that pass through his hands.

The state is also interested in the professional's character. The state may prohibit from fundraising persons convicted of a felony or a misdemeanor involving fiscal wrongdoing, or a breach of fiduciary duty.

Penalties for failing to register and account range from monetary fines to jail terms.

PROFESSIONAL FUNDRAISING CONSULTANT

The professional consultant provides, for compensation, the nonprofit with advice on soliciting contributions. He may plan a fundraising program. He may even prepare direct appeal letters, telemarketing scripts, and advertising materials. However, he does not actually solicit contributions or handle funds. He does not manage or conduct the campaign.

Although he, too, must register with the state, requirements are a little looser. If he fails to register, he may be subject to a monetary fine, but consultants are not usually subjected to criminal penalties.

PROFESSIONAL SOLICITOR

The professional solicitor is paid to actually call potential donors or visit them in their homes, by appointment or door-to-door cold calling. Usually, the professional solicitor is the front-line person who is hired by the professional fundraiser.

EXEMPT INDIVIDUALS

Certain individuals who raise money for an organization may be exempt. This includes volunteers and employees of the charity. Salaried officers of the charity, who maintain permanent offices within a state, are not considered fundraising consultants. The nonprofit's attorney, banker, or investment counselor are also not professional fundraisers.

In most states, these persons are not required to register.

FUNDRAISING CONTRACTS

Many communities mandate that nonprofit organizations must enter into detailed, written contracts with professionals who raise money for them.

The contract must set forth the budget for the fundraising project. It must provide an estimate of the money to be raised. The charity and the fundraiser must disclose the projected expenses. The amount of total donations that will go to the charity must be provided.

Someone in a position of authority must also approve the contract by signing off on it. Often, this is the president and one or more directors. Some laws require approval of fundraising contracts by the entire board of trustees or directors.

In addition, the charity must file the contract with the regulatory body. Some states require filing of the contract by both the charity and the fundraiser.

CONSUMER FRAUD AND DECEPTIVE BUSINESS PRACTICES

Not-for-profit theater companies must be careful that their fundraising activities do not violate their state's consumer fraud and deceptive business practices laws. Common violations include: engaging in unfair methods of competition; deceptive acts or practices; pyramid sales schemes; misrepresentation in any sales of goods and services. Remedies range from monetary fines, to injunctive relief, to class action suits and even criminal penalties.

BOARD MEMBERS

Many people are flattered to be asked to serve on the board of a not-for-profit theater company. Although it is usually a volunteer position, the office brings with it a certain status and prestige. More importantly, it offers a way for people to become involved in their community. Serving on the board of a theater company offers stagestruck individuals a chance to become involved in the arts, even if they lack the desire or talent to actually participate in productions.

Theater companies often select board members for the contributions they can make to the organization. These contributions are usually their fundraising abilities. However, board members may also be selected because they possess legal, accounting, and business skills essential to the company.

Nevertheless, board members—even unpaid volunteers—take on legal responsibilities. Just as directors of for-profit organizations may be held personally liable for certain acts (or failures to act), so too may board members of nonprofits.

RULES FOR EFFECTIVE BOARD MEMBERSHIP

Board members must be proactive. A director who treats her membership as a mere honorary title is shirking her responsibility. Even if she never attends any meetings and never takes an active role in the organization, she is still legally responsible for what the organization does or does not do.

Before accepting a directorship or trusteeship, a person should thoroughly familiarize herself with the company, its purposes, and its artistic and financial goals. Once elected or appointed, she must maintain that knowledge on an ongoing basis. She must discharge her specific responsibilities seriously and thoughtfully.

In most cases, board members cannot materially profit from the organization. The law does allow them to receive reimbursement for any reasonable expenses and costs they incur as a result of their service. But they cannot receive salaries, unless they are also employees. In the latter case, an employee who is also a board member should abstain from any discussions or votes on her compensation.

Many states prohibit loans by the organization to its directors and officers.

Board members must supervise the organization's affairs with a diligent eye. Usually more than good-faith oversight is required. The standard is what an ordinarily prudent person would do under the circumstances.

The board should never act hastily. Each matter that comes before it deserves careful study and due deliberation. If the members do not have enough knowledge and information to make an intelligent decision, they must postpone voting until they do. Each member is charged with having the knowledge that the others have, even if she was absent from the meeting at which the information was disseminated.

Board members oversee the administrative staff, setting the organization's policies, hiring and firing staff, conducting performance reviews, setting salaries, and so on. Although the administrative staff (including the artistic director or chief executive officer) is accountable to the board, the ultimate responsibility for the company rests with the board.

CONFLICTS OF INTEREST

Board members must make loyalty to the organization their mantra. They must put the interests of the company ahead of their own.

Board members, ordinarily, should refrain from conducting business with the organization. They should avoid even the appearance of impropriety.

In the extraordinary case in which it may be permissible for a board member to deal with the nonprofit, she must take certain steps to make sure the transaction can withstand scrutiny.

She should fully disclose her interest in the transaction to the board, including the extent of the benefit she will receive from it. She must fully inform the board of all the circumstances.

The terms of the transaction must be fair to the organization. Prices and other details must be comparable to what the organization would pay if it were dealing with a neutral third party.

The board member should abstain from discussions and from the voting on the matter. A quorum of the board must exist without the member's participation.

It may happen that a board member, either in the course of her service on the board or in her activities outside of the board, may come upon an opportunity that promises great benefit. She is duty-bound to disclose that opportunity to her organization, rather than taking it for herself. It is only after the board (without her participation) turns it down that she may pursue the opportunity for herself.

BOARD DUTIES

The following is by no means an exhaustive list of the board's duties:

- *Establish and monitor the company's organizational policies and practices.*

- *Thoroughly oversee financial records. The staff should, as a matter of course, provide each board member individually with records, books of account, operating statements, annual reports, and so forth. The board should insist on audited statements.*

- *Each board member must review all reports filed with the IRS, state taxing bodies, and the agency that regulates charities. The wise board member keeps copies for her own files.*

- *Retain the necessary independent professionals—attorneys, CPA, investment consultants, and bankers, for example.*

- *Establish and appoint committees to oversee specific activities. Some possible committees: play selection, fundraising, tax oversight, and real estate. The committees should hold regular*

*meetings among themselves and with the appropriate members
of the administrative staff.*

• *Hold regular meetings, as required in the organization's
bylaws and under state laws.*

• *Create the organization's mission statement, and its artistic
and financial goals. Regularly review same to determine how
well the company is fulfilling its mission and meeting its goals.
Amend statement and adopt new goals, if appropriate.*

• *Keep accurate minutes of all board and committee meetings.
Maintain the organization's overall records.*

• *Carefully select new board members, as well as administrative staff members. Set search standards and perimeters, when
new persons must be hired. Thoroughly interview all appli-
cants. Engage new persons by vote.*

• *Set standards for selecting suppliers. Award contracts to the
appropriate persons and entities.*

• *Establish clear-cut policies to avoid conflicts of interest
among board members, as well as staff. Monitor all activities
to make sure conflicts are, in fact, avoided.*

• *Determine the annual budget. Carefully review staff recommendations and requests. Adopt budget. Periodically monitor
financial affairs to make sure the budget is followed.*

• *Find money to carry on the company's affairs. In a nonprofit
theater company, the box office rarely meets budgeting needs.
Income must be drawn from a variety of sources. Explore all
possible avenues of revenue.*

• *Prudently manage and invest company funds. Avoid waste.
Utilize assets in the best possible way, without subjecting them to
substantial risk. See "Imprudent Investments" below.*

• *Set staff compensation at levels that attract competent people, yet do not overwhelm the organization's resources,*

• *In consultation with counsel, make sure the company complies with all federal, state, and local laws.*

• *Supervise all fundraising activities. Contributions must go to the proper purpose. Donations cannot be squandered.*

IMPRUDENT INVESTMENTS

It is often tempting to invest excess funds in stocks or bonds that promise unusually high yields. However, yields are always commensurate with risk. The higher the yield, the more speculative the venture and the greater the chance of loss. Trustees must avoid these "opportunities," especially if they produce no immediate income.

Similarly, board members should avoid purchasing land or buildings purely as an investment and not because the property is needed for operations. Real estate is a very illiquid investment and can often be speculative.

Never buy securities on margin on behalf of the organization. In fact, it's never a good idea to go into any kind of debt for the purpose of speculating on the organization's behalf. This kind of thing produces losses more often than gains.

Remember, the board members may be held personally liable for imprudent investments.

WASTE

Waste occurs when the organization incurs costs (or loses money) that could have been avoided by prudent actions. Penalties are a major form of waste. Penalties arise from building code violations, failing to pay the appropriate amount of taxes, and from not paying bills on time.

Never leave excess cash in a bank account that fails to produce income. And make sure your company receives fair market value whenever it sells assets.

FIDUCIARY STANDARDS

Board members are fiduciaries of the organization they serve. Whether they are called trustees or directors, they hold a position of great trust.

LIABILITY OF UNCOMPENSATED OFFICERS AND DIRECTORS

Under some circumstances, uncompensated officers and trustees will not be held personally liable for their actions while serving on the board of a nonprofit organization. In order for one to avoid liability four conditions must exist:

> *1. Trustees and officers do not receive pay for their services;*
>
> *2. Corporation is tax-exempt under federal law;*
>
> *3. Corporation is organized as not-for-profit;*
>
> *4. Directors and officers must have acted in good faith.*

By itself, "good faith" may not necessarily be enough to protect the officers or directors. Courts ask whether the action or failure to act involved "willful or wanton" conduct. An action can be willful or wanton if:

> • *It shows a deliberate intent to cause harm; or*
>
> • *Even if the action is not intentional, it shows conscious disregard or utter indifference to the safety of others or their property.*

In other words, if a trustee behaves in such a manner toward the organization that he intends to cause it harm or he is so indifferent to its safety, he may be personally liable, even if he serves without pay.

There's another twist to all this: If the uncompensated trustee intentionally, acting with malice, misuses the charity's assets, he may also be subjected to punitive damages. Let's fully understand this one.

Courts may award two kinds of damages. The first kind, compensatory damages, makes the victim whole. If I, as trustee of the Soon to Be Famous Players, act in such a way that I cause the company to lose $10,000, the court may order me to pay compensatory damages. This means I have to pay the Soon to Be Famous Players the sum of $10,000—to make it whole for my misbehavior.

However, if the court finds I intentionally breached my fiduciary duty with malice, it may, in addition to compensatory damages, order me to pay punitive damages to the company. Punitive damages are designed to punish me. Punitive damages can amount to huge dollars, far in excess of the compensatory damages.

Whew!

Except that's not all.

Suppose I deliberately took $10,000 from the Soon to Be Famous Players to pay off my gambling debts to Tony "Break-a U Legs" Mancini. I breached my fiduciary duties. I didn't have legal authority to take the money for my own use. I knew what I was doing.

Under many state laws, I may be guilty of a felony. I might go to jail. The court may also hold me liable civilly to the organization—that is, award compensatory and punitive damages against me.

In short, even though an officer or trustee serves without compensation, he must still act faithfully, with loyalty to his organization's interests.

CHAPTER 8

Joint Ventures

Back in the good old days of the Broadway theater, one man, such as David Merrick, would be the driving force behind a show. Merrick would acquire the property, raise the necessary backing, hire the artistic and business personnel, and shepherd the show to its destination on 42nd Street. But in the Broadway of the twenty-first century, the sole producer has become nearly extinct. Most shows today have two or more producers. (The credits for *The Producers* lists thirteen persons and entities as producers and associate producers.)

Even Hollywood has succumbed to the trend. Today, the list of producers for an average movie or television show goes on and on. (Admittedly, few of these are true producers; in Hollywood, an A-list star can get a producer's credit for her poodle's veterinarian, if she has enough clout and makes enough noise.) And, in the Hollywood of not so long ago, when studio heads were fiercely competitive with each other, it would have been unthinkable for two film companies to jointly produce a movie. Yet, today, the arrangement has become so prevalent it is getting to be the norm. For example, 20th Century Fox and Paramount co-produced *Titanic*.

In the rest of the country, beyond Times Square, it is becoming increasingly common for two or more theater companies to join together to produce a single show. Often, this is done on a broad geographic basis. For instance, several dinner theaters operating in the mid-Atlantic states will band together to produce an original musical that will then play each of their venues.

Of course, the primary reason for all these co-productions is money. With so many different opportunities for consumers to spend their entertainment dollars—movies, theater, sporting events, and concerts—live theater must try much harder than in the past. This often means bigger, costlier, and riskier productions, which are often beyond the resources of a single company.

In the business world, corporations often band together for a single common goal. Perhaps Corporation A owns the patent on a new product, yet it lacks the expertise to market it effectively. It might join together with Company B, whose advertising and sales capabilities are top notch, to form a separate entity to manufacture and distribute the product to consumers. This arrangement is known as a *joint venture*.

REQUIREMENTS

A joint venture requires two or more persons or entities. An entity may be a corporation, a general or limited partnership, or a business trust. The two parties join together to carry out a single business enterprise, with the hope of making a profit.

Usually, each party brings some kind of unique resource to the enterprise. Suppose Grippo and Miller wish to produce a show together. Grippo holds the option on the property *Santa's Children*, and Miller has the money. (He is wealthy himself or he has access to wealthy investors.) We are joined by a third party, Wilbur, who can cajole a major star to appear in our production. This is the most common way in which joint ventures are used in the theater.

Although joint ventures share similarities with partnerships (and indeed they are, for the most part, governed by partnership law), there are significant differences. Ordinarily, if Grippo, Miller, and Wilbur form a general partnership, we will each agree to devote all or at least substantially all of our time and resources to the partnership. It is, for the most part, an exclusive arrangement.

In a joint venture, the parties do not make an exclusive commitment to the enterprise. Each party is free to engage in other businesses, even competing ones. This means that, although I am associated with Miller and Wilbur on our production of *Santa's Children*, I am free to produce other shows, either on my own or with completely different partners. Of course, Miller and Wilbur have the same rights. This is true even though, in my partnership with others, I may produce another Christmas show—even one across the street from the theater in which our show is playing. All that is usually required is that we each commit as much of our time and resources as necessary to produce our production.

Another key difference between partnerships and joint ventures is the scope and duration of the arrangement. Partnerships are ongoing relationships that may involve a complex series of business transactions, and that may go on and on until one of the parties dies or withdraws from the partnership. A joint venture is created for a single, limited purpose and for a certain specific duration.

For instance, Richard Rodgers and Oscar Hammerstein formed a partnership (not a joint venture) to produce all of their shows, like *South Pacific*, *The King and I*, and *The Sound of Music*. It lasted until Hammerstein's death.

Grippo, Miller, and Wilbur can agree to do the same thing. We can form a general partnership that expects to produce several shows over many years, until the first of us dies or withdraws. However, that is not what we have elected to do. We have agreed to form an association for a single, limited purpose: to produce *Santa's Children* in or around Times Square (and all subsequent touring companies). That is our sole purpose for associating. It terminates or dissolves once our production of *Santa's Children* has run its course.

CREATING THE JOINT VENTURE

We create a joint venture by agreeing to create one. Ideally, this agreement should be in writing. It should state clearly all of the terms we have negotiated among ourselves. However, it is possible to create a joint venture by a simple verbal agreement:

MICKEY: I'll tell you what we do. We put on a show!
JUDY: Cool.

We can create a joint venture by our conduct, without expressly agreeing to do so. I have rights to the script of *Santa's Children* and Miller puts up the funds to rent a theater and hire the talent. Meanwhile, Wilbur brings that noted tragedian Ed Booth around to our offices. Booth agrees to play Santa Claus. Although we have not entered into a written instrument nor even verbally agreed to produce the play together, by our conduct, we have created a joint venture.

We must intend, however, to associate together for the purposes of producing a specific show.

GRIPPO: I have rights to a great children's play called *Santa's Children*.
MILLER: I have $10 million in nickels in the top left-hand drawer of my desk.
WILBUR: I bowl every Friday night with Ed Booth. He asked me to find a Christmas show for him.

This conversation among us is merely idle talk. We have not shown any intention of producing the show together.

Once, however, we do agree to form a joint venture to produce the play, the real negotiations must begin in earnest. We must agree on the specific purpose of the enterprise we are forming. In the usual case, producers form a joint venture for the purpose of producing a specific play in a specific location. The joint venture is usually established in order to go on to create the limited partnership that will finance the play. So, when Grippo, Miller, and Wilbur enter into our written joint venture arrangement, we first acknowledge that we have the option on the play. We want to produce the show in New York

City. Now we want to raise the necessary funds. In addition, we three agree to act as the general partners of the limited liability partnership we are organizing: the *Santa's Children* partnership.

It is important to state in the joint venture agreement the specific contributions each of us is making to the enterprise. In my case, I am bringing the rights to the play. Miller is providing the funds through his contacts with wealthy investors. Wilbur will get us our star.

BUDGET

Next, we will propose a budget for the show. It is wise to specify both the maximum dollars we expect to need, as well as the minimum we will accept in order to go forward. Let's say $1,500,000 as a maximum, with $1,450,000 as the bare minimum.

NET PROFITS

In conjunction with the proposed budget, we must also set forth how we intend to divide the net profits of the limited partnership between the limited partners and ourselves as general partners. Commonly, the split is fifty-fifty—the limited partners receive 50 percent of the net profits, while we, the general partners, receive the other 50 percent. To induce parties to invest in the show, it's common to first pay back the investors their capital contributions before splitting net profits with the general partners. (See "Return of Capital to Investors" in chapter 6.)

We must decide how we will split our share of the profits among ourselves. This can become tricky. Miller can argue, justifiably, that since he is the one raising all the funds, he deserves a larger percentage of the general partners' profits. However, Wilbur can contend that his access to Booth gives us a star whose box office draw can mean millions. I can claim that, if I hadn't acquired the rights to the play, there would be no show in the first place.

A variation of this scenario might be one in which all three of us also participate in raising of the funds. Should the party who raises the most cash receive the highest percentage of net profits, in proportion to what he has raised? But what about our respective contributions of play and star? Shouldn't those also count for something?

I can't give you a definitive formula. It must be negotiated among the parties.

LOSSES

And we can't forget losses. In a high-risk business such as the theater, losses are not only possible but quite likely. It is fairest for the limited partners to share losses in the same proportion as they would share in the net profits.

PRODUCERS FEE

In addition to sharing in the net profits, producers are also entitled to a weekly producers fee. This is commonly a percentage of the gross weekly box office receipts. Once the show recoups its investment, this percentage rises. There is no set percentage. It is a negotiable figure, largely dependent on what the limited partners will accept. However 1 to 2 percent is the normal range for the total producers fee, which is then split among the producers.

Similarly, the producers also receive a weekly office overhead fee. (See "Producer Fees" in chapter 6.) The parties to the joint venture must decide how they will share these fees. Usually "equally" seems the most, well, equal way of sharing this money.

BILLING

Of course, we all have egos. Therefore it is important to designate in what order we will each receive producer's billing. Alphabetical is the most logical, yet the producer who raises the most money might argue he should be first. Of course, Grippo found the play . . . and Wilbur got the star . . . so maybe we should . . . well, you get the idea. Deciding on billing credit is almost as sticky as deciding how to share the profits.

The important thing is this: Whatever the order, all producers should receive credit whenever and wherever any of the producers receive credit.

We must also agree on the size and typeface of the billing credits. Ordinarily each producer's name will appear in the same size and style of typeface as the others (regardless of how we have agreed the order is to be).

MANAGEMENT

In a joint venture, all of the parties share equally in the decision-making and management of the enterprise. This is one important difference from the limited partnership. Remember, in a limited partnership, the limited partners cannot participate in the management of the business. Otherwise, they lose their limited liability. In a joint venture, the parties must play an active role in the enterprise.

Now, it is possible that the joint adventurers (and some joint ventures are adventures in themselves) can agree that one of the parties will take on the day-to-day management of the business. For instance, Grippo and Wilbur may be involved in so many different projects that day-to-day administration is impractical for us. In that case, we might give Miller the authority to oversee the daily operations. We must specify the scope of this authority. How far do we want to let him go on his own without consulting us? (Of course, Miller can then argue since he will be undertaking all the day-to-day management responsibilities that therefore he is entitled to an additional share of the profits or the producer's fee.)

We will want to be consulted on major decisions—for instance, sale of the motion picture rights, or a replacement for the star when Booth's contract runs out. Obviously, we want equal say in the decision to close the show or open additional companies. We probably won't care if a replacement dancer must be found for the third gal on the left (unless she's Wilbur's inamorata, in which case—oh, never mind).

And now here's where we must be careful—for our own sakes. Just as in a partnership, all of the partners are agents of each other, so, too, in a joint venture, all of the parties are agents of each other. This means that anything any one of us does on behalf of the joint venture and acting within its scope is binding on the others—even if they did not know or consent to it.

So, if Wilbur, acting on behalf of the joint venture, contracts with Booth to star in our production for, let's say, 50 percent of the gross weekly box office receipts, we are all bound by Wilbur's actions. We might have specifically limited Wilbur's authority to make contracts in our joint venture agreement. However, these terms might be ineffective against third parties, such as Booth, unless they had prior notice of the restrictions on Wilbur's authority.

PERSONAL LIABILITY

Unlike limited partners, our personal liability is unlimited, as far as third parties are concerned. Remember that we said that general partners have unlimited liability to third parties for contracts entered into by one of the general partners on behalf of the partnership. Our liability as joint adventurers is the same.

FIDUCIARY DUTIES

All three of us have a duty to deal with each other in good faith and loyalty. We are fiduciaries to each other. This imposes a very high level of responsibility to act in each other's best interest.

Extreme example: Suppose, after *Santa's Children* opens and is, naturally, the biggest hit since *The Lion King*, Miller receives an offer from I. Gypum, a movie producer, for the motion picture rights. Let's say Gypum offers $1 million. At the same time Universal offers Miller $1.5 million for the rights. Gypum calls Miller back and says: "Look, give me the rights for one million smackaroos and I'll put a hundred grand in your name in cash in a Swiss bank. It'll be between us."

It is Miller's duty as fiduciary to inform both Wilbur and myself that he has received two offers: Gypum's offer for $1 million and Universal's for $1.5 million.

Most likely, of course, we would go with the Universal offer since it means more money—for us and the investors.

If, however, Miller succumbs to greed and tells us only of Gypum's offer (or takes it), without also informing us of Universal's offer or the cash bribe, he is breaching his fiduciary duty to us. (He's not doing the investors any favor either.) In such a case, Miller might be liable to us—his co-producers—for damages, as well as to the investors.

DEADLOCKS

In the production of a show, there are many decisions that must be made, both artistic and financial. Joint adventurers usually agree to make all decisions jointly—at least the major ones. Day-to-day administrative decisions are usually best left to the partner designated to perform those functions. A problem arises, however, when we cannot agree. The last thing any show needs is a deadlock among its producers. Disagreements also often start over the smallest things, but, as egos and people's bank accounts become affected, disagreements have a way of mushrooming until they can paralyze a production. To avoid this problem, it is wise to designate a third party (in your joint venture agreement) to break deadlocks. It is possible to nominate one person to resolve both artistic and business disputes—such as the show's general manager. Or you may name, let's say, the playwright to settle artistic matters, while you allow the show's attorney to break business deadlocks. The important thing is to put a mechanism in place at the outset so that deadlock can be avoided.

It is also wise, at the beginning, to designate in the joint venture agreement the primary personnel the partners will hire for the show. This includes the general manager, the law firm, and accountants.

ASSOCIATE PRODUCERS

Provide for the possibility of bringing in one or more associate producers. An associate producer does not have the status or authority of a full producer. Most often, the associate producer is someone who invests a substantial amount of money in the show but not as much (proportionately) as a full producer. Depending on bargaining power, the associate producer may receive limited rights to put his two cents into the decision-making process, although this doesn't happen often. Even if, at the outset, you don't think you'll need an associate producer, it is a good idea to structure your joint venture agreement to provide for one. As you begin to raise funds, you may find you need the additional investment. Although it is certainly possible to amend your joint venture agreement later, it is much easier to deal with the subject at the beginning.

An associate producer does not receive a full share of the producer's profits. Usually, the associate producer receives a small percentage of the profits, in proportion to the investment he makes.

Associate producers are entitled to billing credit. Usually, this reads as follows:

> Charles Grippo, Jack Miller, and Pete Wilbur
> In association with Fred Scuttlebutt
> present

The size and typeface of the associate producer's credit is usually smaller than that of the producers. However, much depends on how badly the producers need the associate's investment and what they are willing to give up.

FRONT MONEY

One reason to bring in an associate producer may be the producers' need for "front money." (See chapter 6.) Even as producers are selling limited partnership shares and raising the capital necessary to mount a show, they must still expend money in preparing to mount the show. For instance, the producers must pay the author a fee in consideration of the option to produce the work. If the script is based on another copyrighted work (such as a novel), they must purchase the underlying rights for their proposed adaptation. They must retain an attorney, accountant, and a general manager. They will have to give advances to the various artistic personnel, such as the director, choreographer, and star. In the theater of today, producers often hone a script in workshops to get it ready for a full production. Unions require bonds to guarantee their members will get paid. All of these activities require money up front—hence the term "front money."

Often, the producer himself cannot, or is unwilling, to bear these costs himself. Depending on the project, they can easily total several hundred thousand dollars. In addition, it is easy to lose every penny of the investment. Why? It is not recoverable unless the show is produced. And there are lots of reasons why a show may not be produced:

> • *The producer may not be able to raise the full capitalization necessary to mount the show.*
>
> • *After putting the script through the workshop process, the producer realizes the show just isn't working. He decides to throw in the towel.*
>
> • *The show is built around a star who falls ill or simply decides she doesn't want to do this particular play.*

Of course, at the beginning, the producer fully intended to present the script. But since he lacks the money needed to front these bills, he brings in a co-producer or associate producer.

Once the producer raises the full capitalization for the show, and he can begin using investor funds, the producer may reimburse the front money investor. In addition to reimbursement, the front money investor will receive a small percentage of the producer's share of the net profits. This is usually in proportion to the share he could have bought with his money of the limited partner's share.

However, if the front money person leaves his funds in the budget, he also receives a proportionate share of the limited partners' profits. In other words, his money has bought him both a share of the general partner's profits as well as a share of the limited partner's share. This is because, by leaving his money in the capitalization, he has bought himself a share as a limited partner.

SECURITIES LAWS

Only a small number of parties form joint ventures. All of the partners take a significant role in the management and control of the enterprise. These factors exempt joint ventures from the securities laws.

Do not let this confuse you. While a joint venture may not be subject to securities law, the limited partnership it is seeking to organize will be. In other words, Grippo, Miller, and Wilbur create a joint venture for the purpose of raising funds to organize the *Santa's Children* Limited Partnership. Since Grippo, Miller, and Wilbur are actively managing the joint venture, the joint venture among ourselves is not subject to the securities laws. However, remember that we have entered into the joint venture in order to raise money from individual investors and to create the limited partnership. The limited partnership is subject to securities laws.

In other words, we are dealing with two separate animals here: One is subject to securities laws, and one is not.

TAXES

For tax purposes, our joint venture creates a separate tax entity apart from ourselves or any other businesses in which we are engaged. It is necessary to obtain a separate Federal tax ID number for the joint venture.

The joint venture will not pay any income taxes itself. Any income it earns is taxed to each of us as individuals. The joint venture will have to file a partnership tax return.

TERMINATION

The joint venture among Grippo, Miller, and Wilbur will terminate once we organize the limited partnership. Remember: The whole purpose of creating the joint venture was to band together to raise the funds necessary to produce the show. Once we have capitalized the show, the reason for the joint venture has been fulfilled. Therefore it terminates.

The joint venture, like all partnerships, can also terminate if one of the parties dies or withdraws.

Suppose, after putting much effort into wooing investors, we just can't raise the money we need. Maybe our option to produce the play runs out. Maybe Ed Booth backs out, lured by another producer to star in a musical version of *Schindler's List*. For whatever reason, we decide to throw in the towel. Therefore, it is smart to agree in advance that we can choose to abandon the project and terminate the joint venture.

Some time after our play has opened, Grippo, Miller, and Wilbur disagree on whether to close the show. Grippo and Wilbur want to keep it running, but Miller wants to close it. Under our agreement, we have the right to take over the show, while Miller has the right to withdraw. Once Miller withdraws, he gives up all of his interest in the show, except for subsidiary rights. We take control. This means now we are responsible for all of the expenses and liabilities of the show. Of course, we also receive all of the producers' share of the profits. And, although Miller remains liable for any acts of the joint venture taken before his withdrawal, he is not liable for any obligations or activities we undertake after he withdraws.

CHECK-SIGNING AUTHORITY

Of course, it is essential to ensure accountability for the funds of the joint venture. As a practical matter, it might be best to give authority to the day-to-day administering partner to sign routine checks below a certain amount. For checks above a specified dollar amount, it might be wise to require a counter-signature from at least one of the other parties.

JOINT VENTURES BETWEEN THEATER COMPANIES

Organizing a joint venture for the purpose of creating a limited partnership is only one way producers use this form of business enterprise. Another increasingly popular way is when two theater companies bond together to produce a play. Under such a scenario, the purpose is not to raise funds to create a limited partnership. The purpose is to actually produce the play. All of the above rules still apply.

Here, the New Lincoln Theatre Company and Holiday Road Productions have decided to form a joint venture to produce *Santa's Children*. New Lincoln owns the option to produce the play, while Holiday Road has the financial resources and the marketing expertise to reach the play's targeted audience: grade school children and their parents.

New Lincoln Theatre agrees to present the play at its facility for six weeks, beginning in mid-November and continuing through New Year's Day. Holiday Road will put up half of the production budget. It will advertise the play by sending direct mail flyers to families on its mailing list. Both companies will take out display ads in the local media, send brochures to schools, and purchase local radio and television commercials.

The parties are creating a joint venture for a limited purpose and limited duration. Because it is a joint venture and not a general partnership, both New Lincoln and Holiday Road can produce other shows, on their own, or with other partners, during the time period that *Santa's Children* is running. Both parties agree to devote as much of their time and resources as is necessary to produce the show.

New Lincoln and Holiday Road have an equal say in all artistic and business matters. However, at the first meeting over the budget, New Lincoln contends that Holiday Road's allowance for marketing is too low. The parties cannot agree. However, they have previously agreed to leave disputes over business matters to their general manager, Charles Grippo Productions. After hearing arguments for both sides and reviewing the figures, Grippo agrees that Holiday Road's allowance is just right.

The companies hold auditions. Another dispute develops. This one is over the casting of Santa Claus. Holiday Road believes local actor Ebeneezer McScrooge embodies all of the characteristics of Santa Claus. He is a favorite of the Holiday Road contingent. However, the New Lincoln Theatre crowd prefers George Washington Lincoln, a sweet, kindly character actor. Deadlocked again, the parties turn to the director and allow her to make the final choice. She chooses Lincoln.

The parties agree that New Lincoln will administer the day-to-day operations of the show. Both parties will make the major decisions. They give New Lincoln authority to issue day-to-day checks, including salaries. Major expenditures require signatures from the producers of both companies.

Without New Lincoln's knowledge or consent, Holiday Road contracts with local public relations firm, Wally "I MAKE 'EM FAMOUS" Cunningham. Because Holiday Road is acting within the scope of the joint venture, New Lincoln is bound.

Santa's Children opens to excellent reviews and sell-out box office results. Unfortunately, a major snowstorm blankets the city. At the same time, the local newspapers go on strike, interrupting plans for an extensive publicity campaign. Holiday Road decides it is no longer interested in continuing and wants to close the show. New Lincoln, however, believes it has a hit show on its hands. All it needs is a break in the weather and an alternate publicity plan. It wants to keep the show running.

New Lincoln takes over control of the show from Holiday Road. It will pay all of the expenses, make all the decisions, and keep the profits (if any). It gives Holiday Road a written instrument, agreeing to hold it harmless and indemnifying it from any liabilities or obligations New Lincoln incurs from the date of the takeover.

KEY ELEMENTS TO REMEMBER

The key elements to remember in a joint venture are:

- *The parties must intend to create a joint venture, whether by written or oral agreement, or whether by expression or implication.*

- *They must share profits and losses.*

- *The parties must jointly manage and control the enterprise.*

- *The parties must share a common interest—to produce a particular play at a particular time in a particular location.*

- *Each party must contribute something of value to the enterprise—skills, talent, money, the rights to the property, and so forth.*

- *Joint ventures are usually formed by a small number of parties.*

- *Joint ventures terminate like a partnership, either on a certain specified date, the withdrawal or death of one of the parties, or when its purpose has been accomplished.*

- *Parties to a joint venture are mutual agents of each other. They can bind or obligate each other to third parties.*

- *Parties in a joint venture are subject to unlimited liability to third parties for the contracts and actions of any of the other joint adventurers into or undertaken on behalf of the joint venture.*

THE FUTURE

I predict that, in the future, more regional and local producers and companies will form joint ventures to present shows. The increasing costs and risks of producing theater will make it necessary.

CHAPTER 9

Box Office Management

This chapter is about money.

Caught your attention, right?

Specifically, it's about your rights and responsibilities, as producer, toward all that cash that (you hope) is flowing into your box office for each performance. It really doesn't matter who actually runs your box office or handles your finances. In the end, the buck (pun intended) stops with you.

The producer is accountable to a wide variety of persons and entities for all the money that flows into, and out of, his operation. This includes the capital he raises to mount his show, whether from investors or donors. But that kind of money is the subject of a different chapter. For now, we'll just deal with the cash that comes into the box office.

To whom are you accountable? Your investors, if you are in the commercial theater. Your donors—whether individual, corporate, or government—if you are nonprofit. Your board. Your royalty participants—playwright, director, performers. Your employees, whose incomes depend on your box office take. The unions who represent those employees. The IRS, whether you're in the commercial or nonprofit sector. Your suppliers, your—well, get the picture?

And let's not forget your friendly local Attorney General. He's watching you if you raise money through the sale of securities or investment shares in your commercial production. He's also watching you, if you're a nonprofit, soliciting donations from the public.

But perhaps the people to whom an integrity-driven box office counts the most is your audience. For the paying public, your box office is usually the first contact they have with your theater. Therefore, it makes the most significant impression on them, perhaps even more so than what you put on the stage. Anyone forking over money to buy tickets to a show has a right to expect that the box office is well run, able to handle the customers' wishes in a professional manner, and sure to grant the right seats at the right price.

Give him a bad initial experience at the point of purchase, and a theatergoer will already be in a bad mood before your curtain even goes up. He may never come back to another of your shows. He may be unwilling to consider donating money to your nonprofit.

All of these people and entities have a vested interest in how you manage your box office. And you, in turn, have legal obligations to them to manage it in a way that is honest, fair, and professional. If you slip up, you could find yourself personally liable to them. If your actions were deliberate, you may even face criminal penalties.

This chapter is important to you because it will show you how to ensure integrity in your box office operations.

POLICIES AND PROCEDURES MANUAL

You need to establish firm and definite policies and practices. These must be codified in a detailed written manual or handbook, which all box office personnel shall be bound to follow. The most obvious benefit of a policies and procedures manual is to ensure uniform standards in your operations. All sales will be handled alike. Your refund and exchange policies will be clear, both to your personnel and to your patrons. In addition, this helps maintain continuity. Even if your box office personnel change, your practices will remain the same.

Written procedures mean that everyone down the line will understand their responsibilities and the reasons for each action taken, and this will produce constant results from performance to performance and show to show.

In addition, funding sources—whether investors, private donors, foundations, or government sources—will be impressed by knowing you have firm box office policies in place. It will help them to gauge the success of your operations, which in turn guides them in making funding decisions.

And, in case of legal controversy, a written policy manual is strong evidence that you as producer did all you could to maintain an honest and fair box office operation. (In case you haven't guessed by now, I'm a strong believer in protecting yourself at every opportunity. This means you document that you took the appropriate measures.)

If you already operate a theater company, you may wish, in particular, to review this chapter with your box office staff. If you don't already have a written procedures manual in place, this is the perfect time for you and your staff to create one. Even if you already have a policy handbook, it's a good idea to double-check your systems. Perhaps a little fine-tuning—or drastic modification—is in order.

BOX OFFICE MANAGER

We already know that you have way too much work to do yourself, so, if possible, you should delegate box office matters to others.

I highly recommend hiring a general treasurer or business manager, if you can afford one. Even if you are an all-volunteer group, you should place one person in charge of all the money. I know that in an amateur setting you sometimes have to take whomever you can get. (There are always more volunteers who want the glory of the footlights than are willing to do the gritty office work.) But, if you can, you should try to find someone—preferably with an accounting or business background.

Your treasurer will have plenty of work to do, managing and being accountable to you for all the money. He will manage the box office receipts as well as the investment capital you raise, if you are a commercial organization. If you are nonprofit, he will also manage grant money, donations, and other funding. He will keep the books and pay the bills.

Your treasurer may not have enough time to also manage the box office. This is usually a time-consuming position by itself. You may also need to bring in a box office manager.

Don't make the mistake many theaters do of underestimating this position. I know some companies consider it an afterthought, especially those that are artist-driven, in which what goes on before the footlights is usually of more interest than the office work. Yet, every theater depends on its box office for its survival. Even in theaters that receive donations and subsidies, ticket sales often account for a large percentage of revenue. (And donors and governmental agencies usually look to what the box office is doing in making decisions about future funding.)

Therefore, a good box office manager is essential to your continued survival. In addition, his integrity, knowledge, and experience will minimize the risk of legal problems arising out of your ticket sales.

The box office manager may be responsible for having tickets printed up, for accounting for those tickets, and for hiring and supervising the sales staff. He may also be in charge of group and subscription sales. In a small operation, he may even take a turn at selling tickets himself.

If you are leasing space from a theater, often the venue itself will provide box office services and personnel as part of its agreement with you. Even if this is the case, you should have a thorough understanding of common box office practices and procedures. This helps you in two ways: first, before you commit to leasing a particular theater, you can satisfy yourself that its box office is well run. After all, they will be handling your company's money. Second, this is the only way you can be sure the theater gives you the proper share of the box office. You can't hold anyone accountable for demands you have kept to yourself.

BOX OFFICE PERSONNEL

All persons who deal with money should be bonded. A bond is a written promise by an insurance company that, if the bonded person causes you to lose any money, either by a deliberate act (such as a theft) or by negligence, the insurer will reimburse you for your loss. No exceptions. This includes your treasurer, business manager, box office manager, and ticket sellers. The fees of bonding companies are usually quite reasonable, and, in any case, it's money well worth spending. This protects you against embezzlement and even against honest mistakes.

You should perform background checks on anyone seeking a position in which he will handle money. An interview is not enough. At the very least, ask for references and then call those references—preferably previous employers. Especially ask if he handled money.

Today, to avoid being sued for real or perceived defamation, many employers will give you no more than the very bare minimum information about former employees. Often they will only verify that the employer did in fact work for them during the period of time claimed and in the position alleged. There's nothing you can do to elicit more detailed information. However, you can at least document that you took all possible steps in screening potential box office employees.

TICKETS

All tickets should be numbered and dated according to performance. Color-code the tickets to make it easier and quicker for the takers to make sure patrons are attending the appropriate performance. The price of each ticket should appear on its face. Reserved or general seating may be appropriate, depending on your house.

The box office manager should keep a manifest of all tickets printed, for comparison to the total number of seats you have available for each performance. Your treasurer can also match the manifest to the total tickets sold by the box office, as well as the ticket stubs collected by your takers.

LIMITATIONS OF LIABILITY

Put "fine print" on the reverse of your tickets that gives clear notice to your patrons that you are limiting your liability to them under certain circumstances. Here are some examples of the ways you can limit your liability.

"LATECOMERS WILL BE SEATED AT MANAGEMENT'S DISCRETION." This gives you the option of seating anyone who comes after the curtain goes up in a way that will least disturb your actors and the other patrons. Some theaters refuse to seat latecomers until the intermission.

When I presented the Chicago premiere of *Beirut*, because of the intensity and subject matter of the play, the director and I jointly decided that no latecomers would be seated at all. (*Beirut* runs only a little over an hour and is performed without intermission.)

"NO PHOTOGRAPHS, AUDIO, OR VIDEO RECORDINGS MAY BE MADE OF THE PRODUCTION." Flash photography is disturbing both to the actors and the audience, and there is no reason patrons should take pictures of your show. Audio and video recording is, of course, a violation of copyright.

"THIS IS A MERE LICENSE TO ATTEND THE PERFORMANCE ON THE DATE AND TIME STATED. MANAGEMENT RESERVES THE RIGHT TO REVOKE THIS LICENSE—UPON REFUND OF THE FACE VALUE —FOR ANY REASON." This allows you to eject rowdy or misbehaving patrons.

I once attended a production of *Hello, Dolly!* in which Dolly was played by a black actress, while Horace, the character she hopes to marry, was played by a white man. During the performance a totally obnoxious—and possibly drunken—patron began shouting racial epithets at Dolly. Of course, everyone else was horrified, and the ushers quickly and properly threw him out. You want to reserve the right to do the same.

"NO REFUNDS OR EXCHANGES WILL BE MADE." Few theaters give refunds once tickets are sold, but many will exchange tickets for subscribers. Regardless of your policy, this leaves the decision to you, in your sole discretion.

"ARTISTS AND PROGRAMS SUBJECT TO CHANGE WITHOUT NOTICE." This is a little bit tricky. Your patrons presumably bought tickets to see a particular attraction or performer. If you must change the show or if the performer is unable to go on as scheduled, it is only proper that you issue refunds or exchanges. However, keep this right within your discretion.

"TICKETS FOUND TO BE FRAUDULENT OR PURCHASED FROM IMPROPER SOURCES WILL BE VOID, AND MANAGEMENT IS NOT RESPONSIBLE FOR REFUNDS." It may not happen to you, unless you are presenting a real blockbuster hit, but counterfeit tickets do occasionally surface, and you need to protect yourself.

COMPS

Comps are free tickets and are used only on a very limited basis in the commercial theater. The press always gets comps. The producer, director, playwright, and others directly associated with the production should, of course, receive their own seats free. Sometimes, by contract, the artists will obtain a limited number of comps for their friends or professional associates. (As a playwright I always ask for—and thus far have always received—comps for a few select friends and potential professional contacts.)

Obviously, if your production is a showcase, you will want to comp potential investors. If you are a nonprofit, you may comp members of your board and large donors.

As a marketing tool, you may offer comps to certain shows to induce people to buy season subscriptions. For example, if you run a five-play season, you may offer subscribers a "Five-for-four deal," whereby persons who buy a subscription to your entire season get to see one show for free.

Group sales are another source of comps. You may offer a free ticket to anyone who organizes a group of, let's say, twenty-five or more paying patrons.

If you are non-equity, often you will give your actors a limited number of comps. If you can't afford to pay your artists, they are entitled to some inducement for working for you. Often actors will work for free in order to have a showcase for their talents. They will expect you to give them comps so they can invite agents and other (paying) producers who might advance their careers.

Comps may ordinarily be charged to your marketing or fundraising budget, depending on their purpose.

HOUSE SEATS

Ordinarily, house seats are not the same as comps. House seats are not free; they must be paid for. These are usually the best seats in the venue and are reserved for the producer, star, playwright, theater owner, and anyone else who can obtain them in his contracts. They are usually for friends or professional associates. Sometimes the artist himself pays for them and then gifts his friend. Or the friend will simply pay the box office for them directly.

House seats are so common in the Broadway theater that they are a part of the Dramatists Guild Approved Production Contract, and other artists regularly negotiate them into their contracts. Often, the only issue is how many, and that depends on the artist's negotiating power. (See also chapter 4, "Author Comps and House Seats.")

BOX OFFICE REPORTS

Keep detailed box office reports, by the performance, by the week, and by the attraction. Each report should show the potential capacity, number of tickets sold at face value, number of discount tickets, and number of comps and house seats. The report should show how much money was taken in from all sources for each performance. It should account for group sales as well as subscription tickets used.

The box office manager, treasurer, and producer should all sign off on these reports. They must be dated.

You need these reports for your own internal accounting purposes. You also need them for your investors if you are a commercial operation. Your board will want them. The IRS will require them, in case of an audit. Your royalty participants are entitled to them. You must send these reports to the play licensing agencies. The Dramatists Guild also expects them.

In addition, detailed financial reports prove to foundations and other possible sources of grants what kind of business you are doing. Banks will always require them if you are seeking a loan. Finally, your local Attorney General may want to review them if you are a nonprofit and you seek donations.

SPECIAL ACCOUNTING

If you give any kind of discounts, you will need special accounting procedures for these (in addition to your box office statements). You might give discounts to senior citizens, students, or low-income customers. Perhaps you can receive subsidies if you sell lower-cost tickets to certain classes or groups of people, such as the disabled. A subsidy provides the difference between the face value of the ticket and the actual price you charge the targeted individual.

Group sales and subscriptions should also be handled the same way. Pay particular attention to accounting for subscription inducements by which, as I indicated earlier, you might offer a free show to persons who buy tickets to the rest of your season.

TICKET STUBS

After each performance, you should count the ticket stubs you've collected and compare the count with the box office statement. Discrepancies and mistakes should be investigated immediately and the appropriate documentation or notes attached to your records.

YOUR SYSTEM

Your box office system need not be extremely complicated, but it must follow sound accounting procedures and maintain uniform standards. This does more than prevent chaos. In case of an audit by anyone entitled to one—royalty participants, the IRS, your investors, or the board—you can offer concrete evidence that you are conducting your theater's affairs in a lawful, honest manner. Discrepancies will be minimized; and when they occur, your explanations will be backed by credible evidence.

CHAPTER 10

Artistic Staff

Whether the producer presents a single show at a time or an entire season, he will spend a great deal of his time negotiating contracts with his artistic staff. We have already discussed contracts with playwrights. Now we must turn our attention to actors, directors, choreographers, and designers.

Many of these persons are represented by collective bargaining agents, such as Actors' Equity Association or the Society of Stage Directors and Choreographers (see appendix C). If the producer belongs to a major management association—such as the League of American Theatres and Producers—that organization will negotiate contracts on its members' behalf, with the various craft unions.

It is important to remember, however, that union contracts set forth the minimum terms under which their respective members will work and to which producers must adhere. Actors, directors, and other artists will be represented by agents, who will try to better the minimum terms.

ACTORS

Actors may belong to the actors union (Actors' Equity Association), or they may be non-union (non-equity). The difference significantly affects the manner of negotiations the producer will conduct with his performers, as well as the terms of his contracts.

ACTORS' EQUITY ASSOCIATION (AEA)

Actors' Equity Association derives its bargaining power from a current membership of 40,000 actors and stage managers throughout the country. It divides itself into three regions—Eastern, Central, and Western—and five offices. Like all collective bargaining agents, it concerns itself with ensuring minimum salaries and benefits for its members. Its contracts seek to create a safe and dignified work environment and to assure job security. Its agreements cover jobs in the categories of Principal, Chorus, and Stage Manager.

At the present time, Equity negotiates and administers fourteen national and eighteen regional agreements. Its individual contracts are referred to as "rulebooks." Although all of its agreements address the same concerns, the specific terms are determined by the level of production that the particular agreement covers. For instance, its national production agreement covers Broadway, national and international tours, and large performing arts centers, such as the Kennedy Center. Obviously, it requires higher terms than its rulebook for, say, resident dramatic stock productions (Council of Resident Stock Theatres Agreement).

NON-EQUITY ACTORS

Non-equity actors do not belong to Equity. This is not necessarily a reflection of their abilities. They may be performers who are just starting out. They may also be veterans. They simply do not meet eligibility requirements for membership in Actors' Equity.

Non-equity actors are often paid; this at least classifies them as professional. (Amateurs never receive pay.) Their pay may range from a small stipend for each performance to a regular salary.

Most non-equity performers aspire to join the union, sooner or later.

With no one to negotiate on their behalf, non-equity performers must fend for themselves, trying to carve out the best deal and the fairest working conditions they can. They are, however, at the producer's mercy.

Nevertheless, both equity and non-equity performers have the same concerns. As a producer, you will have to deal with these issues when you negotiate performers contracts either with the union or with the individual non-equity performers. To simplify our discussion, I will address the issues both equity and non-equity performers are likely to raise with you.

SALARIES

Equity specifies certain minimum salaries, depending upon the type of production and the standard contract. Remember, however, that these are merely minimums; all actors will try to get you to do better.

One issue that often comes up is the so-called "favored nations" clause. Sometimes this works to the producer's advantage, sometimes not.

Under a "favored nations" clause, performers receive the same salaries as everyone else. In this way, actors who play comparable roles essentially get paid the same.

For example, suppose you're presenting *Annie*. Agents representing the individual children playing the orphans may want to know what you are paying the other "orphans," and expect you to pay their clients the same.

From the producer's point of view, this may be desirable. If an actor (or "orphan" in the *Annie* case) demands more, you can respond that the salary is "X" number of dollars, "favored nations"—that is, every actor playing a comparable role gets the same.

Actors may also seek bonuses if they receive nominations for awards or the awards themselves. This may be well earned, especially if the award is of great significance—such as the Tony. The award may be worth the bonus in terms of the extra box office it brings in.

BILLING

Of course, billing is of extreme importance to actors—perhaps second only to money—and there are those who would argue it is even more important.

In regional, dinner, and stock theater, billing is rarely an issue. All the actors receive equal billing. Sometimes it is alphabetical. Sometimes it is in the order in which their characters appear in the show.

As a producer, I would use billing as a bargaining chip whenever possible. Of course, if you are dealing with a major star with great box office appeal, you would no doubt put her name above the title anyway. Another arrangement, however, calls for use of the word "Starring" or "Also starring" before the performer's name.

However, actors fret about the location of their names in programs, flyers, and advertising. Therefore, you might give away slightly better billing in exchange for paying the actor a lower salary or an otherwise costly perk. Adjusting an actor's billing credit costs you nothing in terms of dollars. Some actors, in fact, will gladly give up extra money in exchange for improved billing.

Equity contracts have specific billing requirements. For example, under the national agreement, chorus members are now guaranteed a biography in the souvenir programs. The bio must be at least four lines, exclusive of the actor's name and the role she plays.

Under Equity rules, a producer must maintain a houseboard listing all of the principal actors' names, either in front of the theater, or, if that is not feasible, then in a prominent place in the lobby. The letters must be at least one-eighth inch high. If an actor leaves the show, the producer must remove her name and pictures, or else face a penalty, which increases by the week.

Billing may follow the tier structure of the play. In *Oklahoma!*, both Ado Annie and Will are the characters in the secondary love story and occupy roughly the same amount of stage time. Therefore, it may be desirable to give them equal billing.

Your bargaining power rests with an actor's natural desire to improve upon the minimum.

DRESSING ROOMS

Negotiating dressing room conditions is often tricky for both the producer and the performer. It is often difficult for a producer to make any guarantees in advance since the producer may not yet have booked the theater at the time he is negotiating the actor's contract.

Of course, a star will make all sorts of demands for her dressing room. No star will share with another performer. A star often expects producers to stock her dressing room with fresh fruit, Evian water, and even chili flown in from her favorite L.A. restaurant. A superstitious star may decide the color of her dressing room walls is bad luck. She may demand that the walls be repainted, more to her liking. Sometimes these extras are negotiated into the actor's contract. However, even for extras that are not, contractually speaking, the producer's responsibility, it is often smarter, in the long run, to accede to the star's demands than to have an unhappy performer.

However, even actors with much less bargaining power may express concerns that you must be prepared to discuss, if not negotiate.

Are the dressing rooms clean? Well lighted? Are they heated in winter and air conditioned in summer? Do they contain showers? Closets? Mirrors? Makeup lights? Bathrooms? Clothing rods? Hooks? Shelves? Chairs?

How far away from the stage are the dressing rooms? Will the actors have to use stairwells to access the dressing rooms from the stage? If so, are the stairwells in good condition and well lighted? Will the distance from stage to dressing room accommodate quick costume changes easily and safely?

Are the dressing rooms in another building? If so, what kind of throughway is available for ingress and egress? An alley? A street? Is the throughway well lighted and safe? Must the actors dodge vehicles passing through? In the winter, is it kept free from ice and snow? Will security be provided?

What about the security of the dressing rooms themselves? Who, besides the actor, has access? Are there locks? What about lockers for personal possessions, such as purses, wallets, photographs, and so on?

Will performers have to share dressing rooms with other members of the cast? If so, how many? Are there separate facilities for men and women?

When I presented a storefront, non-equity production of *Beirut*, the only dressing room facility available was the basement under the storefront theater. The show called for the male and female leads to perform most of the show in their underwear. The only egress and ingress to the stage was outside, through a narrow passageway. It was January in Chicago, and quite cold and snowy. The actors were real troupers—they never complained. But it was not a situation I would want to repeat.

SMOKE AND FOG

Four of the biggest musicals in recent years have required smoke and fog—*Jekyll and Hyde, Les Misérables, Miss Saigon,* and *Phantom of the Opera.* Of course, the use of smoke and fog is nothing new in the theater. Many smaller shows and theaters often use smoke and fog. (I know of one technical director who is so fascinated with the effect—or just likes creating it—that he inserts it into every show, whether it is appropriate or not.)

However, a recent study, commissioned by Actors' Equity and the League of American Theatres and Producers, concluded that smoke and fog may be deleterious to actors' health, particularly their vocal abilities. The study, prepared jointly by the Mt. Sinai School of Medicine and the ENVIRON International Corporation, determined that high levels of glycol smoke and mineral oil (the components of stage smoke and fog) puts actors health at risk.

Accordingly, Equity has issued guidelines (which have been adopted into their national production agreements) to reduce the amount of smoke to a level at which an actor may safely be exposed.

Equity has suggested that productions test the precise amount of smoke being emitted on stage at any given time using highly sophisticated—and expensive—equipment. Because many theaters cannot afford this equipment, ENVIRON, at the request of Equity and the League, developed "Equipment Based Guidelines" to reduce an actor's exposure. The simplest way to protect the actor is through careful blocking and choreography, to keep him away from smoke wherever it is at its peak.

The three levels are:

1. Actors may not be exposed to more than 40 milligrams of glycols per cubic meter (mg_1/m^3).

2. Actors may not be exposed to mineral oil in concentrations greater than 25 mg/m^3.

3. Oil mists should not exceed 5 mg/m^3 as an eight-hour time-weighted average.

As actors become more aware of the potentially harmful effects of smoke, they will demand protections in their contracts. Even non-equity actors are sure to take a stand. Therefore, producers need to address these issues with their technical staffs.

FIREARMS, SWORDS, AND FOILS

Equity contracts demand that producers maintain safe working conditions. When the issue of firearms arises, all performers—union and non-union alike—have a right to demand appropriate care.

If firearms are to be used in a production, the producer should schedule an appropriate number of rehearsals, specifically to make sure the firearms work properly and the actors know how to use them safely. I suggest bringing in a firearms expert to train both the actors and the stage crew that will be handling the guns. The cost cannot be measured against the potential harm that could result from misuse of the firearms. Your local police department can probably help or at least lead you to an expert. (You may also need permits, depending on local ordinances and what you are planning to do.)

One stagehand should be put in charge of cleaning and maintaining guns—even prop facsimiles—as well as the proper storage of ammunition. Remember, even blanks, fired improperly at close range, can kill.

You should advise actors even before you sign them to a contract that firearms will be used in the show and whether they are the ones who will use the guns—or be the onstage targets. You should also inform the actors of the safety measures you are putting into place. As with nudity, actors should have the right to choose whether to participate.

I would not take an actor's word that he is already familiar with guns. All actors should train with your expert.

All of the advice I have given relative to firearms also applies to swords and foils.

STAGE COMBAT AND STUNTS

Stage combat and stunts must always be choreographed by a professional fight choreographer or stunt director. It is not hard to find experts in both specialties, and it is incumbent upon the producer to do so—even if his actors are non-equity.

The producer's first concern here must be the safety of the actors. He should maintain first aid equipment wherever and whenever the actors rehearse or perform fights, stunts, or other potentially dangerous acts. The producer should defer to the safety recommendations of his experts.

In addition, actors who participate in fights or stunts should run through the routine prior to each performance with the fight choreographer or fight captain.

Understudies and replacements are entitled to the same training and rehearsal as the principals.

HOUSE SEATS AND COMPS

We have previously discussed house seats and comps in chapter 4, in relation to playwrights, and in chapter 9, in connection with box office management. Performers will also negotiate with you for house seats or comps.

In non-equity situations, a producer may have to give actors comps to make up for inadequate or even nonexistent pay. However, the producer should establish a clear-cut policy as to the number of comps he is willing to give away. He must state whether the comps are per performance or cumulative over the run of the show. It may be desirable to divide the comps into personal (friends and relatives) and professional (agents and producers). This method, however, may be difficult to enforce. It may also be desirable to set up tiers—that is, principals receive more comps than featured players, who receive more comps than members of the chorus, who receive more comps than extras.

A star always receives house seats, the number of which depends on her bargaining power. The rest of the company may participate in a pool.

WARDROBE AND MAKEUP

The producer always supplies the performers with costumes and wigs. Period costumes may be rented. Contemporary clothing must be new. Wardrobe should be cleaned by a professional laundress, whenever necessary.

It is desirable to keep at least one duplicate of each costume backstage at all times. Rips and tears frequently occur during performances—especially if the role is physical or requires dancing. Often there isn't time for repairs before the costume is needed again.

Even undergarments may be an appropriate subject of negotiation. For years, Walt Disney World furnished underwear to the performers who walked around the park costumed as Mickey Mouse, Goofy, Mary Poppins, and so forth. At the end of each shift, WDW cleaned the underwear before passing it out to another shift. However, performers did not necessarily always get the same underwear back. There were allegations that some of it was not always adequately cleaned (!). The union bargained for—and received—the right for performers to be issued one set of underwear, which they would individually take home and clean themselves.

The producer must supply dancers with footwear, which should be replaced whenever necessary. Worn-out shoes can damage the dancer's feet and impair her performance. If a performer must dance on toe, the producer must provide her with one pair of toe shoes.

Actors supply their own ordinary makeup, but the producer furnishes anything unusual. Linen towels must be provided whenever body makeup must be used for aid in removal.

NUDITY AND SEXUAL SITUATIONS

Some actors have no problem with appearing nude on stage or engaging in (simulated) sexual situations, as part of the script. Others have varying levels of comfort with these matters, and still others will not appear nude under any circumstances.

Both performers and producers are vulnerable, though in different ways. Some unscrupulous producers, claiming nudity and sexual situations are "necessary" to their production, have tried to take advantage of performers, especially those new or naive to the business. By the same token, quite legitimate producers have been victimized by false claims of sexual harassment—or worse—by performers whom they have rejected for jobs.

Requiring nudity or participation in sexual situations in a show is a delicate matter on both sides. Here are some guidelines:

If you require nudity or participation in sexual situations as part of your show:

• *Disclose that nudity is required in all your casting notices. Be as specific as possible: for example, "topless" or "full frontal."*

• *If performers call you, during your phone conversations, make clear your requirements. In that way, performers can decide for themselves if they even wish to audition.*

• *Conduct all of your auditions in a professional manner. Hold auditions in a theater or rehearsal studio. Do not ask or expect performers to meet you at your apartment or the Holiday Inn.*

• *Have at least one other person present at your auditions— preferably of the same sex as the performer. In this regard, make sure that the only other persons present have a legitimate reason to be there—the producer, playwright, choreographer. In Equity situations, either the stage manager or an official from Equity must be present.*

• *Avoid asking performers to strip at the initial auditions. Use the audition to judge them on the basis of their talents (the performing kind) and to weed out those who are unsuitable for the role. Equity actors may not disrobe until after they have been auditioned either as principal actors or chorus singers and dancers.*

• *Do not at any time suggest that sexual contact may help the performer get the part.*

> • *Do not at any time give or withhold a part because the performer is or is not sexually compliant.*
>
> • *Nudity at callbacks is a toss-up. If you expect several rounds of callbacks, I would not require nudity until the finals. Again, you should disclose early in the process that it will be required at callbacks*
>
> • *In truth, unless the performer's physical condition is really, truly essential to the role (be honest!), I wouldn't even require nudity at any step in the casting process. If you do need to see the performer's body before you cast, make sure your need is related to the play.*
>
> • *You must negotiate into the actor's contract the amount of nudity that she will do—for example, "topless."*
>
> • *Actors are entitled to request a copy of the script before they sign contracts requiring nudity.*
>
> • *If an actor has already signed a contract and you require nudity, you must obtain Equity's permission first. The actor must sign a separate rider consenting to the nudity.*
>
> • *Never, ever, ask or expect actors to perform actual sex acts. Equity forbids it. And what kind of theater would you be presenting anyway?*

Closely related to nudity in performance is the photographing of performers in the nude. One use of nude photography may be in connection with publicity for the show. However, the producer may also seek to record all or part of the show either on film or on video.

In all such instances, the performer must be informed in advance and she must give written consent. In the case of photographs, the actor must sign a separate release. The producer must disclose—and the actor must consent to—the specific use of the photograph. And the photograph cannot be used for any other purposes.

If the performer appears nude in any film or videotape of the production, she must first be given the opportunity to view the film or tape. She must give her written consent.

An equity representative must be present at all photographing or filming sessions.

Equity has specific Nude Photograph/Video Release forms, which the performer and the producer must use and file with the union.

The producer must also make sure that no member of the audience enters the stage, performance area, or backstage while the actor is nude.

Equity also forbids artists' renderings of nude actors.

I dwell on this subject at length, because a producer who fails to carefully observe these rules may find himself liable for a lot more than he bargained for. Equity itself can penalize the errant producer. However, the actor—even if she does not belong to the union—may also have the right to sue the producer for invasion of privacy, unless he has made the appropriate disclosures and obtained the proper consents.

OUTS

Actors frequently want "outs" in their contracts—terms that let them leave the show either permanently or temporarily. They dislike being locked into long-term contracts. On the other hand, producers want assurance that performers will stay with the show for the longest possible time.

In the Broadway theater, producers typically want stars to commit to minimum one-year terms (beginning with the later of the first paid performance or the opening). Stars, just as typically, want to sign on for the least possible time they can negotiate.

Under some contracts, actors may leave a show at any time up to two weeks before the first rehearsal. However, thereafter, if an actor wants to leave, he has to buy his way out of the contract.

See "Termination," later in this chapter, for more details.

MORE REMUNERATIVE EMPLOYMENT. Actors often want to leave a show because an opportunity has arisen elsewhere for a higher paying job, such as a film or a TV show. There are two kinds of "more remunerative employment" possibilities.

The first is a short-term opportunity, which Equity defines as employment of no more than three weeks. Long-term employment is, obviously, longer than three weeks.

As a producer, you must either fill the role with the understudy or find a replacement. Of course, this requires additional expense, including rehearsal time with a replacement.

Under equity rules, the actor must give you notice, the length of which depends upon whether the employment is long- or short-term. In addition, actors who are signed to term contracts may not avail themselves of long-term, more remunerative employment opportunities.

TRANSPORTATION

Under Equity Rule 73, there are strict limitations on the amount of travel hours a producer may require of an actor. The Company Manager keeps a "travel log" on which the Deputy must sign off, and which is then submitted to Equity. If an accident or other unforeseen circumstance results in a travel delay, the first half-hour over travel overtime may be excused, but, thereafter, all overtime is due.

Rule 73 also covers such matters as rail, air, and bus transportation as well as the size and amount of baggage that is permitted. It even provides for a replacement bus if the company bus breaks down more than twice.

Of course, non-equity theaters usually don't concern themselves with such matters. In such cases, transportation is up to the actors—except in the case of tours, in which case the producer usually arranges transportation, though not according to Equity rules.

HOUSING

Non-equity theaters—such as regionals, summer stock, and dinner companies—have varying policies regarding actor housing. Some provide a housing allowance, while others do nothing, except perhaps give out-of-town actors a list of real estate management firms in the area. Still others actually provide housing themselves. In the latter case, actors will negotiate many concerns with you.

Is the housing provided on an individual basis for each actor? Or will actors have to share with other members of the company or staff? (In case of nonprofits, sometimes board members provide room and board in their own homes for actors and staff.) Will sharing occur with members of the same sex? Or is the housing co-ed? How many persons will share the facilities? Will actors have private rooms and bath? Is the housing considered part of the actor's compensation? Are the facilities a house or apartment? How far away from the theater is the housing located? Is the area relatively free from crime? If the housing is some distance away from the theater, will transportation be provided? Are the rooms smoking or nonsmoking? Will meals also be provided? What provisions exist for alternate housing if the roommates do not get along? Are pets allowed? If so and Fido damages the facilities, how will the cost of repairs be determined? How far in advance of rehearsals may the actor move in? After the show closes, how soon thereafter must he vacate? Who pays for local telephone calls?

Some companies give out-of-town actors a housing allowance or per diem. Conversely, others may provide housing while deducting "rent" from the actor's paycheck.

ADDITIONAL DUTIES

Under Equity contracts, an actor acts, and that's the extent of his employment. However, in non-equity situations, performers are often called upon to take on extra responsibilities, besides acting.

Some dinner theaters expect actors to also work as servers, busboys, or hosts. Many summer stock, storefront, and regional theater companies require actors to help construct scenery, stage manage, work the box office, distribute publicity flyers, and do just about anything else that's needed. Some companies demand that actors also teach in their adjunct acting schools.

Non-equity producers must determine, in advance, whether they expect performers to take on additional duties. If so, they must disclose these requirements in their casting notices. Some theaters pay the actors extra for this work, while others consider it part of the compensation they are already paying the actor.

DEPUTIES

In Equity productions, the cast elects one of its members to deal with the producer over any actual or alleged breaches of the Equity agreements. There are separate deputies for singers and for dancers.

Even in non-equity productions, I advise producers to ask their casts to elect a deputy to represent them. Although obviously there are no union work rules to observe, a producer can benefit if one of the performers acts as liaison with the cast. The "deputy" can relay complaints and other problems concerning working conditions to the producer and even negotiate corrections. This mechanism is much simpler and more efficient, especially during the press of production, than dealing with each cast member individually.

Of course, the non-equity producer, though not bound by union contracts, must be concerned with the needs of his actors and receptive to improving their working conditions.

PERFORMANCE WEEKS

The contract between the producer and the actors must spell out the number of performances the actor is expected to give over a period of seven consecutive days. Equity contracts hold that a week's work consists of eight performances over six out of seven consecutive days. If the producer requires more than eight performances, he must pay the actors two-eighths of their weekly salary for each performance above eight. Actors who perform less than eight performances a week are nonetheless entitled to a full week's pay.

In non-equity situations, the parties must still agree upon the number of performances per week. It's a good idea to spell out which of these are matinee or evening performances. Of course, if the producer expects the actors to perform additional duties, as discussed above, this requirement should also be detailed in the contract.

Non-equity actors will properly inquire as to the number of hours the producer will be working them each week. These hours include performance, rehearsal, and tech work. It's not unusual, especially in non-equity stock companies, to expect an actor to give a regular evening performance, which finishes at 11:00 P.M., and then expect the actor to work tech until 4:00 or 5:00 A.M.

UNDERSTUDIES

Understudies cover all parts for which the producer issues contracts. The only exceptions are stars and bit players.

Understudies must be present at all performances, unless the producer otherwise excuses them. In musicals, understudies are often drawn from the chorus. Often, more than one understudy covers a particular part; thus, there may be first cover, second cover, and even third cover. Actors covet the first spot, since they are the ones most likely to go on.

General understudies may cover up to five parts. Performing actors may cover up to three parts. All understudies receive extra pay for each role covered—usually one-eighth of their salary each time they perform.

Understudies are entitled to billing. Equity has specific provisions for billing when the understudy performs. As they may work in only one company at a time, the producer must furnish them with their sides and musical materials.

When a show previews out of town (that is, away from its point of origin), the producer must hire understudies not later than two weeks after the first paid public performance.

"AS CAST"

Principals are often hired "as cast." Their part has not been specified or assigned yet; often, they have not even auditioned. Roles will be assigned after they arrive.

If a principal is hired "as cast," then he is only required to perform the part or parts he performs during the first two weeks of the run. Similarly, an "understudy as cast" will only be expected to perform the roles he was assigned to understudy during the earlier of either four weeks after the out-of-town tryout or two weeks after the opening.

If an actor, hired "as cast," wishes to terminate, he may do so without penalty, provided he (1) quits during the rehearsal period; and (2) gives the producer the appropriate notice.

TERMINATION

A producer may terminate an actor in one of several ways:

> • *If the producer must close the whole show, he must pay the performers one week's salary, provided he has also already paid them at least two weeks' salary. In addition, he must remit to them any outstanding rehearsal expense money.*

> • *The producer must give the cast (and Equity) at least one week's written notice that the company is closing. If the company plays Monday through Saturday performances, and the producer posts the notice at or before the end of the Monday performance, it is effective at the end of the following Saturday night. If the company plays Tuesday through Sunday performances, the notice will be effective at the end of Sunday, as long as it is posted before the end of the Tuesday performance.*

> • *After the first public performance, either party may terminate the contract upon giving two weeks notice to the other.*

> • *Sometimes an actor just isn't working out and it is desirable to terminate his services without letting him continue to go on in the role. The producer must pay him immediately and also give him the cost of transportation back to the point of origin.*

> • *If an actor is signed to a run of the play contract, the producer must give him one week's notice of the closing of the show or give him one week's salary.*

> • *When the producer terminates a principal actor, the producer has two weeks after the actor's last performance to sign a contract with a replacement or with the understudy.*

ORIGINAL CAST ALBUMS

There is almost no market or interest in original cast albums for shows that do not play Broadway. If an original cast album is to be made, the producer must hire the actor who sings or verbalizes the part in the show. The appropriate AFTRA (American Federation of Television and Radio Artists) contracts must be signed. The producer must give Equity three days notice.

In any given day, actors may record for a maximum of eight out of nine hours. After the first five hours, they are entitled to a one-hour rest break. If there is an 8:00 P.M. performance, the recording session must terminate not later than 6:30 P.M.

If the recording session goes into overtime, the producer must pay each actor one-eighth of his contractual salary, capped at 250 percent of the production contract minimum for each hour or part thereof.

TELEVISION AND MOTION PICTURES

As I indicated in chapter 4, a show may not be broadcast or recorded, by audio, video, or other means, without violating both the author's copyright and Equity rules. Permission from both the author and Equity must be obtained.

The producer must notify Equity thirty days in advance and negotiate the terms and conditions under which any recordings or broadcasts may be done.

Equity realizes, of course, that television is a powerful medium for promoting a show, thereby extending its run and the employment of Equity actors. For instance, producers highly covet offering an excerpt from the show on the annual Tony Awards telecast. And, in the past two decades or so, producers have also increasingly resorted to television commercials as a means of advertising their shows. Actors must sign the appropriate AFTRA or SAG (Screen Actors Guild) contract. Excerpts from the show may not exceed three minutes in length. Excerpts may also be used in conjunction with television news stories.

Some shows lend themselves to "making of" or "behind the scenes" documentaries. PBS presented an entire documentary on the recording of the original cast album for the Mel Brooks' musical *The Producers*. Of course, a broadcast of this sort serves as the ultimate promotional tool for the stage production of the subject show.

Again, Equity requires that the producers sign the performers to SAG/AFTRA contracts and pay at least the minimums required by those unions. Stars, of course, may demand more.

Non-equity companies also occasionally use commercials. When the Red Barn Theatre in Frankfort, Indiana, presented my play *Sex Marks The Spot*, they asked me for permission to present a brief excerpt—actually about five seconds—during a television commercial promoting their season. Of course, I gave consent, since it was in our mutual interest to publicize the show.

DAYS OFF

Equity requires at least one day off during each week, consisting of seven consecutive days.

Even non-equity actors may expect at least one day off, and, truthfully, it is in your interest to make sure your actors get some rest. Time may be a precious resource, but everyone needs time to recharge.

CODES AND PLANS

Unlike standard Equity agreements, Equity Codes are designed primarily to create opportunities for members to hone their skills and "showcase" themselves in the hope of attracting future jobs. Actors and stage managers work without pay. They are not obligated to remain with a production for any specific period of time. None of the regular benefits or protections of standard agreements exist.

Most showcase-type codes do provide some limited protections, such as future rights guarantees if the production moves to a standard agreement. Seating is limited to no more than ninety-nine seats.

SWING

A "swing" is a performer in the singing and dancing chorus who fills in for absent chorus performers. A swing may also understudy one or more principal roles or chorus parts. A "partial swing" is a performing member of the chorus who substitutes in a specific production number for absent chorus performers.

EXTRA

An "extra" may only be used to provide atmosphere and background. An extra may not be identified as a specific character and may not be required to change makeup. The extra receives a reduced salary—usually 50 percent of the minimum plus benefits.

CHORUS CONTRACT

A chorus contract is used for those actors who are primarily performing chorus work.

BOND

An employer organization signs a security agreement and delivers to Equity a security, usually in the form of a certified check, letter of credit, or a bank letter.

Equity holds this security until the closing of a production, at which time it may deduct any outstanding claims from the bond. Full or partial amounts may either be returned to the producer or rolled over to another production agreement.

Equity's bonding policy was established in the 1920s, a time when actors were often stranded in a strange town after a production unexpectedly closed on the road, or the producer simply disappeared without paying his performers.

As a young vaudevillian, Groucho Marx was once left penniless in a dusty mining town in Colorado when his producer flew the coop. It was this kind of problem that Equity sought to solve.

JUVENILE ACTORS

Okay, so, you've decided to produce *Annie*, and you've got all these little orphan girls that have to be cast. Or you're doing *The Sound of Music* and there are the Von Trapp family kids and you have to provide for them.

Be aware that all states have child labor laws that govern exactly how much you can work the little darlings. The Federal Government also has the Fair Labor Standards Practice Act that also rules what you can and cannot do. And there are special exceptions for children appearing in theatricals.

In some cases, a parent will sit backstage while Junior rehearses or performs. But, in many cases, Mama will drop off her little shining star at the half-hour call and then pick him up after the curtain goes down. In the meantime, you must provide a responsible person to supervise your child performers.

Whenever possible, try to provide separate dressing rooms for male and female juveniles, which are also separate from adult dressing rooms.

Depending on your rehearsal and performance schedule, or whether you are on tour, you may have to provide tutoring for the children. (There are specialty businesses that provide teachers just for this purpose.)

In many communities, you (or the parent or agent) must file working papers for child actors with the appropriate city authorities.

DIRECTORS AND CHOREOGRAPHERS

Directors and choreographers of "First Class" productions are represented by the Society of Stage Directors and Choreographers.

Many directors are also choreographers, such as Susan Stroman and Tommy Tune. When a director wears two such hats, she is entitled to the respective fees and royalties payable under each respective hat.

Directors have many concerns that producers must address.

FEES AND ROYALTIES

A director receives both a flat fee and a royalty. When the director signs the contract, the producer must pay her 25 percent of the flat fee. This portion of the fee is nonrefundable under all circumstances. The balance of the fee is divided into three equal installments, which are paid beginning on the first, second, and third weeks the show goes into rehearsal. Alternatively, the balance is payable not later than one week before the first performance, if that occurs sooner.

Royalties are payable weekly, not more than ten days after the week in which they are due.

If the play is a First Class non-musical, the director receives a minimum of 1.5 percent of the weekly gross box office receipts. The director of a musical receives a minimum of three-quarters of 1 percent of the gross receipts. The choreographer earns 0.5 percent of the gross weekly receipts.

Of course, name directors, such as the ones I listed above, will command higher royalties.

GROSS WEEKLY RECEIPTS

As you might expect, it is necessary to define gross weekly receipts. Generally, these are the total revenues taken in at the box office (which includes mail order, phone, group, and subscription sales) minus certain deductions, such as taxes, sales commissions, pension and welfare deductions coming out of New York's tax abatement program, and the like.

BILLING

Directors and choreographers receive billing on a line separate and apart from anyone else's credit. Name directors may also receive billing on the marquee, usually below the title. The parties will negotiate the size and typeface of the credit. Some directors may demand—and receive—a box around their name on all programs and advertising.

ADDITIONAL COMPANIES

If a producer wants to send out additional companies of the show, he must give the director and choreographer ten days to decide whether to direct or choreograph those companies. If the director or choreographer accepts the employment, the producer must pay her one-half of her original fee for each additional company. In addition, the director or choreographer receives royalties from each additional company she directs or choreographs in the same percentage as the original Broadway production. If either the director or choreographer chooses not to direct any subsequent companies, obviously, she is not entitled to any fees; in addition, her royalty is reduced for each company she does not direct or choreograph.

Director-choreographer options can be very tricky in lesser productions, particularly when the show is a world premiere. Often the director-choreographer of the world premiere will want the option to also direct or choreograph the show if it moves to a higher class of production, or if it moves from a non-profit to a commercial venue.

Here's how the problem presents itself. Suppose the New Lincoln Theatre is presenting the world premiere of a new play, *Salvage Job*, for which it wishes to engage C. B. DeMille, Jr., as director. At this time, New Lincoln does not necessarily know what success the play will have. As a condition of directing New Lincoln's production, DeMille, Jr., wants the option to direct *Salvage Job* if it subsequently has a commercial transfer. Now DeMille, Jr., may be a great director, but by contractually attaching her to the commercial transfer of the show, New Lincoln may be making a mistake.

Suppose the commercial producer, who wants to take *Salvage Job* to Broadway, does not want DeMille, Jr. He may want Jerry Zaks or someone else altogether. If DeMille, Jr., has the option to direct the commercial transfer, the producer may think twice. Either he will have to accept DeMille, Jr., or he may have to buy her out.

Of course, directors of world premieres often attempt to negotiate this right for themselves. Producers are well advised to be very stingy in giving it out.

DISMISSAL

Dismissing a director or choreographer is not an easy proposition, even if the producer has good cause. For instance, the director may simply not be right for the show, or her vision may clash with the playwright's. Nonetheless, the producer who terminates a director or choreographer must make full contractual payment.

LENGTH OF EMPLOYMENT

A director commits to eight consecutive weeks for a straight play and ten weeks for a musical.

In addition, once the show opens, both the director and choreographer must see it at least once every eight weeks. It is their job to maintain the quality and integrity of the production.

It is common for actors, giving the same performance night after night, to get stale or begin improvising things not in the original production. Some actors get completely out of line. It was said that six months into the original *Fiddler on the Roof* run on Broadway, Zero Mostel had improvised and altered his performance so much that it was barely recognizable from opening night. Danny Kaye's antics in *Two by Two*, after he tore ligaments in his ankle, have become the stuff of legend; even producer-composer Richard Rodgers couldn't control him.

In theory, the stage manager is responsible for making sure actors stick to the original performance. In practice, the stage managers often lose. Actors, particularly stars, don't always obey the stage manager.

Consequently, the director and choreographer must come in periodically to maintain the integrity of the show. When necessary, they must call additional rehearsals. They are not entitled to additional compensation.

Furthermore, if the director or choreographer fails to exercise the appropriate, post-opening supervision, her royalties may be reduced by one-half until she gets the job done.

CHOREOGRAPHER'S ASSISTANTS

Choreographers may require assistants, who are employed by the producer. In addition, the choreographer selects both the rehearsal pianist and the dance captain, whose salaries are the producer's responsibility.

TRANSPORTATION AND HOUSING

If the show tries out or previews in a location other than its point of origin, the producer must provide the appropriate transportation and housing for the director and choreographer. Usually this transportation and housing must be comparable to what the producer has arranged for himself. A "star" director may even demand better—or else.

DESIGNERS

Every show needs costume, lighting, and scenic designers. Some designers wear more than one hat—the scenic designer, for example, may also design the lighting plot. In such a case, the producer must negotiate a separate contract with the designer for each job.

SCENIC DESIGNER

The scenic designer's function is to create the physical production—the sets. These may be quite elaborate, as for a musical, or very simple and basic, as for a straight play.

She creates the sketches for the sets, which are then approved by the director (and the producer). She may also construct working models of the settings. The designer prepares the color schemes, determines what materials will be used, and selects the props that will dress the set. She estimates the construction costs. She must concern herself with technical problems that the settings may bring. The helicopter in *Miss Saigon* or the falling chandelier in *Phantom of the Opera* are problems that require the designer's ingenuity. Once the director approves the sketches or working models, the scenic designer works with the construction shop and the carpenters to actually build the sets and physically install them in the theater.

Then she makes sure they are working properly.

LIGHTING DESIGNER

The lighting designer prepares the lighting "plot" for the show. He determines how scenes, and individual moments in scenes, will be lighted. He prepares lighting cues. The designer selects the colors and what equipment will be used. He develops any special lighting effects the show may require. Lighting should be effective, yet unobtrusive, and it should seem perfectly natural for the moment. The lighting designer gives the electricians all the information they need to hang the proper equipment.

COSTUME DESIGNER

The costume designer prepares color sketches of all costumes needed by the characters in each individual scene. She selects the colors and fabrics and furnishes all of the information to the contracting costume shop. She coordinates outfits, including such accessories as footwear, handbags, and jewelry. She is in charge of hair styling, including wigs, beards, and the like.

All of the designers must be present at technical and dress rehearsals; all may call individual rehearsals in their specialties, such as a costume rehearsal.

FEES

Designers are paid particular fees for their work, depending upon whether the show is a straight play or a musical, and whether there is a single set or multiple sets.

The costume designer receives different fees depending upon whether the show is a straight play or a musical, whether it is set in contemporary times (within five years of the current date) or a period piece, and depending on the number of characters she has to dress.

TITLE TO DESIGNS

All designs remain the property of their designers. The designers may exhibit them, but they may not sell them to another production.

The producer may not sell, lease, or license the use of costume, lighting, or scenic designs for use in audio or visual recordings of any kind, without negotiating a separate contract with their respective designers.

If the show is successful, the producer will want to mount additional companies, either to tour the country, or for "sit-down"—that is, non-touring—engagements in other cities. Naturally he will want to maintain the original design of the production, since that is ordinarily one factor in the show's success. Furthermore, road audiences want to see the Broadway production reproduced as faithfully as possible. The producer will ask the original designer to reproduce her designs for each additional company he intends to present. He must give her at least two weeks' notice for each company to accept or decline. If the original designer declines, the producer may bring in a second designer, of whom the first designer must approve. The second designer's fees are deducted from any fees payable to the original designer. The producer himself must be the original producer.

Safety

Of all the producer's concerns, safety must be his highest priority.

Aside from moral considerations, a producer may face substantial legal liability if anyone—patron, employee, or even a trespasser—is injured on his premises.

Even if you simply rent facilities from another producer or corporation, you may still be held liable for injuries to your patrons and others who enter the premises. In personal injury cases, plaintiff's attorneys routinely sue all parties who may even remotely be held liable.

Under most circumstances, liability will be based on the law of torts of the state in which the facilities where the injuries occurred are located. Because each state applies tort law in its own particular way, it is impossible to provide a "one size fits all" guide to tort liability. However, there are certain suggestions I can offer that will help you on an overall basis.

PREMISES LIABILITY

The owner of a business may be held responsible for injuries that occur to persons who are present on his property. He must be at fault or negligent. He may also be liable if his employees were at fault or were negligent. This is the law of "Premises Liability." Its purpose is to protect the public from harm when visiting a business establishment.

A "business owner" means anyone who owns or controls the facilities. Thus you need not own the space in which the injury occurs. You will be held liable even if you are just a renter, even if it's for a one-night performance. For convenience, we will use the term "owner" to designate both the actual owner and the producer who rents or leases the theater.

There are five elements that must be present if an owner is to be found liable:

1. The owner owes a duty to protect people who enter upon his property from harm (this is explained in further detail, below);

2. The harm must be foreseeable;

3. The owner has in some way breached this duty;

4. The breach is the proximate cause of injury to the person; and

5. The person suffers injury of some kind.

Injuries do not have to be physical. Injuries can be mental or emotional. The injuries do not have to occur to the person. They can occur to property she owns. For example, a fender-bender in your parking lot between two patrons' cars may cause harm to the vehicles but not to the physical persons of the owners. Yet, if it can be shown that you failed to prevent the fender-bender, you may be held responsible.

DUTY

How much duty do you owe to third persons? That depends on your state's law. Many states impose different degrees of duty based on whether the third person is:

1. Your invitee;

2. Licensee; or

3. Trespasser.

INVITEES. You owe the highest level of duty to an invitee. These are people you have invited to enter your premises for either a public purpose (that is, the premises are open to the public) or for a business purpose. Your patrons are business invitees. They have bought tickets to enter upon your premises to see your show.

You owe invitees four duties:

1. You must exercise reasonable care to avoid injuring them;

2. You must make an ongoing effort to discover unreasonably dangerous conditions;

3. You must take action to correct unsafe conditions; and

4. You must warn invitees of specific dangers (for instance, you might post a visible sign that warns, "Careful—Loose Ceiling Tiles").

LICENSEE. A business owner owes a lesser degree of duty to a "licensee." This person isn't really doing business with you, but you allow her to use your premises anyway. The person who comes into your lobby to get out of the rain. Or to use your restroom facilities. She isn't there to buy a ticket, but you don't ask her to leave. Chances are, you don't do anything. She just waits there until the rain lets up. Yet, by not ejecting her, you are giving your consent to her continuing presence on your property.

If you know of any dangerous conditions, which would not be obvious, you must warn her. You must tell her of the falling ceiling tiles or otherwise post the sign where she can see it. However, you don't have to warn her of broken glass that is obviously scattered all over the floor. You also don't have to look for unknown dangers. However, you still must exercise reasonable care to avoid doing anything that might injure her.

TRESPASSERS. You owe the least amount of duty to a trespasser. This is someone who comes on your property without your consent. A burglar is the most obvious example. The only duty you owe a trespasser is that you can't willfully or recklessly disregard her safety.

The most extreme example is the business owner who rigs up a booby trap to physically harm the burglar. This is a major No-No.

OTHER FACTORS. Some states do not place different degrees of duty on the status of the injured person as invitee, licensee, or trespasser. Instead, they look at whether you exercised "ordinary reasonable care" under the circumstances to protect third parties from reasonably foreseeable acts of harm. But what constitutes "reasonable care under the circumstances?" Well, that's when the person's status may become important. Reasonable care under the circumstances may be different for an invitee than for a trespasser.

CIVIL AND CRIMINAL PENALTIES

We have all read of million-dollar verdicts in cases in which the business owner has been found to be at fault for injuries to a third person. Huge jury awards can hurt even large corporations. They can devastate a small enterprise, such as a theater company.

There are two kinds of damages common to personal injury cases. "Compensatory" damages pay for the medical expenses of the injured person. They also make up for the past and future earnings her injury causes her to lose. They also compensate her for the pain and suffering she has and will endure due to the injuries.

"Punitive" damages teach the wrongdoer a lesson. They are intended as punishment. They are designed to hurt so much the wrongdoer never misbehaves in that way again. These require a finding of gross negligence or malicious conduct. They are often much greater than compensatory damages.

Courts may award both compensatory and punitive damages in the same case, totaling into the many millions of dollars.

In some cases, when negligence causing injuries is very willful and wanton, the law may impose criminal penalties on the wrongdoer. This means jail time.

PRODUCER, PROTECT THYSELF

Fortunately, the law provides a conscientious producer many ways to reduce his risk and minimize his potential liabilities. Here are my suggestions:

Re-read chapter 1. If you want to insulate your home and personal assets from devastating judgments, consider operating your company as a corporation.

The best way to avoid lawsuits is to prevent injuries to your patrons and employees. Take the time to review your operations now (and I mean now) to determine how safe they are and what still needs to be done to make them as safe as possible.

As part of the policies and procedures manual you give your staff, include a detailed section on safety procedures. Make sure your employees commit it to memory and that they take safety seriously. Safety procedures should be part of your regular employee training.

FIRE

The worst disaster that can befall a theater is a fire during a performance. Within minutes, hundreds of lives can be lost or damaged forever. Liability can mount quickly. There may even be findings of criminal negligence. The resulting guilt can haunt a producer forever, regardless of the legal outcome.

Most fires can be prevented.

> • *Make your facility "nonsmoking" to employees and patrons alike. Most fire codes prohibit smoking in the auditorium, but some permit smoking in the lobby. I would go all the way on this one. Smokers must puff away outside your theater, not inside.*

• *Develop an emergency evacuation plan, for performances when patrons are present, and for all other times when staffers may be present.*

• *Hold regular fire drills for your staff, using your emergency evacuation plan. If a staffer doesn't want to take the drills seriously, because it is too much like grade school, remind him that the life he saves may be his own. Schedule drills as surprises. That way you'll best be able to evaluate how your people will react in a real emergency when they are not expecting a crisis.*

• *Ask your local fire marshal to review your operations and alert you to any potential fire hazards. Don't worry that he may cite you for violating your local fire code. Chances are, he'll be so pleased to work with such a conscientious producer, he won't write you up. And, even if he does, the cost of a citation is peanuts compared to what an actual fire may cost you. Incidentally, the fire marshal will help you develop an emergency evacuation plan and may even conduct your fire drills. I don't know any fire official who wouldn't rather help prevent a fire (especially in a public place) than to fight one.*

• *Flameproof your scenery. Some scene shops will show you a certificate acknowledging they have already done so. You know what? I wouldn't trust 'em. I'd obtain independent certification. Again, your local fire marshal can help, and his services are usually free. Even if the scene shop is telling the truth, flameproofing protections deteriorate over time. Scenery must be treated periodically.*

• *Even if your local code does not require them, install smoke detectors and a thorough sprinkler system throughout your facilities. Periodically examine and test them.*

• *Install fire exits, protected with the proper fire doors.*

• *Keep plenty of extinguishers on hand, to augment your sprinkler system. Maintain them in easily accessible places, where their presence is known to your staff. Periodically check the inspection tags to make sure the dates are still valid and the extinguishers are in good working order.*

• *Designate one person to come out on stage or stand in front of the audience in the event of an emergency. This person should attempt to keep people calm, proffer instructions, and otherwise maintain order.*

• *Keep all parts of the theater free of rubbish.*

• *Avoid, if possible, using hazardous materials in any part of your production. Try to find substitutes. If you absolutely can't avoid using combustible materials, ask your fire marshal for suggestions on how best to deal with them, and, especially, how to dispose of them when they are no longer needed.*

• *Keep all doors and exits free of obstructions at all times.*

• *Conduct regular inspections of all fire exits, to make sure they are always easily accessible.*

• *All fire exits should be identified with clearly marked signs that remain lighted at all times.*

• *Regularly inspect all electrical outlets to make sure they are not overloaded or obstructed.*

• *Repair or replace frayed wiring immediately.*

• *Remove obstructions from heating vents.*

• *Install several fire alarm boxes in easily accessible locations throughout your facility. With your fire department's cooperation, test them occasionally to make sure they are always in good working order.*

The above list is by no means all-inclusive. Your facility may have different needs or special circumstances. Your fire marshal will make recommendations during his inspection.

BOMB THREATS

Always take bomb threats seriously. If you get one by telephone, try to obtain as much information from the caller as possible. The more details you can give the authorities, the better they can handle it.

The police need to know the exact location of the bomb or explosive device, the kind of bomb it is, and when it is supposed to explode. They also need to know how it is set to go off.

Persons making bomb threats can often be coaxed into revealing the specific information the police need. It is even possible, sometimes, to persuade them to reveal their identity and location, and why they have chosen your facility.

Remain calm, as hard as this may be under the circumstances. Don't antagonize the caller. He may be able to trigger the bomb by remote control. If you anger him, he may set off an explosion before you can evacuate the premises.

Obviously, this is not a job for amateurs. Evacuate your facilities as quickly as possible and call the police. Leave it in their hands.

Alert your staff also to the possibility of "letter bombs." It may not always be easy to ascertain whether an otherwise ordinary looking envelope or package contains an explosive device. I would err on the safe side. If you receive any suspicious looking items, especially those without return addresses, notify the police immediately. Do not attempt to open the package yourself. Letter bombs are set off when they are opened. Put the package in a safe place, away from any persons, until the police arrive.

You may be especially vulnerable to bomb threats at certain times:

> • *You are presenting a show that takes one side or another on a political or religious issue.*

> • *A celebrity is starring in your show. The risk of attracting the wrong kind of attention is greatest when the celebrity is controversial or espouses controversial views. Of course, the very fact that you are playing host to a celebrity may serve as a lightning rod for the unstable. What better way to instantly get "fifteen minutes of fame" for oneself or one's cause than by doing or threatening physical harm to a celebrated person?*

Any of these instances may bring the cranks to your door. You should instruct your staff to be particularly on the alert during these times. Take extra security precautions. If need be, hire off-duty police officers to help. Never hesitate to call the authorities if you become aware of suspicious behavior directed toward your facilities or your staff.

PARKING LOT HAZARDS

Rapes, assaults, robberies, and other crimes of violence can happen here. Invest in a good lighting system. Keep the lights on, during evening performances and for a reasonable time afterwards. If you are in a high-crime area, offer your patrons an escort back to their vehicles. (Of course, take care to screen your "escorts" carefully.)

Another way you can reduce potential risk is to offer a valet service, especially if you have a large parking lot or if parking is scarce around your facilities. You can offset some of the costs by charging patrons a reasonable fee or contracting the job out to a professional valet company. The downside? You may be held responsible for damages to vehicles allegedly caused by your valets. (Be prepared for the occasional false claim.)

Vehicles parked in your lot may be vandalized or stolen. The risk is greatest when patrons are inside your facilities for a performance and the vehicles are left unattended. Consider a security patrol.

When the Red Barn Summer Theatre presented *Sex Marks the Spot*, I noticed that the facility had a problem common to many venues: Its parking lot fronted a heavily traveled road that did not have stoplights. Patrons leaving after a performance had to pull into oncoming traffic that had the right of way. To reduce the risk of collisions, producer Martin Henderson had staffers direct patrons safely in and out of the lot. Some theaters hire off-duty police officers for this purpose. As an alternative, you might persuade your municipality to install traffic signals at your exit. A safety study by an independent engineer might convince local officials of the need. Enlist the local police to support your request. Nonprofits can often obtain grants specifically for this purpose, thereby taking the cost off the municipality.

Fender-benders invite lawsuits against you, even though, in most instances, they are not your fault. Make sure you configure your parking lot to allow traffic to move safely. Prohibit "backing into spaces," to reduce possible accidents when the drivers pull out of the spaces later.

Contract with a towing service to remove unauthorized vehicles. They facilitate drug dealing and gang activity. Post signs warning that unauthorized vehicles will be towed.

Keep your lot free of snow and ice. Make sure that lane dividers that jut out of the ground are clearly visible to drivers at all times.

Consider installing speed bumps.

LOBBY AND AUDITORIUM

Your lobby and auditorium will be the scene of most accidents. However, there are steps you can take regularly to minimize risks.

- *Inspect carpeting regularly. Make sure it remains tacked down and there are no holes or tears that could cause anyone to trip.*

- *Wash linoleum or tile floors only when there are no patrons on the premises. Wipe up liquid spills immediately.*

- *Pick up unused and discarded programs as soon as they are noticed, particularly those printed on glossy paper that can be slippery underfoot.*

- *Post "No Smoking" signs in visible locations throughout your facility. In addition, make an announcement in your programs and before the performance. Enforce this policy vigorously.*

- *If you are "in the round," with performers entering and exiting through the aisles, warn patrons to keep their legs, feet, and personal belongings out of the way of the actors.*

- *Outside food and beverages should not be allowed. Do not permit patrons to bring drinks and food from the lobby concession stand into the auditorium.*

- *If you are a dinner theater, food served to patrons must always be stored, prepared, and handled in accordance with local health department regulations. Clean up promptly after the food is consumed.*

- *Maintain first aid kits where they are easily accessible, including the backstage, front of house, and scene shop.*

- *Post emergency numbers in several locations where your staff can find them quickly.*

- *Periodically hire licensed experts to inspect furnaces, air conditioning systems, elevators, and moving escalators. Do not procrastinate needed repairs. Find the money.*

- *Never allow patrons to watch the show by sitting on the stairs in the mezzanine or balcony. "Standing Room Only" is a wonderful marketing device, but it exposes you to a variety of risks.*

- *Configure accessibility for the physically challenged so that wheelchairs and walkers do not obstruct entrances and exits.*

- *Ushers must have working flashlights at all times.*

- *Do not allow latecomers to find their seats on their own after the curtain has gone up and the auditorium is dark. Ushers should escort them. Train your ushers to find any seat in the house in the darkness.*

- *Keep all house lights in good, working condition, especially those that illuminate the public areas of your facilities.*

- *Install safety banisters on all staircases.*

- *Inspect guardrails regularly, to make sure they are secure and sturdy.*

- *Install nonslip bath mats in the dressing room showers.*

- *Train your staff in emergency procedures. Especially make sure they know how to handle apparent heart attacks and slip-and-fall cases.*

- *If an incident occurs, your staff should call in expert help immediately. They should also prepare a contemporaneous report for your records, and, if necessary, for your insurance company.*

No one can guard against every harm that could conceivably occur in operating a theater. However, by establishing an ongoing safety program, you can reduce many of your risks.

Such a program helps in several ways. It's a wonderful public relations tool. It will likely reduce your insurance costs. In the event of a lawsuit, it may mitigate fault or damages. It may even prevent a lawsuit.

EMPLOYEE INCENTIVES

Your best protection against liability claims is your own staff. Involving your employees in safety issues is a smart, cost-free move that may save you big dollars.

Review your operations periodically with all members of your staff. They know their departments better than anyone (including yourself). For instance, your ushers can tell you more about the condition of the carpeting in your auditorium than anyone else. Your stagehands know what hazards lurk backstage. Your actors can tell you if your dressing rooms facilitate safe and quick costume changes.

Create a safety committee consisting of both management and staff. Give employees a voice in safety matters. Take their concerns seriously. Keeping workers constantly aware of potential safety hazards reduces the risk of accidents to themselves, thereby minimizing workers' compensation claims as well as downtime due to injuries. In addition, employees can be on the lookout for potential dangers to your patrons.

Run safety contests. Reward employees who uncover potential hazards. (You can give them a $25 savings bond.) You will be glad you did.

CHAPTER 12

Taxes

Regardless of the form of organization you have selected for your theater company, you will have to face the issue of taxes, in one form or another. Of course, the more sophisticated and complex your business arrangement is, the more complicated the tax rules are that will apply to you.

It should go without saying, therefore, that in this area in particular you need the help of both a good tax lawyer and an accountant. This is not a field for amateurs. Moreover, it is impossible to cover all the tax laws to which you are subject in just one chapter in this book. Dozens of volumes have been written about even just one topic, such as "Employee Taxes." However, I can give you an overview of the issues you will confront in your daily operations. With that in mind, let's plunge in.

SOLE PROPRIETORSHIPS

As I indicated in chapter 1, the sole proprietorship is the most basic form of business and the easiest to start up. For tax purposes, it is also the simplest kind of business to report. This holds true whether the sole proprietorship is a one-person operation or employs many workers. (If the sole proprietor employs even one person, the owner must comply with the payroll tax laws, which are discussed later in this chapter.) It is equally true whether the business earns $1,000, $10 million, or loses money altogether.

Unlike a corporation, the tax authorities do not recognize the sole proprietorship as an entity separate and apart from its owner. (That is one reason the sole proprietorship can never obtain tax-exempt status.) As far as the IRS and local taxing authorities are concerned, the sole proprietorship is one person who is in business for herself.

Therefore, the sole proprietor reports all business income on a separate schedule (Schedule C—Profit or Loss from Business), which she attaches to her own individual income tax return, the 1040. She will use both her personal Social Security Number and her business's Employer ID Number. She adds business profits and losses to any other income she might have—such as wages, dividends, and interest. This means, of course, that all of this income is taxed according to whatever tax bracket it brings her into. The good news about business profits is that they are profits; the bad news is, they will likely push the sole proprietor into a higher tax bracket. The bad news about business losses is that they are losses; the good news is, they offset income from other sources, so they will likely move her into a lower tax bracket.

If you have ever worked as an employee for others and you then start your own business, the tax authorities have a surprise in store for you. As an employee, your employer deducted your federal and state income tax payments out of your check every pay period, according to a set schedule, along with your share of Social Security and Medicare taxes. But, as a sole proprietor, you are now responsible for paying your own taxes on the business income. You must make estimated tax payments to the IRS four times each year—April 15, June 15, September 15, and January 15 of the following year. You can't simply wait until April 15 of the following year and pay everything in one lump sum; if you do, you will incur penalties.

This gets tricky, because you have to estimate the profits you are taking each quarter and then figure out how much tax you owe on them. If you estimate too high, you are giving the IRS an interest-free loan of your money until the following April 15, when you discover you have overpaid your taxes and you apply for a refund. But, if you underestimate your taxes, the IRS will charge you a substantial penalty for not paying enough taxes during the year. So you have to make sure your estimates are pretty accurate.

Remember that, as a sole proprietor now, you are also paying your own Social Security and Medicare Taxes (Self-Employment Taxes). These must also be included in your quarterly tax estimates, along with your income taxes.

In all states that have their own income taxes, you must do the same, or else face penalties there, too.

PARTNERSHIPS

Partnership taxation is extremely difficult to explain in any simplified way. Unfortunately, it becomes even more difficult when one enters the world of theatrical limited partnerships. In fact, this is one area in which the need for expert legal and accounting advice is absolutely critical.

I can, however, offer some general principles.

Unlike shareholder-employees of a closely held corporation, partners are not paid in wages or salaries. They are not employees of the business. Instead, partners agree to periodically withdraw money out of the business. However, these withdrawals are not always necessarily taxable.

Let's suppose that on January 1, 2000, Jim, Mary, and Dick are theater arts majors, who, after graduation, decide to form a partnership called the JMD Theatre Company to produce plays. Jim will serve as producer, Mary as artistic director, and Dick as technical director. Using the suggestions I gave in chapter 1, they draw up a partnership agreement, whereby they will split profits and bear losses equally.

Each contributes $3,000, so that the JMD Theatre Company can produce its first show on a budget of $9,000. This money goes into each partner's "capital account." This is an account which sets out each partner's contributions, withdrawals, and annual share of profits and losses. So, at the outset, the capital accounts for the JMD Theatre Company look like this:

> Jim: $3,000
> Mary: $3,000
> Dick: $3,000
> _____
> Total Capital Accounts: $9,000

Seems simple so far?

Yeah. So far.

Wait.

The value of each person's contribution is called his tax "basis" in the partnership—that is, each partner has a tax basis of $3,000 in the partnership.

Suppose the JMD Theatre Company operates quite successfully. In October 2000, Mary takes a "distributive share" out of the business in the amount of $1,000.

What is a "distributive share?" That's a partner's share of the business's profit or loss. In this case, the partners have agreed to share profits and losses equally. However, they could have agreed to "unequal distributive shares." These are called "special allocations." This means that the partners will receive shares of profits and losses that are disproportionate to their ownership interest. In other words, although it seems as though Jim, Mary, and Dick each own 33.333 percent of JMD Theatre Company, they might have agreed that Jim will receive 20 percent of the profits and losses, Dick will receive 10 percent, and Mary will receive 70 percent. Why would they agree to such unequal distributions? Perhaps Mary devotes her energies full time to working for the company, while Jim and Dick have other jobs and so can only commit to lesser amounts of time. It doesn't matter. The partners must pay tax on the amounts they are each *deemed* to have received from the partnership.

Just to complicate matters further, as we have said, Mary withdraws $1,000 from her capital account. This money is tax-free to her.

Why?

It is considered a withdrawal of her capital contribution, or the money she contributed when the partners formed their partnership. All she is doing is taking back part of her own money.

By withdrawing this money, Mary also reduces her tax basis in the partnership. Now the capital accounts (or tax bases) look like this:

Jim: $3,000
Mary: $2,000
Dick: $3,000

Mary can continue withdrawing money tax-free until she has withdrawn all of her capital contributions—or the balance of $2,000. She can take her account down to zero, tax-free. It is only after the account reaches zero that any further withdrawals Mary makes are subject to tax.

Suppose Mary does continue to withdraw funds until her account is down to zero.

Jim: $3,000
Mary: $0
Dick: $3,000

Now, in 2001, JMD Theatre Company has a banner year, earning profits of $12,000. (To keep our example simple, the partners still share profits and losses equally.) Each receives 33.333 percent of the profits, or $4,000. So now, the capital accounts are as follows:

Jim: $7,000 ($3,000 + $4,000)
Mary: $4,000
Dick: $7,000 ($3,000 + $4,000)

Jim withdraws $7,000—his original $3,000 plus his share of the profits. Jim does not pay taxes on the original $3,000. However, the balance of $4,000 is taxable. Dick does the same and has the same tax liabilities. Since Mary had previously withdrawn all of her capital contributions, she will pay taxes on her withdrawal of $4,000.

Are we clear?

Okay, then, let's add a further wrinkle. But first let's look at the capital accounts as of December 31, 2001

Jim: $0
Mary: $0
Dick: $0

In the year 2002 the JMD Theater Company presents *Grease* for twelve performances, taking a net profit of $15,000. Now the capital accounts look like this:

Jim: $5,000
Mary: $5,000
Dick: $5,000

The partners decide that, since their little company is growing, it would be best to leave the profits in the business, to help them produce an even bigger show next year. None of them took any of the cash that is now in their capital accounts, as shown above.

Unfortunately, the IRS has other ideas. Although they haven't taken out any cash, Jim, Mary, and Dick must nevertheless pay taxes on their individual proportionate shares of the money. They must pay the taxes with cash from another source.

But, instead of taking a profit, suppose *Grease* showed a loss of $15,000. Now (keeping in mind the partners' capital accounts had been down to zero), after the show closes, their accounts look like this:

Jim: ($5,000)
Mary: ($5,000)
Dick: ($5,000)

Now each of the partners can report a loss on his individual tax return. They can use those losses to offset income from other sources. For instance, Jim works days as a waiter, and, in 2001, his wages and tips totaled $20,000. He can use his loss to offset his waiter's income, thereby reducing it by $5,000.

(Cautionary note: Only the partners who are actively involved in the business can deduct unlimited losses. Passive investors—the limited partners in a theatrical partnership—are strictly limited in the amount of losses they can take in any single year.)

Partners may sell their interests to one of the other partners, or, if the partnership agreement permits, to a third party altogether. The sale by one partner of his interest to anyone does not affect the partnership's taxes. The partnership merely has to report the sale to the IRS on its Form 8308 (Report of Sale or Exchange of Certain Partnership Interests).

The selling partner has to report a gain or loss, depending on his basis in his partnership interest. To compute gain (or loss) the partner must first determine her basis in the business.

Mary decides to sell her interest to Dick. Originally, she contributed $3,000 to the partnership. One year later, she put up an additional $1,000 to help fund the company's production of *West Side Story*. But six months ago, she withdrew $2,000. Dick has offered her $6,000 for her interest.

Mary determines her adjusted basis, as follows:

Original Basis: $3,000
Additional Contribution: +$1,000
Withdrawal: –$2,000

_____

Mary's Adjusted Basis: $2,000.00

Mary sells to Dick for $6,000. She subtracts her adjusted basis of $2,000. This leaves her with a taxable gain of $4,000.

Jim, Mary, and Dick are not sharing a unique experience. Many artists, especially recent college graduates, band together as partners to form small theater companies. It is important for anyone—organizers of shoestring companies to sophisticated investors buying shares in a multimillion-dollar Broadway musical—to understand at least the rudiments of partnership taxation.

C CORPORATION

Most small commercial (in other words, for-profit) theater companies are C Corporations, even those that act as general partners for the limited liability partnership. (Don't worry about the letter "C"; it just refers to the subchapter of the IRS Code that applies to this kind of corporation.)

A C Corporation is taxed separately and apart from its owners (stockholders). It is a legally distinct entity—sometimes called an "artificial person."

One disadvantage of a C Corporation is that the IRS taxes its profits twice. First, the corporation must pay taxes on its net earnings at the corporate rate, before it can distribute any of those earnings to its stockholders. Then, when it pays out its after-tax earnings (dividends) to the stockholders, the stockholders must include these dividends in their personal income on their 1040s, as taxable individual income.

However, it is possible to avoid much of this double taxation in a small, closely held corporation. A "closely held" corporation has fewer than thirty-five shareholders, many of whom either work in the business or are sophisticated investors. It sells its stock privately, not to the general public. Since many of its stockholders are also employees, it simply pays out most of its earnings to them as wages and benefits.

Another way to avoid or at least minimize double taxation is called "income splitting." The corporation simply retains part of its earnings in the business, paying out only a portion to its shareholders. This helps, at least up to a point, because initial corporate tax rates tend to be lower than the individual rates its owners will pay.

Be aware, however, that C Corporations are also frequently subject to certain additional taxes:

- *Accumulated earnings tax: Up to a point, the Tax Code will allow a C Corporation to accumulate earnings for the purpose of expanding and growing its business. However, once the corporation accumulates earnings exceeding $250,000, it will become subject to an accumulated earnings tax.*

- *Corporate Alternative Minimum Tax: This operates to make sure that every corporation pays at least some taxes, no matter how many loopholes in the Tax Code it attempts to fit itself through.*

- *Personal Holding Company Tax: This most likely won't affect your theater company, since producing shows is an active business. This is a tax on corporations that are basically passive investment vehicles, that is, they earn most of their income from dividends and royalties.*

Be careful in your own business dealings with your corporation. The IRS scrutinizes dealings between closely held corporations and their shareholders carefully. This is because the stockholders have great opportunities to use their corporate entity to abuse the Tax Code.

First, if you are also an employee of your corporation, make sure the compensation it pays you is "reasonable." The IRS loves to look for corporations that are paying their stockholder-employees what it deems "unreasonable compensation for personal services." The IRS will deem the excess as "dividends" and disallow the corporation its deduction. Make sure you can demonstrate your wages are reasonable and fair for the services you perform; if possible, get comparable figures from similar businesses. Avoid relating your salary to corporate profits.

There's nothing inherently wrong if a closely held corporation makes a legitimate loan to its shareholders. But there must be an actual debt, not a sham. The best way to handle a loan is for the corporation to treat the shareholder as if she were a third party. That is, obtain a credit report on her and put it in the files. Make her sign a promissory note, which calls for repayment in full by a certain date with periodic (for instance, monthly) payments in between. The law allows the corporation to make the loan interest free, as long as it is under $10,000. I would charge interest on a loan of any size, however, just to be extra sure. Make the interest rate the same as a commercial bank would charge. Give the corporation the right to sue in the event of default—and proceed to suit if it becomes necessary. Require collateral to secure the note. Do not show favoritism in any way.

If you sell or lease property to the corporation, make the transaction as close to "arms length" as you can. "Arms length" means that you treat it with the same terms and conditions as you would apply to a transaction with a third, unrelated party. Prices, fees, and charges should be comparable to what strangers should charge or pay to each other. All arrangements should be set forth in writing, signed by an officer of the corporation acting on its behalf, and the shareholder. Whenever possible, obtain independent reports or analysis from local experts that describe what the terms would be in the open market between strangers.

SUBCHAPTER S CORPORATIONS

A Subchapter S Corporation combines the limited liability advantages of the corporate form with the tax advantages of a partnership. In other words, shareholders of an "S" can protect their personal assets from the business liabilities, but, instead of the corporation itself paying taxes, the individual shareholders pay taxes, as they would if they were members of a general partnership. Obviously, this eliminates the problem of double taxation with the corporate form.

Business profits flow to the shareholders, who add their proportionate share to their income, in the same way partners do. Similarly, business losses flow (proportionately) to the shareholders, who may use these to offset other income from taxes. (However, only shareholders who "materially participate"—that is, actively manage and work—in the business may deduct losses.)

One additional benefit of "S" status allows shareholders to deduct certain items on their individual income tax returns. The shareholder may "separately state" these items, so that she may benefit from the special tax treatment these items get.

Here's an example. Suppose Jim, Mary, and Dick are the shareholders of the JMD Theatre Corporation, Inc. (an "S" Corporation), each owning equal shares. JMD sells a portion of real estate, which it presently uses as a parking lot, for a gain of $24,000. Since it has owned this land for more than one year, the profit is a capital gain. JMD passes its profit on to Jim, Mary, and Dick in equal shares: each receives $8,000. Because JMD earned this profit as a capital gain, Jim, Mary, and Dick can "separately state" their respective shares as a capital gain on their individual income tax returns. Capital gains are taxed at lower rates than ordinary income. Thus, Jim, Mary, and Dick will each save taxes on their profits by being able to treat them in this way.

One problem with "S" Corporations, however, is that any earnings it wants to retain in the business will be fully taxed as if they had flowed to the shareholders. Hence, if the corporation does retain these earnings, the shareholders must pay taxes on cash they haven't personally received.

In addition, S Corporations can't provide fringe benefits to its shareholders in the same way C Corporations can.

A C Corporation can elect to become an S Corporation as long as it qualifies. It must file an election with the IRS. An S Corporation can revoke its status (becoming a C Corporation) as long as shareholders owning 50 percent or more of its shares vote to do so.

NONPROFIT EXEMPT CORPORATIONS

Many theaters are organized as nonprofits. However, it is unlikely that their administrators and board members really understand what that means. This is one of those topics that may seem of importance only to their attorneys and the IRS. I believe it is equally important to their board members, administrators, and managers.

Legally, a nonprofit is a corporation that does not distribute any of its income or profit to its members, directors, or officers. Unlike for-profit corporations, a nonprofit does not issue ownership shares. In other words, you can buy ownership shares in Microsoft (a for-profit corporation), but you can't buy ownership in the Mark Taper Forum (a nonprofit corporation).

Some lawyers attempt to distinguish between "nonprofit" and "not-for-profit" corporations. They argue that a nonprofit can attempt to make a profit, just as long as it uses those profits only to support its nonprofit purposes. In other words, a theater company is a "nonprofit" even though it operates an adjoining restaurant, as long as the restaurant's profits support the company's productions. These are legal semantics, which I mention only because I knew you would ask.

ALTRUISTIC MOTIVE

The key to determining whether a corporation deserves nonprofit status is the motive of its organizers and officers. As long as that motive is primarily "altruistic," it's likely the authorities will grant it nonprofit status.

Nonprofits must fall into at least one of three categories:

1. The public benefit: Most theater companies will fit in here very nicely.

2. Mutual benefit: Two or more theater companies band together to form a trade association.

3. **Private benefit:** *This is difficult, though not impossible, for a theater company. A nontheatrical example would be a low-cost housing development.*

A nonprofit's members cannot have any interest in its assets, except under very limited conditions.

TAX-EXEMPT STATUS

As we discussed in chapter 1, the chief advantage of organizing as a nonprofit is the opportunity to seek tax-exempt status.

Notice I said the "opportunity to seek" tax-exempt status. Many people mistakenly believe that when a corporation is organized as "nonprofit" it also automatically achieves tax-exempt status. Nothing could be further from the truth. Organizers of a nonprofit must take active measures to obtain tax exemption.

FEDERAL TAX EXEMPTION

Organizers of a nonprofit should first seek exemption from federal taxes. They must lay the necessary groundwork in the articles of incorporation, which they must file with the state.

This is for two reasons: first, a nonprofit must be organized as such from the outset; secondly, the Internal Revenue Code specifically requires it.

Most corporations seek tax-exempt status under Internal Revenue Code 501 (c) (3). To qualify, the corporation must have been "organized and operated exclusively for religious, charitable, scientific, testing for public safety, literary, or educational purposes, or to foster national or international amateur sports competition, or for the prevention of cruelty to children or animals."

The accompanying IRS regulations require that the corporation's articles of incorporation expressly limit the organization's purposes to one or more of the above exempt purposes. The articles cannot expressly give the corporation the power to engage in any activities that don't further the exempt purposes. The IRS does allow an exception if the nonexempt activities are not substantial.

If your company's purpose fits within one or more of the above exempt purposes (and most theater companies do), the next step is to file an application for tax-exempt status with the director of the district where your principal office or place of business is located. There are different forms, depending on the basis you are claiming for your exemption. Forms 1023, 1024, and 1028 are available from your local IRS office, by mail, fax, and over the Internet from the IRS Web site.

You must attach the following documents to your application:

- *A conformed copy of your articles of incorporation;*

- *Your latest financial statement; and*

- *A written declaration that it is made under penalty of perjury.*

The IRS will review your organizing documents carefully to make sure you have not given your organization any powers that are not permitted.

You must also submit an Application for an Employer Identification Number (Form SS-4) and a power of attorney authorizing either your attorney or another person to represent you before the IRS.

If, for any reason, you decide to withdraw your application, you must do so before the IRS rules on your request. Be aware, though, that once you submit your application, the information contained therein goes into Your Permanent Record with the IRS, which can use that information in any subsequent audits. (Now, do you understand why your teachers always told you to keep your permanent record clean?)

Oh, and one more teensy-weensy detail: You must pay a filing fee when you apply.

RETROACTIVE EXEMPTION

In most instances, you will want to have your exemption apply retroactively to the date when you organized your corporation. Therefore, you must file your application not later than fifteen months from the end of the month in which you created your organization.

Retroactive exemption can greatly benefit your company. Here's how it works.

You organize the Soon to be Famous Theatre Company, Inc., by filing articles of incorporation with your state on June 2, 2001. On August 1, 2001, you present your first show, *Camelot*. The production turns a tidy profit of $10,000. On December 31, 2001, a leading member of your community, impressed by the cultural benefits you are providing, donates $5,000 to your company. On September 30, 2002, you file Form 1023 with the director of the IRS district in which your company is located. The IRS grants tax-exempt status to your organization, which relates back to June 2, 2001. In other words, the IRS recognizes you as a tax-exempt entity as of June 2, 2001.

Your timely filing benefits you in two ways. You do not have to pay taxes on the profit you made from *Camelot*. Your kindly donor can deduct his gift of $5,000 from his taxes. You took your profits, and your donor made his gift after the IRS recognized you as tax-exempt.

Just remember to observe the deadline.

MAILING TIP

I never rely on the U.S. Postal Service when I file IRS documents, especially when timely filing is essential. Instead, I take the original documents directly to the nearest IRS office, together with at least one copy. I file the originals in person, getting the date stamped before my eyes. I ask the clerk to date-stamp my copy. This gives me the strongest possible record of the date I actually filed.

UNTIMELY FILING

What happens if you don't file on time? Your tax-exempt status begins only on the date you actually filed your application. It does not apply retroactively. Using the above example, if you don't file for tax exemption until October 1, 2002, your status as tax exempt begins on October 1, 2002. You have to pay taxes on the *Camelot* profits, and your donor cannot deduct his gift as a charitable contribution to you.

DETERMINATION LETTER

Once you have submitted all of the necessary documents, one of several events will happen:

> • *The IRS will issue a ruling or determination letter recognizing you as an exempt organization.*

> • *The IRS may insist that you make changes in your operations, to conform with the appropriate tax-exempt purposes. In that case, it may not grant your exemption until such later date as it is satisfied you have made the requested changes.*

> • *It may deny your application through an "adverse determination." You have thirty days after receiving the adverse determination to request consideration by the Appeals Office. You can request an in-person conference with the Appeals Office.*

> • *After exhausting all of your administrative remedies within the IRS itself, you may seek judicial remedies. This means you can ask either the U.S. Tax Court or the district court for the District of Columbia to issue a declaratory judgment that your organization is exempt from tax. If the court agrees, the IRS will issue a favorable determination, provided you have filed an application for exemption, and provided you can show both the facts and the law have not changed since the whole rigmarole began.*

> • *The IRS must issue its determination letter or adverse determination within 270 days after you file Form 1023. If it does not do so, you also have the right to ask the court for a declaratory judgment.*

If your organization has not yet begun operations, you can ask the IRS to give you an advance ruling on its exempt status before you open your doors. You must describe in full the kinds of activities in which you plan to engage. These must meet the requirements in the category in which you are seeking exemption. You must also detail your sources of expected funds, as well as your anticipated expenses. The IRS can still demand that you first provide a record of actual operations before it will give you a determination letter.

Did you really think this was going to be easy?

And wait! We're just getting to the really fun stuff.

LOSING YOUR EXEMPTION

Yup! That's right. What the IRS giveth, the IRS can also taketh away.

Just because the IRS issues a final determination that your organization is tax-exempt, doesn't mean the determination is—well, final.

You *can* lose your exemption.

At any time.

This means you. Yes, you, the producer who has read through the foregoing and thought, "Well, none of that applies to my company. We've been tax-exempt since 1985. So what do I care about determination letters?"

Boy, are you in for a shock!

I'll put it another way. The IRS can revoke or modify its determination letter recognizing your organization's tax-exempt status *at any time*. It doesn't matter if the IRS issued your determination letter yesterday, or in 1985, or in 1965. It can revoke your exemption if you give it the proper cause.

So, heed my words carefully.

The most common reason the IRS revokes an organization's tax-exempt status is that the corporation fails to operate exclusively for exempt purposes. Sometimes, as an organization grows and expands, it strays away from its original purposes, the very basis for its tax exemption in the first place.

One way this happens is when the corporation begins involving itself too heavily in political activities, including lobbying for or against legislation or political candidates. If the corporation's political activities are too substantial in relation to its other activities, it may lose its exempt status.

A corporation may indirectly lose its tax-exempt status by making political contributions or expenditures on behalf of a candidate. Both the IRS

Section 4955 (d) and the Omnibus Budget Reconciliation Act of 1987 (OBRA) impose taxes on such contributions or expenditures.

Discriminating in violation of the Civil Rights laws can cost an organization its exempt status.

Of course, filing false yearly tax returns on Form 990 is a big No-No. In addition, if the organization deliberately omits or misstates a material fact in its application for exemption and other filings, the IRS can revoke its tax-exempt status.

A corporation can lose its exempt status if the IRS determines it is in fact operating to benefit private interests. For example, the organization may be paying out too much of its income to its organizers or officers.

The most difficult problems relate to "unrelated trade or business" activities.

Income that results directly from the organization's exempt purpose is not taxed. Thus, profits from the sale of tickets to your production of *Camelot* are not taxable. However, if you also operate a gift shop adjacent to your lobby, the profits from the gift shop will be taxed, even though you use these profits to support your productions.

Here is where you have to be very careful. Do not allow the gift shop to play too big a part in your operations, regardless of how profitable it might be. If the IRS decides you are no longer operating exclusively for exempt purposes, it may very well revoke your exempt status.

STATE TAX EXEMPTION

Being recognized as tax-exempt by the IRS shields a nonprofit from paying federal taxes on income it derives from its exempt purpose. It also has the effect of shielding the same income from most state income taxes. States commonly base their definitions of taxable income on income that is taxable at the federal level. Therefore, it follows that if the federal government does not tax income derived from exempt activities, the states will not tax it either.

But, in addition to income taxes, states commonly impose other taxes on corporations. A mere nonprofit may be subject to certain of these taxes. A nonprofit that is organized as a charity may, on the other hand, be exempted from many state taxes.

If that isn't confusing enough, there's more to come. Even within one state, a charity might be exempt from one tax, yet not be exempt from another. It all depends on how the statute for each particular tax determines which organizations are exempt. Obviously, this fact makes it impossible to construct a general rule that will fit all taxes in all states.

Making matters even more complicated is the great number of taxes imposed by individual municipalities within a state.

STATE BUSINESS TAXES

The following are the most common taxes states impose on businesses.

• ***Organization tax:*** *Most states impose a tax on the capital stock that a corporation issues when it is organized. (If, later in its existence, the corporation issues additional stock, as many do, it will have to pay taxes on these additional shares as well.)*

Nonprofits do not issue stock. Therefore, nonprofits do not have to pay organization taxes.

• ***Franchise tax:*** *States may impose franchise taxes for the privilege of doing business within its borders—even if the corporation doesn't exercise the privilege. Nonprofits are exempt from franchise taxes.*

• ***Amusement tax:*** *Tax authorities impose amusement taxes to amuse themselves. (Just kidding!) In truth, many communities impose amusement taxes on various forms of entertainment, such as movie theaters, stage shows, and concerts. It is a tax the public pays when it wants to be entertained. It is usually charged on each ticket sold, often as a percentage of the face value. Such a tax can be hefty and produce substantial revenue for the municipality.*

Most producers charge the amusement tax as part of the total ticket prices. Whether nonprofits are exempt from this tax depends upon local ordinance.

• ***Sales tax:*** *Communities impose sales taxes on sales out of concession stands—such as food, beverages, and show merchandise. These are usually charged to the patron. In some communities, as long as the profit is going to support the purposes of the charity and not to any private individuals, the charity's sales to patrons may be exempt from taxes.*

Similarly, commercial theater companies pay sales taxes on equipment and other products they purchase for their own use, just as individuals do. Charities are often exempt from paying these taxes. To obtain this exemption, they ordinarily must provide the merchant with their tax exemption information.

If your company only occasionally sells merchandise and you are not otherwise engaged in business, your sales may be exempt. For instance, if you hold an occasional bake sale to raise money for your organization, in many communities, it is not necessary to charge sales taxes to your customers.

• **Use tax:** *If I purchase goods within the borders of my state, I must pay sales taxes on my purchase to my state. However, if my neighbor purchased the same goods in an adjoining state, he did not pay sales taxes to our home state. Yet he is getting the enjoyment of his purchases within our state. Thus the state may impose a use tax on him for—what else?—using the goods within its borders.*

Charitable organizations are usually exempt from use taxes.

• **Property tax:** *States impose taxes on property that is owned within their respective borders. Property may include real estate or other tangible or intangible personal property. Charitable organizations are often exempt from these taxes.*

EMPLOYER TAXES

All employers, regardless of their "for-profit" status, are responsible for depositing the so-called "payroll taxes" imposed by the federal government and by many state and municipal governments. There is no such thing as being exempt from these taxes. In addition to depositing the actual taxes with the appropriate agency, the employer must also file certain reports.

The law imposes four duties on employers. The employer must:

1. Withhold payroll taxes from employee wages;

2. Deposit these with the IRS;

3. Deposit the employer's share of the taxes; and

4. File certain employment tax reports with the IRS by certain specific dates.

WITHHOLDING INCOME TAXES

All of your employees have a duty to pay taxes on their wages. However, decades ago, the government devised a system whereby employers, rather than their employees, actually deposit these taxes on behalf of the employees. Each pay period, the employer withholds "X" number of dollars from the employee's paycheck. The exact amount depends on the size of the employee's salary, the number of withholding exemptions she claims, and a table of withholding issued yearly by the IRS.

By January 31 of the year following the period for which you withheld wages, you must furnish your employee with an IRS W-2 form, which shows how much you paid the employee in full, as well as all withholdings from her wages. This allows the employee to prepare her income tax return for the year. She must file one copy of the W-2 with her federal 1040, another with her state income tax return, and, in some communities, with her municipal income tax return.

In addition to withholding income taxes from the employee's wages, the employer must also withhold the employee's share of Social Security and Medicare taxes (FICA). The employer must pay an equal share of these amounts.

Once a year, the employer must pay Federal Unemployment Taxes (FUTA), which supports the federal unemployment insurance system.

PAYROLL TAX DEPOSITS

The employer is responsible for depositing the employees' withheld income and FICA taxes with the IRS. Most banks have the authority to accept these deposits. Small businesses must deposit these on a monthly basis. However, if the total deposit is $500 or less, the deposits may be made quarterly.

The employer must file three employment tax reports with the IRS:

1. Employers Quarterly Federal Tax Return (Form 941): You report the number of employees you had during the quarter, the total wages you paid, and the amounts you withheld for federal income taxes, Medicare, and Social Security.

2. IRS Federal Tax Deposit Coupon (Form 8109-B): This accompanies each monthly payroll tax deposit.

3. Employer's Annual Federal Unemployment Tax Return (Form 940): This report shows how much federal unemployment tax you owe.

WORKER CLASSIFICATIONS

As if all of this hasn't been enough fun already, you should be aware of a slight (ha!) complication in the law.

It is possible to classify your workers into four distinct categories. How you (and the IRS) classify workers can make a big difference in your payroll tax obligations, as well as in the amount and kind of reporting you have to do.

COMMON LAW EMPLOYEE. A common law employee is a worker who performs services under your control. You dictate what work she will do and how she will do it. You train the worker, furnish the tools and equipment she will use on the job, and pay for her business and travel expenses. You set the hours she will work. Usually, she works on your premises. You require her to devote her time substantially to your business. You can fire her at any time, and she can quit at will (or by the terms of your written contract with her).

The key element here is the degree of control you have the right to exercise (or actually do exercise) over the services she performs, regardless of whether you also give her certain freedoms of action.

This is the classic employer-employee relationship. You are responsible for paying her taxes. You must also pay your share of FICA taxes, as well as both federal and state unemployment insurance.

Your actors, technical staff, and office help are common law employees.

INDEPENDENT CONTRACTOR. An independent contractor basically operates her own business. Your lawyer, dentist, and accountant are independent contractors. So is the playwright whose script you are producing.

An independent contractor usually performs services for many people or entities at the same time. (You are not your lawyer's only client or your dentist's only patient.) She assumes the risks of her business, either making a profit or taking a loss. Usually, she works out of her own facilities, and you pay her on a job-by-job basis. She chooses when she wants to work and how she will do the work. She also selects her own clients. You can't fire an independent contractor. You can only stop doing business with her, and, in such an event, the independent contractor cannot file a claim for unemployment compensation.

An independent contractor pays her own taxes and files her own reports. You do not withhold income on FICA taxes on her behalf.

There is an exception to the reporting requirements, however. If you pay the unincorporated independent contractor more than $600 in non-employee compensation in a single year, you must report the payment on Form 1099. You must furnish a copy to the independent contractor not later than January 31 of the following year. Then, not later than February 28 of the year following the payment, you must send the IRS a copy of the 1099, together with a summary and transmittal form (Form 1096).

Using independent contractors as much as possible can save a theater company a great deal of money in taxes, as well as eliminate many reporting requirements. Many businesses seek to classify workers as independent contractors.

Tread carefully here. If the IRS audits you, regardless of what triggered the audit, it will as a matter of course consider how you classify your workers. In fact, the IRS uses special audit teams—the Employment Tax Examinations Unit—just for this purpose. If the IRS finds you misclassified employees as independent contractors, the penalties will be steep. You have to pay all the back taxes, plus interest, plus penalties that can go as high as 35 percent of the tax bill (but not lower than 12 percent).

Worst of all, the IRS may also notify your state tax authorities (and vice versa). You might also become responsible for state payroll taxes, interest, and penalties.

Make sure the worker is a "true" independent contractor. Reduce your arrangement to a written agreement, which clearly establishes the worker is in business for herself and is not your employee. Have her bill you for her services, on her own letterhead, clearly showing she operates her own business. Make sure she has other clients besides yourself (or is making efforts to get others). Pay her by the job. Allow her to choose when and how she will work. Even if you pay her less than $600 in one year, report the payment anyway on a 1099. Arrange things so she does most, if not all of her work, on her own premises.

STATUTORY EMPLOYEES. Statutory employees are not common law employees, yet under certain conditions, you must, nevertheless, treat them as employees for Social Security, Medicare, and FUTA tax purposes. Here are some examples:

- *A full-time insurance salesperson;*

- *An agent (or commission driver) who delivers food or laundry products;*

- *Full-time sales people, such as manufacturers representatives, who deal with other businesses;*

- *Home workers who work according to specific guidelines, using materials furnished by the business. An example would be someone who stuffs flyers furnished by a business into envelopes addressed to customers of that business.*

Statutory employees are a creation of a specific Federal law: IRC 3121 (d) (3). Except for the envelope stuffers, who may address mailings to subscribers, the media, and potential patrons, most of these are not likely to be used by a theater company.

STATUTORY NON-EMPLOYEES. Again, these are not likely to be found in a theater company. These are direct sellers and licensed real estate agents who are paid by commission.

Question: Do you use telemarketers to sell season subscriptions or solicit donations on behalf of your company? Under which classification do they fall?

Answer: There is no answer I can give you. It all depends on the facts and circumstances of your operation. I pose the question merely to suggest that you and your attorney review your telemarketing system to determine whether you are complying with the payroll tax laws.

EMPLOYER LIABILITY

I cannot stress enough how important it is for you to file all reports and to make all payments to the taxing authorities on time. The interest and penalties, both at the federal and state level, can cripple and even destroy a business.

You cannot escape them. Payroll taxes are not dischargeable in bankruptcy.

Even worse, the owners of a small business are personally liable for its payroll tax obligations. For that purpose, the taxing authorities define "owner" very broadly to include sole proprietors, general partners, limited liability company members, and the directors and officers of a corporation, regardless of whether they were also shareholders. This is one instance in which the corporate shield does not protect one from unlimited liability.

The taxing authorities may also hold certain employees personally responsible, even though they did not own a piece of the business. An example might be a bookkeeper responsible for paying the taxes on time. Outsiders, such as accountants and attorneys, may also be found to be responsible.

The government's theory for imposing such broad-based responsibility is that all of these persons—the owners, directors, and accountants—are in the best position to make sure their organization meets its payroll obligations. Even if the managers delegate payroll tax duties to another person, such as a bookkeeper, it is the managers' job to supervise the bookkeeper and make sure he complies with the law. If the bookkeeper fails to do so—whether out of negligence or a deliberate act—the "owner" (as broadly defined) is ultimately the one who pays the price.

FACTORS THAT DETERMINE RESPONSIBILITY

The IRS looks at several factors to determine who is ultimately responsible.

- *Who signs the company's checks?*

- *Who gives the order to pay (or not pay) the company's bills?*

- *Whose duties include paying and reporting the taxes?*

- *Who has the authority to decide financial matters for the firm?*

Furthermore, the employer is deemed to be a trustee for the employee payroll taxes. (Bet you didn't know you were working as an unpaid trustee for the IRS.) There are two elements the IRS must find before it can charge you with these taxes:

1. You were responsible to make sure your company paid its taxes on time.

2. Your conduct in not paying the taxes on time was willful. "Willful" is such a broad based term that the IRS can find just about any kind of conduct as being "willful."

PENALTIES

The IRS can come after you or your business any time up to ten years (!) after the taxes become due. This holds true even if you leave the company or if it goes belly up in the intervening time. It can seize your personal residence, bank accounts, inheritances, and wages. It'll take just about anything from you—except your mother-in-law (sorry, guys).

You will be held responsible for all the income taxes you should have withheld from the employee's wages for the period in which you were delinquent. (That's right: now you are paying your employee's income taxes out of your own pocket.) In addition, you must pay one half of the FICA taxes (7.65 percent of the employee's wages).

If the IRS does find you liable for a Trust Fund Recovery Penalty, don't panic (yet). Presumably, you sought legal counsel when you received the first notice of delinquency from the IRS. You do have the right to appeal, and, occasionally, the IRS Appeals Officers will reverse a Revenue Officer's findings. If you are still not satisfied after the Appeals Office has issued its finding, you can take the matter to the U.S. Tax Court.

PRODUCER, PROTECT THYSELF

Your best defense: make sure your company's payroll taxes are paid on time. Period.

If you are a member of a general partnership or a stockholder in a small corporation, make sure all of your partners are aware of the firm's responsibilities—even those partners and officers whose duties do not include payroll matters. Make sure everyone understands his potential personal liability. Stress the necessity for complying fully with the law, including the need for timely reporting and depositing of taxes due.

I would go one step further. Include an indemnification clause in your partnership agreement specifically for any payroll tax penalties. Each of the partners agrees to pay his proportionate share of delinquent payroll obligations. If one partner is held liable for these penalties, the others agree to reimburse him for any amounts above his proportionate share.

In addition, all partners share, proportionately, the costs of attorneys and accountants fees incurred as a result of contesting the matter with the IRS.

CHAPTER 13

Wrapping Up

At some point, a producer may find it necessary to discontinue operations. Perhaps he was presenting a single show and now the time has come to close the production. Or perhaps the producer and the members of his company have decided to move on to other things. In the worst case, the commercial producer may simply run out of money.

Nonprofits often close down because of lack of interest. Often, local theaters are run by a core group of driven volunteers. But when they can no longer devote the time to put on their shows, they may not have successors in waiting. Nonprofits may also close up if their sources of funding dry up.

Unfortunately, many companies operate on an informal basis. When it comes time to wrap up their business, their managers believe that since informality worked so well in the past, it will work just as well when they close their doors.

This is a dangerous misconception.

Of course, it is true that one can operate a business of any kind informally and never see negative consequences. It is also true that one can deliberately underreport one's income to the tax authorities and never get audited. It is equally true that one can commit murder and never get caught. One can play the odds in almost anything.

However, when the odds do catch up, the consequences are often severe.

To attempt to close up a theater operation without taking the appropriate steps to tie up all the legal loose ends is downright foolish. It is not that difficult to wrap up business in the proper way. The peace of mind and security it brings are well worth the trouble.

This chapter will show you the proper way to close up shop, under various scenarios.

CORPORATIONS

A theater company that has been organized as a corporation can dissolve (terminate) in one of several ways. (Unless otherwise noted, the same rules apply both to commercial corporations and nonprofits, and "stockholders" shall also refer to "members.")

VOLUNTARY DISSOLUTION WITHOUT COURT SUPERVISION

A corporation may dissolve by a vote of its stockholders. Depending on the state, this vote may be by two-thirds majority, a simple majority, or unanimity. If the corporation has been adjudicated a bankrupt, or has not begun operations, or its stated duration has expired, some states permit dissolution upon a majority vote of directors.

The corporation's charter or bylaws may restrict the right to dissolve.

In any event, the decision to dissolve must be made in good faith. In the event anyone challenges the dissolution legally, a judge will look at the circumstances behind the decision. Was fraud involved? Was the decision oppressive to the majority or minority?

If you want to dissolve, voluntarily, without seeking court supervision, you must follow these steps:

1. The directors must call a meeting for the purpose of voting on dissolution.

2. The stockholders must vote in favor of dissolution, according to the voting rules discussed above. In other words, they must adopt the resolution to dissolve.

3. In some states, the directors don't have to call a meeting. The directors first adopt the resolution to dissolve. They submit it to the stockholders. The members sign the resolution, thereby consenting to dissolution.

4. Management must file executed articles of dissolution with the appropriate state authorities. These must be properly prepared according to the state's law.

5. Many states require that a local official approve the dissolution. The official is often a judge, who signifies approval by affixing his signature or seal to the articles of dissolution.

6. The managers must notify creditors of the pending dissolution. The best way of notifying creditors is by personal service—that is, by physically giving or mailing the creditor notice of the dissolution.

7. There may be creditors whose identities and locations are not known to the managers. Yet they are also entitled to notice. The law requires the managers to publish a notice to any unknown creditors (or other interested parties) in a newspaper that the state supreme court says may publish legal notices. In each state, court rules specify how many times the notice must appear.

8. The managers must also notify the appropriate local tax authorities. If the authorities are satisfied that the company does not owe any local taxes, they must issue a certificate of clearance. (Remember, even nonprofits owe payroll taxes as well as taxes on income from unrelated operations.)

9. The corporation will continue to exist while its officers wind up its affairs. This means it must pay legitimate creditors' claims, dispose of its property, and otherwise terminate its operations.

I caution that you must follow your state's requirements very exactly. Many of these rules are detailed and quite specific.

VOLUNTARY DISSOLUTION WITH COURT SUPERVISION

Sometimes, it is desirable to petition the local court to supervise the voluntary dissolution of a corporation. Any interested party can ask for court supervision.

Often, creditors call in the courts. They are concerned that if the managers dissolve the corporation voluntarily, their rights may be affected adversely. Creditors may even seek to nullify a dissolution, if they believe they have a good cause.

A leading cause of dissolution is political civil war among the stockholders. Often, the unrest makes running the business difficult if not impossible. Stockholders may split into factions, each of which attempts to pursue its own agenda. In such cases, it is wise to seek court supervision.

The advantages are many. The court will make sure that the managers give the appropriate legal notices. If state law so requires, the judge may call in a local authority to have her say, such as an objective expert like the Attorney General. The court will hear claims. It will decide whether dissolution will benefit the stockholders.

FORFEITURE OF CHARTER

A state's grant of a corporate charter carries with it certain obligations. If the corporation abuses or neglects its duties, the state itself may bring action to forfeit the corporate charter.

Often, the Attorney General receives a complaint from an interested party, which prompts her to start an investigation into the allegations against the corporation.

Occasionally, authorities will discover that the organizers or managers have made misrepresentations or fraudulent statements in the corporation's annual reports to the state or even in its articles of incorporation.

Some states will suspend a corporation's charter, if it is delinquent in its tax payments. Other states take away the corporation's right to sue others in the state's courts. In most instances, if the corporation brings its payments up to date, it may pay a fee to have its charter reinstated. However, if it fails to do so altogether, the Attorney General may bring action before a court to annul the charter.

If there is a prolonged period in which the corporation fails to actively use its powers, the Attorney General may seek to terminate its charter. In most states, this inactivity must be continuous for a period of two years. In some states, creditors may continue to press claims against the corporation until it is officially dissolved. However, in other states, it isn't necessary to bring dissolution proceedings. Prolonged inactivity results in an automatic surrender of the corporate charter.

INVOLUNTARY DISSOLUTION

A corporation may be dissolved on an involuntary basis. There are many possible causes:

> • *If you attempt to incorporate a business and corporate status is not achieved, the Attorney General or secretary of state may seek to dissolve the corporation. These are called "quo warranto proceedings." Fraud is the most common cause. However, often, the organizers just don't follow through and complete all the steps that are necessary to properly organize the corporation. Many states do give you a chance to remedy the situation before dissolving your corporation.*

> • *The corporation may fail in its stated objectives. Or it may abandon its goals.*

- *Sometimes the state grants a corporate charter for a certain limited period of time. If no one takes action to extend this period, the corporation will die automatically.*

- *Statutes permit courts to dissolve corporations, when directors or officers so mismanage the business it can no longer effectively operate.*

- *Since states are particularly concerned about corporate fundraising (whether nonprofit or otherwise), improper solicitation of funds may be grounds for dissolving a corporation. Perhaps money was solicited or used fraudulently. Or funds solicited were never used for the purpose for which they were raised.*

- *States permit courts to dissolve a corporation when it has substantially and willfully violated consumer fraud or deceptive business laws.*

- *The directors misapply or waste corporate assets.*

- *The directors and shareholders are deadlocked so hopelessly their disagreement will irreparably injure the corporation.*

HOW TO LIQUIDATE A CORPORATION

As I stated earlier, once proceedings begin to dissolve a corporation, it nevertheless continues to exist during the period it takes to wrap up its affairs. Its business continues as it winds down.

DISSOLUTION VERSUS LIQUIDATION. Technically speaking, "liquidation" and "dissolution" are not the same thing. When a corporation is dissolved, its legal existence ends. When a corporation is liquidated, the managers (or trustees) collect corporate assets, pay expenses, satisfy creditors' claims, and distribute whatever is left to its stockholders.

In some states, the corporation first files an "intent to dissolve" with the appropriate authorities. Then the managers liquidate the company. Finally the corporation is dissolved.

In other states, the corporation dissolves first. Then the managers liquidate the business. Finally, the corporation's existence terminates.

CORPORATE ASSETS. Corporate assets are treated as trust funds. That is, the managers are under a special trust to protect assets for the benefit of creditors and shareholders. The managers must gather together all assets. They must collect all accounts receivable and pursue any claims that the corporation might have against other parties. They must obtain independent valuations of corporate assets. The managers must not squander or waste corporate property. They must hold all assets so that they are available for eventual distribution.

LEGAL ACTIONS. During dissolution, the corporation may sue to collect money owed to it. At the time of the filing of the certificate of dissolution, the corporation may already be a party to legal proceedings. It may have been pursuing claims against others or it may have been defending itself against claims by others. In either event, absent a court order to the contrary, these proceedings may continue all the way to judgment.

GIFTS TO NONPROFITS. Many noncharitable nonprofits often receive gifts of property instead of money. For example, supporters may donate sound systems, seats, and computers to their favorite theater company. However, when the company faces dissolution, such property may be subject to special treatment.

There are three distinct positions on donated property:

1. Gifts must be returned to the donors or their heirs.

2. The property is forfeited (escheated) to the state.

3. Donated property goes to the members.

Unfortunately, I must oversimplify here. This area of law is called the "cypres" doctrine, and it's as difficult to summarize as it is to pronounce. Furthermore, different courts have different opinions as to how these gifts must be handled. Many courts take this position:

Look, when Charles Grippo donated his lighting board to the XYZ Theatre Company, he intended the board to be used for live stage performances. If XYZ is now going out of business, then we should give the board to another theater company, because that's what Grippo would have wanted.

Other states say the assets must be forfeited to the state. (You ask: Just what will the bureaucrats in my state do with a lighting board? Don't ask.)

The key is this: In the case of a nonprofit that was organized for a charitable purpose (religious, educational, or the like), the members cannot take the property for themselves.

SALE OF ASSETS. Corporate assets must be sold off for the best possible price. After the sale, the proceeds must be used to pay off the parties who have an interest in the business.

INSOLVENCY

The XYZ Theatre Company finds it cannot pay its bills on time, in the regular course of putting on its productions. Maybe it has produced a series of shows that have flopped at the box office. Or maybe its expenses are much higher than its income from ticket sales and grants. It may be a temporary condition or it may be more serious. In any case, XYZ is in trouble and its creditors are anxious. Either its managers or creditors look to its state's insolvency laws for help.

This is called "equity insolvency."

CREDITORS AGREEMENT. Under one scenario, XYZ agrees to pay its creditors less than the full amount it owes each of them. Creditors don't have to participate. Many will, however, on the theory that "something is better than nothing." This is an informal arrangement. No one has to go to court. This is the simplest, least expensive, and least time-consuming procedure.

ASSIGNMENT FOR THE BENEFIT OF CREDITORS. Unfortunately, not all of XYZ's creditors are willing to accept a "creditor's agreement." Instead, they insist that XYZ transfer all of its property to a third party, who will act as trustee. This trustee will sell XYZ's property and distribute the proceeds to the creditors. This is an assignment for the benefit of creditors.

RECEIVERSHIP. Even an "assignment" does not satisfy all of XYZ's creditors. (They are merciless, aren't they?) Well, to be fair, the creditors have legitimate cause for concern. In an assignment, the trustee can act pretty much as he wants. Without a court to watch over him, he can sell and divide up the proceeds in whatever way he wishes. There's no guarantee he will treat all the creditors the same.

So, instead, the creditors begin "receivership" proceedings in the local court. The judge appoints a "receiver" who takes possession of XYZ's assets and distributes them to the creditors. The court decides when and how to distribute the assets and then tells the receiver what to do. A receivership is best used when there is an emergency or for the purpose of gaining some time.

GRIPPO'S RECOMMENDATION. If your company is facing insolvency, I would put the matter in the hands of the court. I realize that informal plans such as the "creditor's agreement" may seem quick and less embarrassing. However, as I indicated, some of your creditors are bound to grumble, especially those that believe they have not been treated equally.

More importantly—and I am thinking of you here—court proceedings protect you and your board from claims by creditors (or others) that you are not acting properly.

Here's what I mean. Suppose you are faced with a transaction that isn't part of your regular course of business. Should you go ahead and sign the contract? But, if you do, your creditors might accuse you of squandering precious corporate funds. However, suppose the contract promises a good potential return, thereby actually improving your cash flow. If you don't sign the contract, your creditors may complain that you blew a good opportunity.

So, you can be damned if you do and damned if you don't.

Go to court. You'll have your say. Your creditors will have their say. The judge will make the decision. She will order you to sign the contract or deep-six it. In any case, her order will protect you, no matter what happens.

BANKRUPTCY

Bankruptcy insolvency means that the value of all of the assets of the XYZ Theatre Company is not enough to pay all of its debts.

Bankruptcy is a matter of Federal law. The Constitution gives Congress the authority to establish bankruptcy laws for the entire country. This is to assure uniformity wherever the debtor (the party who owes the money) lives or does business. Unlike insolvency proceedings, which are a matter of state law and therefore heard in state court, bankruptcy proceedings take place in the Federal court.

VOLUNTARY BANKRUPTCY. The debtor decides it cannot deal with its creditors on its own anymore. It directs its attorney to file a petition for bankruptcy.

You do need an attorney to file your written petition for bankruptcy for your organization. If you yourself file on its behalf, the Court may decide you are engaged in the unauthorized practice of law. It may dismiss your company's petition.

Once your attorney initiates bankruptcy proceedings on your behalf, the court is likely to designate a referee to supervise the proceedings. Creditors elect a trustee, who will take charge of all your assets.

The moment you file the petition for bankruptcy, you are under the protection of the Court. Creditors cannot harass you for payments. They are given a deadline to file written claims with the court for whatever sums they allege you owe them.

Your bankruptcy petition may also affect your pending contracts. If you have a contract with the "Build 'Em Right" Scene Studios to construct flats for your next show, the studio may anticipate that you will breach your contract with it. Therefore, they may stop working on your project. If you owe them money, they may file their own claim with the Court.

Corporations use the Bankruptcy Act to reorganize in such a way that they can continue to operate. The corporation submits a plan to the Court that rearranges its debts and the claims that have been filed against it. Its creditors continue to maintain an interest in its assets, though usually for less than what they originally had claimed. The interests of creditors take precedent over the interests of the shareholders.

INVOLUNTARY BANKRUPTCY. A creditor can force the issue of possible corporate insolvency by filing a petition with the court seeking to declare the corporate debtor a bankrupt. This is an "involuntary" bankruptcy.

This may be done only with "for-profit" corporations. Creditors cannot subject a nonprofit to involuntary bankruptcy.

GRIPPO'S RECOMMENDATION. Bankruptcy is a very drastic measure. It should only be used as a last resort. Given the choice between voluntary and involuntary, the commercial producer is likely to fare better if he files for voluntary bankruptcy.

AVOIDING INSOLVENCY AND BANKRUPTCY

Each situation is different, of course, but there are steps producers can take to avoid insolvency and bankruptcy. If you are constantly sweating over inadequate cash flow, I suggest you review the following suggestions to help you solve your problems and keep your company going.

> • *Do your shows constantly cost more to produce than you have budgeted? If so, either your budget estimates are wrong or you don't know how to say "No" to your budget-breaking requests— like new sets or costumes—from your artistic personnel.*

> • *Are you producing shows that are too rich for your budget? It may be necessary to scale down your productions.*

• *Related to the foregoing, consider this: Musicals cost more money to produce than modest comedies and dramas. Yet musicals often gross more ticket dollars than straight plays. Review your last two seasons and compare the costs of your musicals versus the cash flow they generated, against the costs and cash flow of your straight plays. Perhaps you need to readjust your mix of shows to bring your costs and cash flow more into line.*

• *Are you producing shows that your audiences want to see? This raises the age-old question of art versus commerce. Your mission may be to produce very esoteric or avant-garde pieces. But are you drawing enough audiences to keep your doors open? You may have to swallow your artistic bent and produce instead more commercial fare, at least once or twice each season, to subsidize the more artsy material. Or you may have to rethink your marketing strategy. Perhaps you are marketing to the wrong people.*

• *If you are a nonprofit, are you fully looking into all sources of funds that may be available to you? For instance, are there foundations, corporations, community organizations, and government agencies whom you have not yet approached for funding help? If so, what are you waiting for?*

• *Nonprofits may also find wealthy patrons of the arts who may be willing to assist them financially through cash flow problems. Are there any such persons in your community?*

• *Have you overextended yourself? Are you trying to do too much with insufficient resources? Many companies try to produce too many shows in one season. Or they engage in outreach programs to schools and other children's organizations. Can you really afford to conduct these programs? Again, there is often special funding available for certain programs. Are you fully tapping into these sources?*

• *Are your facilities costing too much? Do you really need all that office and performance space? Can you move your offices to a less expensive part of town? Are you keeping your per-formance space occupied enough to justify the overhead cost? Would you save money by licensing a performance venue on a show-by-show basis? Can you rehearse in cheaper space? During your dark times, is it feasible to license your space to other producers to generate some cash flow?*

• Related to the questions above: is it possible to share facilities with another theater company in your town? While space sharing opens up a host of issues—from who takes priority to whose ego may get bruised—often two or more performing arts companies will find it advantageous to share the same facilities. This reduces overall costs. A theater company can, of course, match up with another theater company. However, other possible partners include opera compa-nies, symphony orchestras, dance companies, and others.

• Do you really need all those employees? This is a tough ques-tion. No one likes layoffs. But take a good hard look at your pay-roll costs. Often they are higher than they need to be. Perhaps you do have too many people. Perhaps you might ask your employees to take a pay cut. Or to shoulder some of the costs of health insur-ance themselves. Perhaps some functions may be outsourced. I know this is a very painful subject to bring up, but if you are facing a cash flow crisis, you may need to take drastic measures.

• In a cash flow crisis, ask your creditors for extended payment terms. Of course, creditors don't like these requests. But, given the choice between insolvency or bankruptcy proceedings in which they may (if they are lucky) see only a fraction of what you owe them, many creditors will gladly work with you.

• If you are fortunate enough to produce a hit show, don't go hog wild with all the excess cash the show is generating. Don't think you have to use it all to expand your operations. Instead, put a portion of it aside into a cash reserve for times when money is tight. Invest your reserves prudently and in such a way that you can get at them quickly if you need to.

LIMITED PARTNERSHIPS

Most theatrical limited partnerships are created for the purpose of producing one show. Once that show closes, the producer–general partner must wrap up his operations.

TIME

The time for terminating the partnership depends a great deal on its original goals. The intent may have been to produce the play in one company (including replacement actors) within a specific geographic region until a certain specific date. Or the goal may have been "run of the play." Once either the specific date has come and gone, or the play has exhausted its box office appeal, the show closes. The partnership terminates.

PRODUCER'S DECISION

The producer reserves the sole right to decide when to close the play. He must make the decision to abandon any intentions of continuing to produce the show.

This is not as straightforward as it sounds.

Often, the author has granted the producer the right to present the play in more than one specific place. For example, the producer may have the right to initially present the play off-Broadway. However, he may also have the right to present other companies that will tour the United States. It is standard in Broadway and off-Broadway deals for the author to grant the producer the right to also produce the play in the British Isles and Canada. (Remember, once the limited partnership is formed, the producer, in turn, transfers these rights to it.)

If the show is a hit, the producer, on behalf of the partnership, will surely organize additional companies to tour the United States. Or he may license the production to other presenters on a regional basis. Of course, he will exploit any other rights he has, such as those for the British Isles and Canada. Thus, the partnership may maintain an interest in keeping companies of the play running for a very long time.

It is only when the last of these companies closes that the producer may decide he has exhausted any further possibilities for the play. He will terminate the partnership.

PROCEDURE

First, the producer must use whatever cash is on hand to pay off the partnership debts. These may include royalties or any other money owed to artists, unions, theater owners, and others associated with the various companies. Of course, he will need some money to remove the physical production from the theater in which it was last playing. He must pay any taxes that are still due, as well as any other obligations of the partnership.

Whenever any business winds down, there are always unforeseen obligations that creep up. The producer must set aside money to cover these expenses. If the show has not yet repaid its investors, they are next in line to receive back their investment capital.

It is often possible to sell off the scenery and costumes. The Broadway company may close, but another producer may want to tour the show in a more scaled-down, non-union production—or the bus and truck tour. He may wish to purchase the scenery and costumes. Costume and scenery rental houses may also be likely buyers. In some cases, the original producer (as general partner) or one of the limited partners may buy the physical assets of the partnership. They must do so at a fair price. Thus the original partnership may recover part of its costs.

The partnership will also have an interest in such subsidiary rights as stock and amateur licensing, foreign language productions, original cast albums, and motion picture rights. Except for the motion picture rights, the general partner may ordinarily sell the partnership's interests in these rights. Again, either the general partner or any of the limited partners may be the purchaser, as long as the price is fair.

Finally, the general partner will distribute profits (if any) to the partnership. The exact share of the profits the general partner and the limited partners receive are determined by the formula set forth in the partnership agreement.

ABANDONMENT BEFORE OPENING

Sometimes, a producer may decide that a show is just not working as well as he hoped. Ticket sales are poor. Audiences are walking out of the previews. Perhaps the show is built around a star and the star falls ill during rehearsal. A suitable replacement cannot be found. Whatever the reason, the producer believes it is best to abandon the show even before it opens. In that event, the producer will liquidate its assets and distribute whatever funds are left in the same way as if the show had opened.

FINALE ULTIMO

When a show closes, or a producer must wind up his company's operations, there is always a feeling of sadness. Even if the show has had a long run, or if the company has operated for several good seasons, there is always a letdown.

The morning after the closing always brings with it a feeling of emptiness, like a part of one's life is gone.

Fortunately, show people are a hearty lot. When a show or company closes, the participants scatter. Most go on to other shows, other opportunities in the theater. A few do leave the business altogether.

Forgive me if I sound a little prejudiced, but actually, I believe the producer is the heartiest of the lot. He initiated the project or founded the company, raised the money, made the tough decisions, and had the lion's share of the headaches and the stomach ulcers. He seldom receives any glory, unless his show wins an award. Even then, however, he may have his moment in the sun, but the truth is, everyone will remember his actors, playwright, and director long after they have forgotten him. Of course, if he's lucky, he's made some money.

But still the producer goes on, looking for that next hot project . . . or hoping to open another theater company real soon.

And he'll have to make all the decisions all over again. What form of organization should his company take? Should he license performance space for a single show, take a lease, or purchase a venue? How should he raise money? What terms should he include in his contracts?

Oh, well, that's life upon the wicked stage.

Play Licensors

One can obtain a license to present almost every published play through one of the dozens of play licensing houses that exist specifically for this purpose.

The following is a list of the major play licensing sources. (There are also dozens of other smaller enterprises.) A few charge a token fee for their catalogs, which are usually updated annually.

Baker's Plays
100 Chauncy Street
Boston, Massachusetts
 02111–1783
(617) 482–1280

Broadway Play Publishing, Inc.
56 East 81st Street
New York, New York 10028–0202
(212) 772–8334

Contemporary Drama Service
Merriwether Publishing, Ltd.
885 Elkton Drive
Colorado Springs, Colorado 80907
(719) 594–4422

Dramatic Publishing Company
311 Washington Street
P.O. Box 129
Woodstock, Illinois 60098
(815) 338–7170

Dramatists Play Service
440 Park Avenue South
New York, New York 10016
(212) 683–8690

Eldridge Publishing Co., Inc.
P.O. Box 1595
Venice, Florida 34284
(800) 447–8243

Encore Performance
P.O. Box 692
Orem, Utah 84059
(801) 225–0605

Heuer Publishing Company
P.O. Box 248
Cedar Rapids, Iowa 52406
(319) 364–6311

Music Theatre International
421 West 54th Street

New York, New York 10019
(212) 541–4684

Pioneer Drama Service, Inc.
P.O. Box 4267
Englewood, Colorado 80155
(303) 779–4035

Rodgers and Hammerstein Theatre Library
For *amateur*
 performance rights:
229 West 28th Street
New York, New York 10001
(212) 564–4000

For *professional* performance rights:
1633 Broadway, Suite 3801
New York, New York 10019–6746
(212) 541–6600

Samuel French, Inc.
45 West 25th Street
New York, New York 10010–2751
Non-musicals: (212) 206–8990
Musicals: (212) 206–8125

Tams-Witmark Music Library, Inc.
560 Lexington Avenue
New York, New York 10126–0394
(800) 221–7196 or (212) 688–2525

The Dramatists Guild

THE FOLLOWING IS A CURRENT LIST OF THE DRAMATISTS GUILD MODEL FORM CONTRACTS:

- *Approved Production Contract for Musicals (Broadway/First Class)*

- *Approved Production Contract for Plays (Broadway/First Class)*

- *Model League of Regional Theatres Agreement (LORT)*

- *99 Seat Theatre Contract (Los Angeles)*

- *Showcase Contract (New York City)*

- *Small Theatre Contract (National)*

- *Collaboration Agreement (Musicals)*

- *Collaboration Agreement (Plays)*

- *Commission Agreement (Musicals)*

- *Commission Agreement (Plays)*

- *Option Underlying Rights (Musicals)*

- *Option Underlying Rights (Plays)*

- *Licensing Agreement*

FOR MORE INFORMATION ABOUT THESE OR TO CONTACT THE GUILD:

The Dramatists Guild
1501 Broadway, Suite 701
New York, New York 10036
(212) 398–9366
Fax: (212) 944–0420

APPENDIX C

Collective Bargaining Agents

For simplicity's sake, I have listed only the national offices of these various unions. Most have regional and local offices throughout the country. The national office can refer you to the local in your community.

Actors' Equity Association
165 West 46th Street
New York, New York 10036
(212) 869–8530
Fax: (212) 719–9815
Represents actors and stage managers who work in the legitimate theater.

American Federation of Musicians (AFM)
1501 Broadway, Suite 600
New York, New York 10036
(212) 869–1330
Fax: (212) 764–6134
www.afm.org
Represents musicians.

American Federation of Television and Radio Artists
260 Madison Avenue
New York, New York 10016
(212) 532–0800
Fax: (212) 545–1238

www.aftra.org
Represents performers and news people in videotape, television, radio, comercials, and phonograph recordings.

American Guild of Musical Artists (AGMA)
727 Broadway
New York, New York 10019–5284
(212) 265–3687
Fax: (212) 262–9088
Represents concert performers, ballet dancers, and opera singers.

International Alliance of Theatrical Stage Employees (IA or IATSE)
1515 Broadway, Suite 601
New York, New York 10036
(212) 730–1770
Represents technicians, artisans, and craftspeople, in live theater, film, television, and trade shows.

Screen Actors Guild (SAG)
5757 Wilshire Blvd.
Los Angeles, California 90036
(213) 954–1600
www.sage.com
Represents professional screen actors who appear in theatrical motion picture, prime-time television, commercials, industrial films, and videos.

Society of Stage Directors and Choreographers (SSDC)
1501 Broadway, Suite 1701
New York, New York 10036
(212) 391–1071
Represents directors and choreographers.

United Scenic Artists Local 829, IATSE
16 West 61st Street, 11th Floor
New York, New York 10023
(212) 736–4498
Fax: (212) 977–2011
Represents scenic, costume, and lighting designers, as well as assistant designers.

Index

BOOKS FROM ALLWORTH PRESS

Building the Successful Theater Company
by Lisa Mulcahy (paperback, 6 × 9, 240 pages, $19.95)

The Business of Theatrical Design
by James L Moody (paperback, 6 × 9, 288 pages, $19.95)

Producing Your Own Showcase
by Paul Harris (paperback, 6 × 9, 224 pages, $18.95,

Technical Theater for Nontechnical People
by Drew Campbell (paperback, 6 × 9, 256 pages, $18.95)

The Health & Safety Guide for Film, TV & Theater
by Monona Rossol (paperback, 6 × 9, 256 pages, $19.95)

Booking and Tour Management for the Performing Arts, Third Edition
by Rena Shagan (paperback, 6 × 9, 288 pages, $19.95)

Career Solutions for Creative People
by Dr. Rhonda Ormont (paperback, 6 × 9, 320 pages, $19.95)

Movement for Actors
by Nicole Potter (paperback, 6 × 9, 288 pages, $19.95)

An Actor's Guide—Making It in New York City
by Glenn Alterman (paperback, 6 × 9, 288 pages, $19.95)

Clues to Acting Shakespeare
by Wesley Van Tassel (paperback, 6 × 9, 208 pages, $16.95)

Creating Your Own Monologue
by Glenn Alterman (paperback, 6 × 9, 192 pages, $14.95)

Promoting Your Acting Career
by Glen Alterman (paperback, 6 × 9, 224 pages, $18.95)

Casting Director's Secrets: Inside Tips for Successful Auditions
by Ginger Howard Friedman (paperback, 6 × 9, 208 pages, $16.95)

Please write to request our free catalog. To order by credit card, call 1-800-491-2808 or send a check or money order to Allworth Press, 10 East 23rd Street, Suite 510, New York, NY 10010. Include $5 for shipping and handling for the first book ordered and $1 for each additional book. Ten dollars plus $1 for each additional book if ordering from Canada. New York State residents must add sales tax.

To see our complete catalog on the World Wide Web, or to order online, you can find us at *www.allworth.com*.